Strategic Supply Chain Management

Preface

This book provides an analysis of an approach to modelling supply chains and their management with distinctive practical application. It incorporates elements of multi-dimensionality, optimisation and interaction within business and consequently is practical, realistic and meaningful both theoretically and to the industry.

Following discussion of the development of supply chain management it provides a usable and practical model for supply chains and which is evaluated in the real-life context of a major international car manufacturer with whom the authors have closely worked.

As a result it attempts to satisfy the demand from industry for guidance in the complex world of supply chain modelling in the logistics and supply chain management business sector that has become highly significant and continues to grow.

Acknowledgements

From Safaa

My appreciation goes to my mother, sisters and to my brother and special thanks to my Godmother Miss Patricia Lee and my father Professor Hassan Sindi, who never stopped believing in my abilities and pushed me to become better. I admire him greatly and hope to become as accomplished as he is.

I would like to express my gratitude to my close friends, especially Dr Roger Woodman who helped me greatly, encouraged and supported me through the hardest part of this process.

I would also like to thank Plymouth University for the support of their academic staff during my studies at Plymouth. In addition a special thanks to the Saudi Arabian Ministry of Higher Education and the Saudi Cultural Office for their financial sponsorship throughout my studies, and the support given to me during my academic years in the United Kingdom.

And from Michael

As always my thanks go to Charlton Athletic for limitless entertainment, but more especially to Liz, Joe and Siân without whom none of this would be possible.

Contents

1 Introduction to Strategic Supply Chain Modelling   1

2 The Evolution of Supply Chains and Logistics   7

3 A Theoretical and Conceptual Framework for Strategic Supply Chains   27

4 A Methodology for the Strategic Supply Chain Model   101

5 Data Collection for Strategic Supply Chain Modelling   109

6 The Application of Fuzzy Delphi to Strategic Supply Chain Modelling   131

7 Data Analysis for Strategic Supply Chain Management   179

8 Testing and Implementing the Strategic Supply Chain Model   223

9 Conclusions – What Next for Strategic Supply Chain Modelling?   249

Appendix 1: Era Definitions   255

Appendix 2: Panel Contact Details   261

Index   267

List of Abbreviations

APS	Advanced planning and scheduling
BSC	Basic supply chain
CLM	Council of logistics management
ECR	Efficient consumer response
EDI	Electronic data interchange
ERP	Enterprise resource planning
JIT	Just in time
MDM	Multi-dimensional matrix
MRP	Material requirement planning
SME	Small and medium size enterprise
TPS	Toyota's production system
TQM	Total quality management

List of Figures

Fig. 1.1   Supply chain eras   4
Fig. 2.1   The scheduling of MRP (adapted from Chen
            and Ji 2007)   9
Fig. 2.2   Four elements of supply chain functions (adapted from
            Porter 1980)   16
Fig. 2.3   Customer order decoupling points (adapted from Olhager
            2011)   17
Fig. 3.1   Integrating key decision processes (adapted from Lambert
            and Cooper 2000)   37
Fig. 3.2   Integrating business processes across the supply chain
            (adapted from Lambert and Cooper 2000)   41
Fig. 3.3   Lean automotive model (adapted from James-Moore
            and Gibbons 1997)   67
Fig. 3.4   "Market qualifiers" matrix (adapted from
            Jones et al. 2000)   72
Fig. 3.5   Conceptual framework of the study   77
Fig. 3.6   Conceptual framework for the multi-dimensional matrix   82
Fig. 3.7   Interactive multi-dimensional matrix   90
Fig. 5.1   Delphi study feedback loops   110
Fig. 5.2   Combining Delphi and fuzzy controller into Fuzzy Delphi   125
Fig. 6.1   Cost and JIT variable Crisp Sets   132
Fig. 6.2   Cost and lean variable pilot Delphi Fuzzy sets   135
Fig. 6.3   Preliminary MDM   137

Fig. 6.4   Fuzzy Delphi round one MDM   141
Fig. 6.5   Cost and JIT lean variable round one Fuzzy Delphi   142
Fig. 6.6   Cost and lean variable round 2 Fuzzy Delphi   148
Fig. 6.7   Preliminary interactive MDM   149
Fig. 6.8   Variety of consensus (adapted from Gracht 2012)   150
Fig. 6.9   Cost variable functions   156
Fig. 6.10   Lean variable functions   157
Fig. 6.11   Delivery to request variable function   159
Fig. 6.12   Tactical distribution variable function   160
Fig. 6.13   Innovative product variable function   161
Fig. 6.14   High-end product variable function   162
Fig. 7.1   Cost vs frequency variables   203
Fig. 7.2   Cost vs. frequency and JIT lean vs. frequency variables   205
Fig. 7.3   Delivery to request and JIT lean scatter diagram   206
Fig. 7.4   Delivery to request and cost scatter diagram   207
Fig. 7.5   Innovative product and JIT lean scatter diagram   207
Fig. 7.6   Manufacturing lead-time vs. JIT lean scatter diagram   209
Fig. 7.7   Manufacturing lead-time vs. cost scatter diagram   210
Fig. 7.8   Innovative product vs. JIT lean scatter diagram   213
Fig. 7.9   Innovative product vs. Cost scatter diagram   214
Fig. 7.10   Interactive MDM home-page   216
Fig. 7.11   Interactive MDM home and logistics strategy pages   216
Fig. 7.12   Interactive MDM supply chain strategy and 21–30%
            JIT vs. 0–10% Cost   217
Fig. 7.13   Interactive MDM (>90% JIT lean vs. 0–10% cost)   218
Fig. 8.1   NSC invoice trigger nodes   229
Fig. 8.2   NSC strategies   231
Fig. 8.3   NSC, testing "off assembly" node   232
Fig. 8.4   Manufacturing lead-time ≤ 10% cost and >90% JIT lean   233
Fig. 8.5   NSC, testing "accepted by sales"   234
Fig. 8.6   Supply chain and logistics strategies. Push system
            and operational and strategic distribution   235
Fig. 8.7   Delivery to commit date and delivery to request   238
Fig. 8.8   Importer Non-EU countries invoice trigger   239
Fig. 8.9   Importing EU invoice trigger   241
Fig. 8.10   Tactical distribution <10% cost and >90% JIT lean   245

List of Tables

Table 3.1	The four strategies and six approaches of supply chains	76
Table 4.1	The chosen methodological approaches and their application	102
Table 4.2	Methodological stages of the research	104
Table 4.3	Advantages and disadvantages of fuzzy Delphi	105
Table 5.1	Types of Delphi techniques	118
Table 5.2	Advantages and disadvantages of various Delphi techniques	120
Table 6.1	Consensus type and calculation	154
Table 6.2	Fuzzy Delphi variable functions	165
Table 6.3	The interactive MDM chosen variable functions	173
Table 6.4	Category groups of the chosen variables	175
Table 7.1	Cost variables	182
Table 7.2	JIT lean variables	184
Table 7.3	Operational distribution variable	185
Table 7.4	Strategic distribution variable	186
Table 7.5	Tactical distribution variable	187
Table 7.6	Delivery to commit date variable	188
Table 7.7	Delivery to request variable	188
Table 7.8	Order fill lead time variables	189
Table 7.9	Manufacturing lead-time variables	190
Table 7.10	Innovative product variable	192
Table 7.11	Functional product variable	193

Table 7.12   Innovative functional product variables   194
Table 7.13   High-end product variables   195
Table 7.14   Self-customised product variable   197
Table 7.15   Push system variable   198
Table 7.16   Summary of frequency variables converted into
             percentages   200
Table 7.17   Cost and JIT lean frequency converted into percentage   202
Table 7.18   Manufacturing lead-time fuzzy rules summary   211
Table 7.19   Manufacturing lead-time of 0–10% JIT lean vs. cost   212
Table 7.20   Innovative product fuzzy rules summary   212
Table 8.1   Major automotive companies manufacturing in the UK
             (adapted from Automotive Council UK, 2016)   224
Table 9.1   Advantages and disadvantage of game theory
             (adapted from Foss 1999)   252
Table 9.2   Advantages and disadvantages of hybrid
             intelligent systems   253

1

Introduction to Strategic Supply Chain Modelling

The earliest outbreak in supply chains can be seen with the first industrial revolution in Britain in the late eighteenth century through the mechanisation of the textile industry. Tasks previously done by hand in weavers' cottages were brought together in a single cotton mill and the factory was born (Handfield and Nichols 1999). This resulted in the need for sophisticated coordination of raw materials, production and the delivery of finished products (Baldwin 2012). This sophistication of material flow became apparent with the second industrial revolution in the early twentieth century when Henry Ford mastered the moving assembly line, hence the age of mass production. The first two industrial revolutions made people richer and more urban (Lee and Billington 1995). According to early research on the creation of supply chains by Georgia Tech Supply Chain and Logistics Institute (2010), logistics was a term used almost exclusively to describe military movements. However, in the 1940s and 1950s, after the industrial revolution, the focus was on logistics research due to evolving machinery. The aim was to improve labour intensive processes such as material handling and to maximise the utilisation of space by the use of efficient racking and warehouse design improvement.

© The Author(s) 2017
S. Sindi, M. Roe, *Strategic Supply Chain Management*,
DOI 10.1007/978-3-319-54843-2_1

In the mid-1950s, the "unitised load" concept became popular in shipping especially with regard to container ships. This concept was extended to transportation such as trains and trucks that deals with these containers (Georgia Tech Supply Chain and Logistics Institute 2010). The third technological revolution has come with digital integration that revolutionised supply chains. For example, a number of technologies such as clever web-based software services, novel materials, more dextrous robots, three-dimensional printing and a range of services aiming to create a fast and responsive supply chain that can satisfy the increasingly volatile market (The Economist 2012). This third technological revolution not only affected how things are made, but where. Factories moved to low-wage countries to cut labour costs. However, due to markets becoming highly fluctuating, companies preferred to set up additional manufacturing plants closer to their customers in order to respond faster to changes in demand (Friedman 2005). This can be seen with specialised and sophisticated products, as it helped designers and production to be close to their market, for example high-end watches and jewellery. Although consumers preferred the new age of better products and swiftly delivered goods, governments often found it harder due to their obligation to protect home-industries and companies, hence subsidising old factories in an attempt to minimise production moving abroad (Friedman 2005). Seeing that the old method of production has proven to be inefficient due to intensive labour activities, the factory of the future will focus on mass customisation as a product can be designed on a computer and printed on a 3D printer to be sent to the manufacturer for mass production (Pearce et al. 2010). 3D printing creates a solid object by building up successive layers of material and can make many things which are too complex for a traditional factory to handle. Furthermore, 3D printing creates new horizons for supply chain sustainability, as with reduced logistic distribution comes a reduction in carbon emissions (Pearce et al. 2010). Digital design and 3D printing will further revolutionise the supply chain of the future, as "where" production occurs will no longer matter as it can take place from any location resulting in an increase in decentralisation (Jalwan and Israel 2014). The factories of the future will be uncluttered, sophisticated and almost deserted, as jobs will not be on the factory floor but in the management offices close to the market, which will be full of specialist workers such as designers, software engineers, logistics experts, marketing staff and other professionals.

With the increase in competition and advances in technology, large companies as well as small and medium enterprises (SMEs) face the challenging issue of selecting an optimal supply chain strategy. Never before has the distinction of which supply chain model to incorporate within the business strategy been of such importance to business success. The confusion of which strategy to implement is due to the many supply chain models and definitions developed over the years (Cagliano et al. 2004). One objective of this book is to establish a clear understanding of these choices. From this, a model will be developed to help companies understand the position of their supply chain in the market, as well as be able to identify the best suited strategy for their business.

The Knowledge Gap

The evolution of the supply chain can be traced back to the 1940s; the "Creation Era". The problematic issue facing many businesses is to decide which supply chain model to incorporate within their business strategy (Cagliano et al. 2004). To help to do this we go on to identify and analyse the different evolutionary stages of supply chains with their relevant models and definitions. This framework is divided into seven eras, each representing a period of evolution. The phrase "Era" is well suited to describing certain periods of evolution, as it denotes events before and after they change significantly. Due to the slow pace of change in some business activities, and due to overlapping economic effects, the phrase "Era" is appropriate as it is not confined by a time constraint (Kumar et al. 2008). These supply chain models and strategies will be incorporated into a multi-dimensional model to help firms diagnose their position in the market and identify the best suited strategy for their business structure and speciality. This multi-dimensional matrix (MDM) will generate recommendations and choices for firms to select. Their preferred strategy can then be integrated into their business structure through supply chain re-engineering to maximise efficiency of the end-to-end distribution processes whereby customer value is prioritised.

Era name	Time period
One: Creation	1940–1980
Two: Integration	1970–2000
Three: Globalisation	1980–2000
Four: Specialisation	1990–2008
Five: Specialised globalisation	2008–2011
Six: Multi-dimensional strategies	2011–2016
Seven: Interactivity and automation	Forecast

Fig. 1.1 Supply chain eras

The central feature of this book is to investigate the issues facing SMEs and corporations in diagnosing their position in the market and choosing a suitable supply chain strategy for their business structure. This will mitigate complexity by identifying a full range of supply chain strategies and allocating them into "Eras" (Fig. 1.1). The strategies have been selected according to the emerging definitions arising in each era, and highlight the issues faced by companies through the evolution of supply chains. The aim of developing the MDM is to help firms identify and allocate their strategy in accordance with the company's speciality and market. Furthermore, the model will aim to provide firms with opportunities to shorten their lead-time, add value and reduce costs, as the model acts as a diagnostic tool that can generate recommendations as well as options for the firm to choose from. To ensure the model has sufficient capabilities to survive in a digitalised era, the model will be interactive and able to be further improved and tailored by the company.

We continue by providing a background to supply chain development acting as the basis for a discussion of supply chain eras. This is followed by a conceptual framework for the MDM matrix. Methodological issues are then examined to guide a suitable data collection process. Once the data collection is completed, the MDM matrix will be constructed including its interactive capability. Finally, the capability and applicability of the MDM matrix will be tested in the context of an established automobile manufacturing firm in the UK.

References

Baldwin, R. (2012). *Global supply chains: Why they emerged, why they matter and where they are going.* Geneva: University of Geneva, No. DP9103 (1), 1–37.

Cagliano, R., Caniato, F., & Spina, G. (2004). Lean, Agile and traditional supply: How do they impact manufacturing performance?. *Journal of Purchasing and Supply Management, 10*(4), 151–164.

Friedman, T. (2005). *The world is flat: The globalized world in the twenty-first century.* London: Penguin Books. 137–166.

Georgia Tech Supply Chain and Logistics Institute. (2010). The evolution of the supply chain and logistics. http://www.scl.gatech.edu/scl-evolution.php.

Handfield, R. B., & Nichols, E. L. (1999). *Introduction to supply chain management.* New Jersey: Prentice-Hall. 1–183.

Jalwan, H., & Israel, G. (2014). 3D printing your supply chain. *Transportation and Logistics-MIT, 1*(1), 10–40.

Kumar, V., Lavassani, K., & Movahedi, B. (2008). Transition to B2B e-marketplace enabled supply chain: Readiness assessment and success factors. *International Journal of Technology, 5*(3), 75–88.

Lee, H. L., & Billington, C. (1995). The evolution of supply chain management models and practice at Hewlett-Packard. *Interfaces, 25*(5), 42–63.

Pearce, J. M., Blair, C., Laciak, K., Andrews, R., Nosrat, A., & Zelenika-Zovko, I. (2010). 3-D printing of open source appropriate technologies for self-directed sustainable development. *Journal of Sustainable Development, 3*(4), 17–29.

The Economist. (2012). *The third industrial revolution, the digitisation of manufacturing will transform the way goods are made and change the politics of jobs too.* http://www.economist.com/node/21553017.

2

The Evolution of Supply Chains and Logistics

The Emergence of Supply Chains and Logistics

The emergence of personalised computers in the 1980s changed logistics in terms of graphical planning, flexible spreadsheets, mapping interfaces and optimisation models for supply chain design and distribution planning (Garcı´a-Dastugue and Lambert 2003). The Georgia Tech Production and Distribution Research Centre was the earliest innovation leader in combining map interfaces with optimisation models for supply chain design and distribution planning, while the Material Handling Research Centre (MHRC) provided leadership in developing new control technology for material handling automation. The Computational Optimisation Centre developed new large-scale optimisation algorithms that enabled solution of previously intractable airfreight scheduling problems. Much of the technological development began to find its way rapidly into commercial industry, giving logistics and supply chains increased recognition from business executives (Georgia Tech Supply Chain and Logistics Institute 2010). Therefore, resources were invested in the development of logistics to improve significantly their supply chain and business strategies. Moreover, in

© The Author(s) 2017
S. Sindi, M. Roe, *Strategic Supply Chain Management*,
DOI 10.1007/978-3-319-54843-2_2

the mid-1980s Material Requirement Planning (MRP) systems were developed in an attempt to integrate multiple company databases that exist in companies and encourage them to communicate with each other (Lambert et al. 1998). This resulted in 1985 in the technological revolution that led the National Council of Physical Distribution Management (NCPDM) to change its name to the Council of Logistics Management (CLM). This was said to reflect the evolving discipline including the integration of inbound, outbound and reverse flows of products, services and related information (Harland and Lamming 1999).

The Introduction of Supply Chains and Logistics

In early years logistics was a term that had been used almost exclusively to describe the support of military movements. This shifted in the 1940s and 1950s to focus upon how to use machinery to improve the labour intensive processes of material handling and utilise warehousing design layout (Harland and Lamming 1999). Although the terms "warehousing" and "materials handling" were used to describe many of these activities, fundamentally it was viewed as part of industrial engineering rather than a discipline on its own (Cooper et al. 1997).

By the 1960s the term "Physical Distribution" emerged as a result of freight transportation shifting to truck rather than rail (Tan 2001). Hence the NCPDM was formed in 1963 focusing on satisfying the growing logistics' industries' needs. All transactions were recorded manually until the arrival of commercialised computers in the 1970s. This led to the creation of the Georgia Tech Production and Distribution Research Centre and the Computational Optimisation Centre at Columbia University. These centres focused on opening doors to the innovation of supply chains, logistics and distribution, such as optimising inventory and route tracing (Georgia Tech Supply Chain and Logistics Institute 2010).

Technological Impact on Supply Chains and Logistics

Logistics and supply chain management became more accepted in industry and increased in 1990 through the emergence of enterprise resource planning (ERP), which improved data availability and accuracy (Lummus and Vokurka 1999). The ERP system was an expansion on the MRP systems developed in the 1970s and 1980s, further increasing recognition of the need for better planning and integration among logistics databases and components. The aim of the MRP system was to integrate the multiple databases in almost all companies that seldom talked to each other (Lummus and Vokurka, *ibid*). MRP follows a top-down hierarchical approach (Fig. 2.1). It begins with the Master Production Schedule (MPS) orders for the final products by quantity and date which are then translated into a specific planned start and due dates for all components based on the product structure, resulting in a detailed scheduling solution to meet them. Unfortunately, MRP does not accommodate capacity constraints and assumes lead times are fixed, creating problems in production and increases in bottlenecks (Chen and Ji 2007).

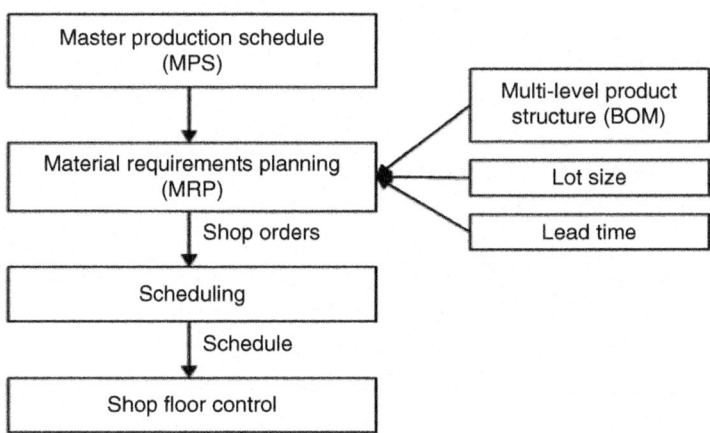

Fig. 2.1 The scheduling of MRP (adapted from Chen and Ji 2007)

These issues resulted in the creation of ERP. With globalisation, companies recognised the need for better planning and integration among logistics components and hence worked hard towards improving ERP, resulting in a new generation of advanced planning and scheduling (APS) software (Kim and Kogut 1996). This software contains a range of capabilities such as capacity scheduling, constraint-base planning and allowing companies to optimise their supply chain resources and reduce costs. It aims to improve product margins, lower inventory and increase manufacturing throughout by helping companies decide when to build each order, in what operation sequence, and with what equipment in order to meet the required due date (Lee et al. 2002).

Globalisation Influences on Supply Chains and Logistics

The increase of globalisation and development of technology are changing supply chains. Product designers, marketers and manufacturers that were previously housed in a single facility are now spread over several continents forcing businesses to integrate with different cultures, languages and business objectives (Johnson 2006). The globalisation of manufacturing, particularly in China has increased the amount of outsourcing, off-shore suppliers, distribution and shipping capacity since the mid-1990s. This has increased the widespread use of the term "supply chain" as a result of globalisation increasing the need for logistics strategies to deal with complex networks spanning multiple continents (Cooper et al. 1997). The term "supply chain" arose to refer to strategic issues while the term "logistics" began to refer to tactical and operational issues (Tan 2001). This resulted in the Council of Logistics Management changing its name again to Council of Supply Chain Management Professionals. This marked the distinction that logistics is part of a supply chain process that plans, implements and controls the efficient, effective forward and reverse flow of goods, storage, services, customer requirements and related information between the point of origin and point of consumption (Cooper et al. 1997). Globalisation has brought new risks and challenges, such as short product life cycles and uncertain demand. This has led companies to invest in technologies and approaches for enhancing supply chains in order to gain competitive advantage (Cavinato 1992). With supply chain complexity leading to new risks, efficiency, price discrimination and low-cost resources, out-sourcing jobs has become increasingly common, although it has created global winners and losers (Johnson 2006).

There are now two distinctive supply chain strategies "Lean Supply Chain and Agile Supply Chain". "Lean Supply Chain" was initiated by the Japanese business method. The term "lean supply" implies the use of lean production that aims to eliminate waste and enhance customer value with the continuous improvement of manufacturing system, prac-tices and techniques (Ugochukwu 2012). This gained popularity in manufacturing companies. However, to create a successful Lean Supply Chain, companies must adopt "leanness" through their entire business structure, resulting in the integration of lean concepts within every node, such as suppliers, focal organisations, distributors and cus-tomers (Ugochukwu, *ibid*). A lean supply chain was recognised by companies to have many benefits (Li et al. 2006; Gereffi 1999b) includ-ing improved quality, reduced cost, improved delivery, high flexibility and reduced shortage. It was further distinguished by having the follow-ing competitive advantage attributes: long-term relations with suppliers, effective communication and information sharing, integrated supply chain members, continuous improvements and predictability. However, although lean supply chains reduce inventory costs, they are susceptible to shocks such as natural disasters or global pandemics (Bullington 2005).

The second distinctive strategy is known as "Agile Supply Chain". With globalisation giving birth to an era of a time-based competition as customers insist on shorter delivery times, it became critical for supply chains to be flexible and synchronise to meet peaks and troughs of demand (Mansor et al. 2011). Agility requires a business-wide integra-tion of flexibility in all nodes of the supply chain's organisational structures, information systems, logistics processes and manufacturing. Having an agile supply chain with flexible manufacturing systems has its disadvantages. For agile management to ensure flexibility and customer satisfaction, the customer must be clear about the expected project output, otherwise a risk arises in the output of manufacturing (Mansor *et al., ibid*). For agility to succeed it requires adaptability to the changing market environment, both time consuming and expensive, contradicting the low cost and lead time requirements of customers (Macheridis 2014). This has resulted in the creation of a Leagile concept that combines the strength of Lean and Agile as it improves on their weaknesses. Leagile supply chain strategy combines Lean and Agile with the use of decoupling point, which uses an agile strategy to respond to a volatile demand downstream yet uses a lean strategy to provide high-level scheduling upstream from the marketplace. This makes Leagile the perfect system for supply chains to adopt in order to survive in any market.

Globalisation has created some challenges for supply chains such as de-centralised management, outsourcing of raw materials, manufacturing and jobs to countries such as China and India (Gereffi 1999b). This has redirected companies' energy to research and develop new information technologies, such as radio frequency identification (RFID) and tools that enable enterprise integration and collaboration to enable them to gain competitive advantage (Hayes 2001). Furthermore, globalisation has increased competition in consumer pricing, supplier contact and negotiations, adding further strain on the economic forces within and between companies' supply chains. Risk management has become key, as demand volatility makes supply chains more complex and leads companies to further explore product life-cycle management, planned obsolescence, post-sale service and reverse logistics in the case of product recovery, all of which contribute to the changing environment that awaits the future of supply chains (Chandak et al. 2014).

Forecasting Supply Chains and Logistics

Technology continues to move at a fast pace, with communication capabilities made extremely easy, and has re-shaped the way information sharing is perceived. This technological advance provides tremendous value in addressing supply chain and logistics issues such as warehousing, distribution, transportation and manufacturing logistics (Lummus and Vokurka 1999). Supply chains and logistics planning are based on distribution models simulated by software. Today interactive software tools have become crucial for systematic, strategic and tactical coordination of logistics functions within a company and across its suppliers for the purpose of improving the long term performance of the business and its supply chain as a whole (Tan et al. 1998). Moreover, the technology of 3D printing has challenged manufacturing systems as it is cost-effective, efficient and environmentally friendly. The use of 3D printing for manufacturing in many locations can be low cost and very beneficial for a global logistics network (Kaltenbrunner 2014), while businesses need to station local manufacturing centres increasingly closer to strategic markets to reduce the length of the supply chain and transportation costs and help towards a reduced carbon footprint (Pearce et al. 2010). In a world of next-day delivery where consumers want products fast, 3D printing helps tackle inventory concerns, especially for industrial spare parts as regional manufacturing can easily implement leanness. 3D printing technology will enable manufacturers to readily produce goods to order, helping save money and minimise waste (Jalwan and Israel 2014). It also helps the implementation of agile systems, to reflect constant changes in consumer taste. 3D printing is a tool for selling highly customised products in the tightest lead-times.

However, there are many new branches of supply chain that are being addressed (e.g. agricultural, medical, humanitarian) each of which has become a focal point in expanding modelling systems beyond traditional boundaries (Lummus and Vokurka 1999). The expansion brought by globalisation has in turn created confusion as to how a supply chain can be initiated within a company to incorporate a suitable business structure for its market and commodities that can expand in future (Johnson 2006). With the volatility of the global integrated market, supply chains face several issues in the future including cost adaptation to the market and visibility with the rapid increase in information. Additionally, there are issues in risk management as well as customer intimacy, where despite the drive towards demand, companies prefer to create better connections with their suppliers than with their customers (IBM 2009).

Initiating Supply Chains

Supply chain management has emerged as one of the major areas for companies to gain a competitive edge. Managing supply chains effectively is a complex and challenging task, encompassing the end-to-end flow of information, products and money (La Londe and Masters 1994). The effects of globalisation have resulted in trends of expanding product variety, short product life cycle, increasing outsourcing and continuous advances in information technology with the support of the internet. With it, companies in a supply chain can be connected in real time with information and knowledge shared continuously (Garcı´a-Dastugue and Lambert 2003). New products and services can be designed to fit special market segments, increasing needs and opportunities to develop supply chain management to serve customers' new-found requirements (Mentzer et al. 2001). The pressures a company's supply chain faces are excessive inventory, outsourced customer service, escalating costs and declining profits. Ability to cope with challenges and opportunities in new markets strongly affects an organisation's competitiveness in such areas as product cost, working capital requirements, speed to market and service perception (Cavinato 1992). For that reason, proper alignment of the supply chain with business strategy is essential to ensure a high level of business performance. In order to achieve a successful alignment, the right supply chain strategy to implement depends on a number of factors (Lee 2002):

- The strategy needs to be tailored to meet specific needs of the customers.
- A product with a stable demand and a reliable source of supply should not be managed in the same way as one with a highly unpredictable demand and an unreliable source of supply.
- The Internet can be a powerful tool for supporting or enabling supply chain strategies for products with different demand and supply uncertainties. Software modelling is the new tool to support supply chain strategies based on a "one-size-fits-all" as they can be programmed to be tailored to fit the needs of the company as it has all the options required for a firm to choose from.

According to Lee (2002), there are two key uncertainties, product demand and product supply. The "uncertainty framework" was further expanded by Fisher (1997), to introduce supply chain strategies to the right level of demand uncertainties of the product. This is achieved by linking the demand uncertainty to the predictability of the product demand. Fisher (*ibid*) divided product demand into three types. First, functional products that have long product life cycle and therefore stable demand, such as household consumable items, basic foods, oil and gas and basic clothing. Secondly, innovative products (Britoa et al. 2008) with short life cycles resulting in highly unpredictable demand, such as the fashion industry. Other examples of high-end products are computers and specialised sports equipment. Lastly, innovative functional products, which are a combination of necessary daily products that require innovation, for example mass-customised goods such as the automobile industry.

Supply Chain Characteristics

An organisation's supply chain strategy is shaped by four main elements (Fig. 2.2). The industry framework (the marketplace); the organisation's unique value proposal (its competitive positioning); internal processes (supply chain processes); and managerial focus (the linkage among supply chain processes and business strategy) (Porter 1980).

With these product categories in mind, a company must consider the four elements of supply chain strategy before achieving a successful alignment. According to Porter (1991), the reason why firms succeed or fail is the central question in strategy. Supply chain strategy defines the connection and combination of activities and functions throughout the value chain. In order to fulfil business value, operational efficiency is needed to achieve excellence in activities and functions to satisfy the customers across the marketplace.

Industry framework refers to the interaction of suppliers, customers, technological developments and economic factors that affect competition in any marketplace (Porter 1991). The main drivers affecting the

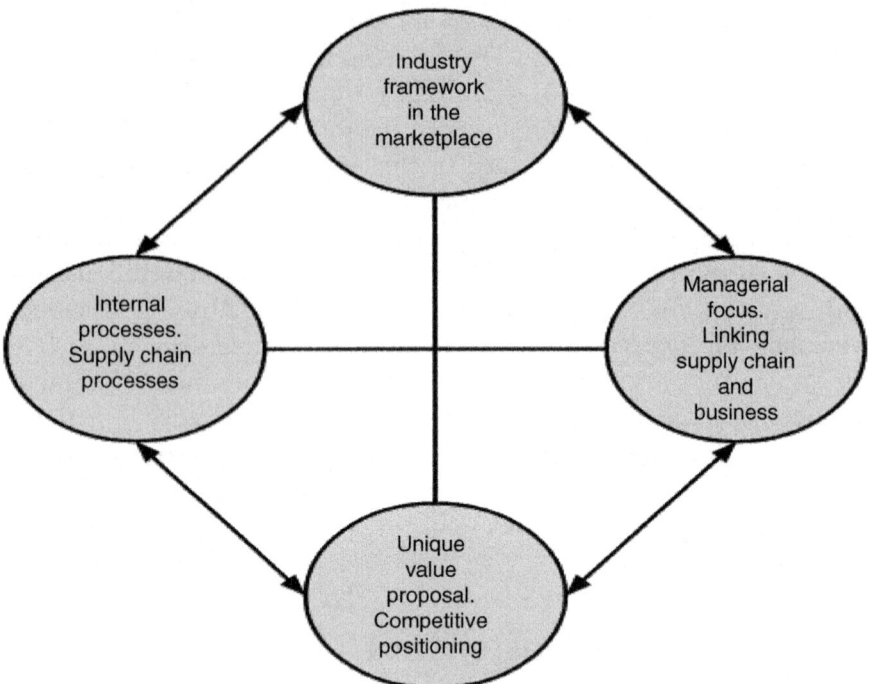

Fig. 2.2   Four elements of supply chain functions (adapted from Porter 1980)

industry's supply chain design are: demand variation, market mediation costs associated with the imbalance of demand and supply and product lifecycle, which is continually getting shorter in response to the speed of change in technology, fashion and obsolescence (Britoa et al. 2008). All of these push companies to increase the speed of product development and responsiveness to unexpected demand.

Unique value proposal requires the business to clearly understand its supply chain's competitive position (Li et al. 2006). For example, recognising the main product features and service will help a company determine if it is competing with a functional, innovative or innovative functional product (Porter 1980).

Managerial focus links supply chain process and business strategy by ensuring coherence between supply chain execution and a business's unique value proposal. This approach encourages companies to focus

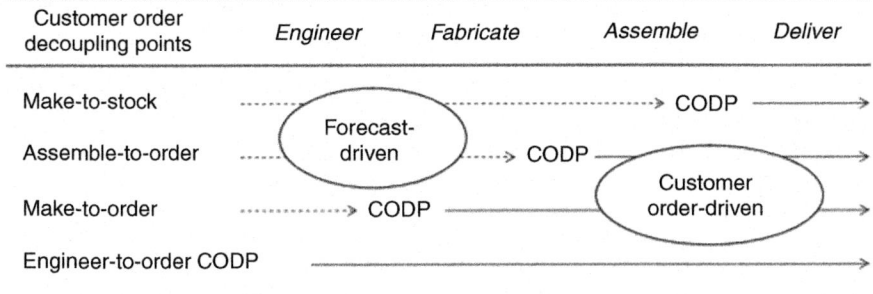

Fig. 2.3 Customer order decoupling points (adapted from Olhager 2011)

on seeking local efficiencies such as identifying cost-effectiveness with in-house manufacturing, distribution and identifying the process that can be cost-effective by outsourcing (Ketchen and Hult 2007).

Internal processes provide connection and integration within the supply chain activities that fall under the categories of source, make and deliver. The most important element in the internal process according to Olhager (2011) is the location of the decoupling point linked to the material flow where the product is tied to a specific customer order, the basic choices being make-to-stock, assemble-to-order, make-to-order and engineer-to order. Each material flow requires a different position for the decoupling point (Fig. 2.3). The decoupling point divides the operations stages that are forecast-driven (upstream) from those that are customer order-driven (downstream). The decoupling point is also the last point at which inventory is held, and should be located at the end of the transformation process or at least, at the output point for the most relevant manufacturing asset in terms of cost (Christopher and Gattorna 2005). Prior to the decoupling point is a "push" system, leading the production cycle to be long in order to increase production efficiency. After the decoupling point is a "pull" system, where the chain is driven by demand and is therefore highly variable, and the production cycle tends to be shorter in order to reduce the order cycle time and increase customers' positive perception of service (Christopher et al. 2006). When the decoupling point is located farthest from the customer's end of the supply chain, product customisation increases, while when the decoupling point is located towards the customer's end, product customisation diminishes, such as the make-to-order and engineer-to-order (Olhager 2011). Therefore, the demand buffering should be supported by excess capacity.

In addition, Novack and Simco (1991) state that collaborative relationships with customers become more useful as they help to reduce demand uncertainty. Consequently, the minimum size of the order does not depend on the size of the manufacturing batch, and minimum order size is governed by the relevance of transportation cost to the total cost. Identifying the decoupling point is of utmost importance to the selection of the best suited supply chain strategy. The location of the pull and push system will determine if a company will implement a lean, agile or Leagile strategy (Christopher and Gattorna 2005).

Although each of these four elements includes multiple factors, some are relevant drivers for the formulation of a supply chain strategy matrix model to help companies identify the best strategy for their marketplace. The aim of the matrix is to create a multi-dimensional matrix (MDM) that can account for the four main elements to help a company shape its own supply chain and tailor it to its specific needs with regard to uncertainty in the marketplace. In addition, it aims to help companies mitigate the four issues of globalisation (cost, visibility, risk and customer intimacy).

Definition of Supply Chains

Cagliano et al. (2004) expressed the need for a unified definition of supply chain strategy that extends to manufacturing and operations strategy in upstream management. Supply strategies are generally defined on the basis of either supplier selection criteria or integration mechanisms, although various studies consider supplier selection criteria as the link between competitive strategies and aligning the supply chain with the firm's objectives. Companies are increasingly attempting competitive success through integration of internal business processes and strategic alignment of internal functions but also through the integration and alignment of inter-company processes. According to Mentzer et al. (2001) the evolution of the supply chain resulted in the creation of many definitions which complicated the selection of the most relevant strategy. The difficulty firms faced in defining their supply chain resulted in misinterpretation of what their business requires in order to compete in the marketplace. The overlaps between each time frame of supply chain evolution created a diverse range of definitions. The lack of a single interpretation created the need to adopt one unified definition which would add sophistication to research and practice. Appendix 1 outlines the most significant definition of supply chains and logistics and allocates them into "Eras". The use of the term "Era" is to allow flexibility of overlap in time and to help identify each evolution period to which they relate.

Appendix 1 also shows how different institutes, centres and councils were created throughout the supply chain evolution. The NCPDM was formed in 1963 while the Georgia Tech Production and Distribution Research Centre, and the Computational Optimisation Centre were initiated in the 1970s. The CLM emerged in 1985 with the commercialisation of personalised computers, globalisation and technology, to cater for the fast development in supply chain and logistics management (Mentzer et al. 2001). Furthermore, the recognition of the importance of supply chains and their relation to business strategy is reflected by the CLM as it changed its name to the Council of Supply Chain Management Professionals (CSCMP) in 2005. This resulted in a surge of research including Fisher (1997) who introduced the concept of supply chain segmentation that caused several academics and consultants, including Lee (2002), Christopher and Gattorna (2005) and Ketchen and Hult (2007) to propose several models regarding the formulation of supply chain strategy.

Large firms also developed a keen interest and took advantage of emerging innovation in business strategy to develop their own unique supply chain systems. For example, Motorola's pursuit to achieve Six Sigma performance since 1986 has led to the company achieving its very own efficient performance metric to drive improvement, innovation and optimisation which later developed into a software "Digital Six Sigma" to cater for technological development (Supply Chain Digital 2011). Another example is the Toyota Production System (TPS) developing out of necessity in response to the market. Between 1936 and 1956 management at TPS worked to formulate a sophisticated supply chain and logistics system by developing the Seven Wastes, Standardisation, kaizen-5S continuous improvement, quality control error proofing and Kanban system, to create a responsive chain that can tap into various markets (Sugimori et al. 1977).

During the 1990s, many third party suppliers such as manufacturers of spare parts and service providers, realised the fierce competition facing them in winning projects from large firms and formed an alliance with their own suppliers to upgrade their management functions to share information in order to gain a competitive advantage over other supply chains (Lambert and Cooper 2000). Meanwhile, rivalry in the marketplace changed dramatically from completion of "firm versus firm", to battles of "supply chain versus supply chain". Within this context, value supply chains are emerging as a means to create competitive advantages and superior performance (Li et al. 2006). Traditional supply chains often focus primarily on one key outcome such as speed or cost; therefore integration was required to merge the best attributes of both the traditional and value supply chains to cover an array of uniquely integrated priorities such as cost, quality, speed, customer intimacy and flexibility (Ketchen and Hult 2007).

With increasing competition, companies that are unable to define supply chain strategy tend to be at a disadvantage. To do this it is important to select a suitable definition for supply chains and logistics where the latter is used to refer to strategic issues, while the former refers to tactical and operational issues such as high due date reliability, short delivery times, low inventory level and high capacity utilisation, which in turn can be divided into two segments (Mangan et al. 2008):

1. Inbound logistics which is one of the primary processes concentrating on purchasing and arranging inbound movement of materials, parts and/or finished inventory from suppliers to manufacturing or assembly plants, warehouses or retail stores.
2. Outbound logistics which is the process related to the storage and movement of the final product and the related information flows from the end of the production line to the end user.

The CSCMP definitions are highly relevant and adaptable: logistics is part of the supply chain process that plans, implements and controls the efficient, effective forward and reverse flow, storage of goods, services and related information between the point of origin and the point of consumption in order to meet customers' requirements, while supply chain management is the systemic, strategic coordination of the traditional business functions and the tactics across these business functions within a particular company and across businesses within the supply chain for the purposes of improving the long-term performance of the individual companies and the supply chain as a whole (Georgia Tech Supply Chain and Logistics Institute 2010).

The Problem Statement

The issue facing many firms is the distinction of which supply chain model to incorporate within their business strategy. This is due to the many models and definitions developed over the years obscuring the key elements that companies need to identify the strategy that best suits their supply chain to help it overcome the challenges it faces in the marketplace. Assembling a sample of definitions and allocating them into Eras can help the development of an MDM for business that aims to diagnose and tailor strategies. The term MDM is chosen due to the variety of dimensions needed in creating the model, for example the supply chain's four elements (industry framework, unique value proposal, managerial focus and internal processes). In addition, the strategies lean, agile and Leagile form a series of dimensions that should be considered. We will go on to select the most relevant supply chain elements and strategy in order to build an MDM capable of mitigating the challenges of globalisation (cost, visibility, risk and customer intimacy). The increase in technological progress will require the MDM model to adapt to ever-increasing automation through creating an interactive tool that can be accessed on a website and developed as software, enabling companies to upgrade it for continuous progress in diagnosing the alignment of their supply chain strategy with the market. Allocating each development into an era will help examine the supply chain models that have been created and establish a conceptual framework to build the MDM on the basis of the collective models as they have developed through time.

According to Cagliano et al. (2004), supply chain research reflects a lack of multiple dimension supply strategies which could provide a more complete picture of the options available to managers for shaping the supply strategy in different contexts and help to align them with companies' goals. This will be addressed by collecting data through expert opinion and combining statistical analysis with deductive reasoning to establish the various suitable strategies that can be incorporated into the MDM, in addition to providing options that companies can favour to create their tailored approach. The MDM model can then be tested for its interactive capability with an established firm to investigate its applicability and suitability.

References

Britoa, M., Carboneb, A., & Blanquartd, C. (2008). Towards a sustainable fashion retail supply chain in Europe: Organisation and performance. *International Journal of Production Economics, 114*(1), 534–553.

Bullington, K. (2005). Lean supply strategies: Applying 5S tools to supply chain management. *International Supply Management, 90*(1), 1–5.

Cagliano, R., Caniato, F., & Spina, G. (2004). Lean, Agile and traditional supply: How do they impact manufacturing performance? *Journal of Purchasing and Supply Management, 10*(4), 151–164.

Cavinato, J. (1992). A total cost/value model for supply chain competitiveness. *Journal of Business Logistics, 13*(2), 285–301.

Chandak, S., Chandak, A., & Sharma, A. (2014). Globalisation of supply chain management for an automotive industry-future perspective. *International Review of Applied Engineering Research, 4*(2), 155–164.

Chen, K., & Ji, P. (2007). A mixed integer programming model for advanced planning and scheduling (APS). *European Journal of Operational Research, 181*(5), 515–522.

Christopher, M. G., & Gattorna, J. (2005). Supply chain cost management and value-based pricing. *Industrial Marketing Management, 34*(2), 115–121.

Christopher, M. G., Peck, H., & Towill, D. R. (2006). A taxonomy for selecting global supply chain strategies. *The International Journal of Logistic Management, 17*(2), 277–287.

Cooper, M. C., Douglas, M. L., & Janus, D. P. (1997). Supply chain management: More than a new name for logistics. *The International Journal of Logistics Management, 8*(1), 1–14.

Fisher, M. (1997). What is the right supply chain for your product?. *Harvard Business Review, 1*(3), 105–116.

Garcı́a-Dastugue, S., & Lambert, D. (2003). Internet-enabled coordination in the supply chain. *Industrial Marketing Management, 32*(3), 251–263.

Georgia Tech Supply Chain and Logistics Institute. (2010). The evolution of the supply chain and logistics. http://www.scl.gatech.edu/scl-evolution.php.

Gereffi, G. (1999b). International trade and industrial upgrading in the apparel commodity chain. *Journal of International Economics, 48*(1), 37–70.

Harland, C. M., & Lamming, R. C. (1999). Developing the concept of supply strategy. *International Journal of Operations and Production Management, 19*(7), 650–673.

Hayes, D. (2001). Market reaction to ERP implementation announcement. *Journal of Information Systems, 15*(1), 3–18.

IBM. (2009). The smarter supply chain of the future. *Global Chief Supply Chain Officer Study, 1*(1), 2–50.

Jalwan, H., & Israel, G. (2014). 3D printing your supply chain. *Transportation and Logistics, 1*(1), 10–40.

Johnson, M. (2006). Supply chain management: Technology, globalization and policy at a crossroads. *Interfaces, 36*(3), 191–193.

Kaltenbrunner, H. (2014). How 3D printing is set to shake up manufacturing supply chains. http://www.theguardian.com/sustainable-business/2014/nov/25/how-3d-printing-is-set-to-shake-up-manufacturing-supply-chains.

Ketchen, D., & Hult, T. (2007). Bridging organization theory and supply chain management: The case of best value supply chains. *Journal of Operations Management, 25*(7), 573–580.

Kim, D., & Kogut, B. (1996). Technological platforms and diversification. *Institute for Operations Research and Management Sciences, 7*(3), 283–301.

La Londe, B. J., & Masters, J. M. (1994). Emerging logistics strategies: Blueprints for the next century. *International Journal for Physical Distribution and Logistics Management, 24*(7), 35–47.

Lambert, D. M., & Cooper, M. (2000). Issues in supply chain management. *Industrial Marketing Management, 29*(1), 65–83.

Lambert, D. M., Stock, J. R., & Ellram, L. M. (1998). *Fundamentals of logistics management*. London: Irwin/McGraw-Hill. 9–328.

Lee, H. L. (2002). Aligning supply chain strategies with product uncertainties. *California Management Review, 44*(3), 105–119.

Lee, Y., Jeong, C., & Moon, C. (2002). Advanced planning and scheduling with outsourcing in manufacturing supply chain. *Computer and Industrial Engineering, 43*(3), 351–374.

Li, S., Nathan, B., Nathan, T., & Rao, S. (2006). The impact of supply chain management practices on competitive advantage and organizational performance. *The International Journal of Management Science, 34*(4), 107–124.

Lummus, R., & Vokurka, R. (1999). Defining supply chain management: A historical perspective and practical guidelines. *Industrial Management and Data Systems, 99*(1), 11–17.

Macheridis, N. (2014). Managing projects: A template for an agile approach. *Lund Institute of Economics Research, 2*(1), 6–14.

Mangan, J., Lalwani, C., & Butcher, T. (2008). *Global logistics and supply chain management*. Chichester: John Wiley and Sons Ltd. 57–335.

Mansor, Z., Yahya, S., & Arshad, N. (2011). Towards the development of success determinants charter for agile development methodology. *International Journal of Information Technology and Engineering, 2*(1), 1–7.

Mentzer, J. T., DeWitt, W., Keebler, J., Min, S., Nix, N., Smith, C., & Zacharia, Z. (2001). Defining supply chain management. *Journal of Business Logistics, 22*(2), 1–25.

Novack, R.A., & Simco, S.W. (1991). The industrial procurement process: A supply chain perspective. *Journal of Business Logistics, 12*(1), 145–167.

Olhager, J. (2011). *Contributions to management science: The role of decoupling points in value chain management*. Linkoping, Sweden: Physica-Verlag HD. 37–47.

Pearce, J. M., Blair, C., Laciak, K., Andrews, R., Nosrat, A., & Zelenika-Zovko, I. (2010). 3-D printing of open source appropriate technologies for self-directed sustainable development. *Journal of Sustainable Development, 3*(4), 17–29.

Porter, M. (1980). *Competitive strategy techniques for analysing industries and competitors*. New York: Simon and Schuster Inc. 5–340.

Porter, M. (1991). Towards a dynamic theory of strategy. *Strategic Management Journal, 12*(2), 95–117.

Sugimori, Y., Kusunoki, K., Cho, F., & Uchikawa, S. (1977). Toyota production system and Kanban system materialization of just-in-time and respect-for human system. *International Journal of Production Research, 15*(6), 553–564.

Supply Chain Digital. (2011). *Motorola's Six Sigma Journey: In pursuit of perfection.* http://www.supplychaindigital.com/procurement/2068/ Motorolas-Six-Sigma-Journey:-In-pursuit-of-perfection.

Tan, K. C. (2001). A framework of supply chain management literature. *European Journal of Purchasing and Supply Management, 7*(2), 39–48.

Tan, K. C., Kannan, V., & Handfield, R. (1998). Supply chain management: Supplier performance and firm performance. *International Journal of Purchasing and Materials Management, 34*(3), 2–9.

Ugochukwu, P. (2012). Lean in the supply chain: Research and practice. *Quality Technology and Management, 1*(1), 1–60.

3

A Theoretical and Conceptual Framework for Strategic Supply Chains

This chapter will present a theoretical and conceptual framework for supply chains and potential solutions to the problems that are identified. Both frameworks are based on the identification of key concepts, and the relationships among them will be seen to have emerged from the historical review of supply chain eras which follows. The theoretical framework will commence by creating a historical timeline where supply chain developments are allocated into "Eras" to mark the evolution of the concept. This will ease the categorisation of developed theories and aid the investigation of why supply chain models were created and how they can be integrated to form a conceptual framework that will mitigate the difficulty for firms in diagnosing the most suitable strategy for their marketplace.

The conceptual framework embodies the direction which analysing these chains will take, describing the relationship between specific variables identified in the study. It also outlines the inputs, processes and outputs for the investigation of supply chains; hence it plays a key role in mapping the research paradigm (Imenda 2014).

The developments of supply chains though the first five eras of evolution will be integrated with the concepts and variables found in

© The Author(s) 2017

S. Sindi, M. Roe, *Strategic Supply Chain Management*,
DOI 10.1007/978-3-319-54843-2_3

the last two eras in order to create a preliminary design of the multi-dimensional matrix (MDM) model. The conceptual framework will map the path selecting the most relevant methods in order for the final model to be put forward in the analysis and its applicability to be tested with a well-established firm.

Era One: Creation (1940s–1980s)

This section will look at the emergence of the supply chain discipline and the breakthrough in understanding how industrial company success depends on the interactions between the flows of information, materials, money, manpower and capital equipment (Forrester 1958). Theories were initiated for distribution management that integrated system dynamics with organisational relationships to maximise performance, product development, engineering, sales, promotion and marketing.

Since World War II, trade agreements have been established to bring countries together. In 1946 governments took measures to eliminate trade barriers to free the movement of finance through international agreements such as the General Agreement on Tariffs and Trade (GATT) (Crowley 2003). In 1982 the International Maritime Organisation (IMO) continued to produce new and updated procedures across a variety of maritime issues as well as focusing on sustainability such as emissions from ships and the Safety of Life at Sea (SOLAS) treaty, which covers maritime security.

From the 1950s to 1960, manufacturing emphasised mass production in order to reduce the cost of unit production as there was little flexibility in operations strategy. Manufacturing relied exclusively on in-house technology and capacity, which resulted in slow new product development (Shukla et al. 2011). In the 1960s, the terms "warehousing" and "materials handling" were commonly used to describe many logistics efforts. However, the increasing shift to freight transportation by truck rather than rail, led to the development of the logistic term, "physical distribution" to join "warehousing", "material handling" and "freight transportation", which came under the NCPDM formed in 1963 (Lambert and Cooper 2000). The start of mass customisation by manufacturers initiated material requirement planning (MRP) in 1970, due to inventory management requiring large investments in areas such as "Work In Process" (WIP), crucial for cost reduction, quality, product development and delivery lead-time. The MRP and WIP aided mass customisation by information sharing between companies, its consumers and suppliers in order to reduce inventory costs (Croom et al. 2000). However, sharing technology, information and expertise with customers or suppliers was considered risky, thus little emphasis was placed on cooperative and strategic buyer-supplier partnerships (Tan 2001).

Academic research followed growing industry recognition, especially with regards to the computer revolution in the early 1970s. This in turn marked the beginning of supply chain globalisation to be discussed in Era three. In the 1980s logistics was recognised as being very expensive, important and complex (Forrester 1958). Company executives realised that opportunity came if they significantly improved logistics, investing in trained professionals and new technology. This was also noted in 1985 by the NCPDM when it integrated the various evolving aspects of supply chains, such as services, information flows, in-bound, outbound and reverse flows of products that led it to change its name to the Council of Logistics Management (CLM) (Georgia Tech Supply Chain and Logistics Institute 2010).

Implementation and Coordination Mechanisms

The supply chain is not only a single business-to-business chain but rather multiple integrated relationships, such as marketing networks. This means it cannot be left to one department alone but needs to be incorporated in each element of the business framework (Forrester 1958). To reduce further complications in a business, CLM divided and integrated logistic processes throughout the management of key business processes within the supply chain. In 1982, the management of multiple relationships across the supply chain was referred to as Supply Chain Management (SCM) (Persson 1997). The emergence of supply chains was due to the recession of the late 1980s and early 1990s;

this gave industrial managers the opportunity to improve supply chain models and cost reduction processes at business strategic level (Chiu and Lin 2004). The complexity of managing all the products and suppliers back to the point of origin requires SCM and logistics to operate as independent yet interlinked sectors. Firms are required to establish a department designated to the coordination of suppliers and another logistics department that coordinates the intra and inter-logistic movement of goods (Forrester 1958). This led in 1998 to CLM redefining logistics, categorising it as part of SCM: "Logistics is that part of supply chain process that plans, implements and controls the efficient, effective flow and storage of goods, services and related information from the point of origin to the point of consumption in order to meet customers' requirements" (Lambert and Cooper 2000). The rise of technological planning created a globalised market that changed the nature of competition from "business vs. business" to "supply chain vs. supply chain". The survival of a supply chain rested upon its value and management which is reflected in how a firm can use its supply chains as a strategic weapon to gain advantages over its peers. This allowed the traditional supply chain concept to incorporate "value-added" into the traditional concept of "cost reduction" and integrate customer fulfilment throughout the organisational process (Harland and Lamming 1999). This resulted in the traditional concept of supply chain, including warehousing, material handling and freight transportation being expanded to include technological developments such as MRP and WIP in addition to value added enabling it to cope with the marketplace. Hence the traditional supply chain gained a basic array of uniquely integrated priorities in addition to its cost reduction such as quality, speed, customer intimacy and flexibility (Ketchen and Hult 2007).

In 1997, the popularity of this traditional basic supply chain concept was noted at the Annual Conference of the CLM as 22% of the sessions contained the term (Christopher 1992). Due to its increasing popularity in recent years, several other definitions and models have arisen. Christopher (*ibid*) summarises supply chains as multiple firms, both upstream (i.e. supply) and downstream (i.e. distribution) and their integration of different processes and values in the form of products and services, that can be delivered efficiently to the end consumer. Meanwhile, other definitions were established, such as La Londe and Masters (1994) who defined supply chains as a set of firms that pass materials forward (i.e. upstream). Lambert et al. (1998), stated that supply chains include the alignment of firms that bring services or products to the market and finally to the consumer (i.e. downstream). From these definitions it is clear that technological progress is further leading the traditional basic supply chain to evolve into a new era of integration in order to link different processes that meet the new demands of consumers, in addition to the need for an alignment between the business framework and supply chain strategy to ensure optimal performance (Kim and Kogut 1996). The need to align SCM strategies is to increase the competitive advantage of companies with a strategic plan of purchasing, providing benefits to the overall network performance of the company (Cagliano et al. 2004).

Era Two: Integration (1970–2000)

In the movement from Era one to Era two, successful supply chains required the management of cross-functional integration of key business processes within the firm and across the network of the firm (Lambert 2000). Supply chains have been defined by Lee and Billington (1995) as the integration of procurement, manufacturing and distribution. In order to optimise performance of the chain, Finch (2004) states that companies should add as much value as possible for the least cost possible. The challenge is to fully integrate external and internal processes in order to determine and achieve successful inter-network competition. In the quest to fully integrate external and internal processes upon the chain, Georgia Tech Institute aimed to understand the issues facing this challenge by better linking research, education and practice, hence Georgia Tech Research and Professional Education merged into The Logistics Institute in 1992 (Georgia Tech Supply Chain and Logistics Institute 2010). This marked an historic event in which integration capabilities and development became a crucial area for strategy. This led to the findings of the four base-line strategies which firms adopted in order to take a detailed approach to integrating supply chains with their business framework (Stevens 1989).

Stage one "Baseline": Companies designed a plan to be reactive for the very short term to counter the company's vulnerability due to the effects of change on the supply chain's demand patterns (Jayaram et al. 2010b). The supply chain responsibility is divided across nodes to form the baseline. These nodes carry the inventory responsibility to integrate and synchronise activities across the control system to manage information of sales, manufacturing, material control (raw material flow through to finished goods), production control and purchasing (Frohlich and Westbrook 2001).

Stage two "Functional Integration": This focuses on the inward flow of goods and combines time-phased planning with materials and manufacturing management, using MRP with the distribution network, hence allowing the demand to be aggregated and avoiding poor visibility of demand which leads to inadequate planning (Stevens 1989). This increase in visibility aims to reduce risk and cost by implementing buffers in the inventory for demand fluctuation. Focused on improving performance, plant utilisation will increase efficiency as well as reduce costs (Frohlich and Westbrook 2001). Functional integration between the nodes of the supply chain allows for a reactive approach towards customer service, that can be improved by acquiring internal integration of customer intimacy into its core culture (Jayaram et al. 2010b).

Stage three "Internal Integration": Focuses on the management of goods to the customer, by integrating customer intimacy directly into the supply chain. Internal integration is characterised by a comprehensive integrated planning and control system (Das et al. 2006). Typically companies in the third stage will use distribution resource planning (DRP) integrated with MRP for material management, as well as just in time (JIT) for manufacturing to ensure full integration of systems such as visibility from distribution through to purchasing, efficiency, synchronisation and full utilisation focused on tactical rather than strategic approaches to achieve cost effectiveness (Sugimori et al. 1977). Additionally, extensive use of electronic data interchange (EDI) to integrate customers with faster response, leading to a better reaction to customer demand rather than "managing" the customer (Kim and Kogut 1996).

Stage four "External Integration": By applying these four steps, companies will attain full integration by extending their scope outside the company to embrace suppliers and customers, moving away from being product to being customer-orientated, hence understanding the products, culture, market and organisation (Das et al. 2006). This ensures a change in the company's attitude by adhering to the customer's needs and requirements, creating a foundation by which the company can mitigate the issues of cost, visibility, risk and customer intimacy brought by globalisation (Kim and Kogut 1996).

Call for Integration

The four baseline stages taken by firms to establish integration were made possible by the technological tools that aided the alignment of the various nodes of the chain with the business framework. In the 1970s, MRP was a technological tool that integrated management with manufacturing in order to reduce the cost of new product development and reduce the lead-time of the WIP (Kim and Kogut 1996). The aim was to improve the outcome for customers by standardising transactions and transferring information in order to increase organisational efficiency based on integrating the marketing concept, the "4 P's" (Product, Price, Promotion and Place). Hence, integrating marketing with supply chain processes commenced, aiming to:

1. Identify the members of the marketing chain
2. Coordinate the marketing chain
3. Structure and illustrate the marketing chain process (Lambert 2000)

However, the contribution of the third party suppliers and manufacturers had not been accounted for as it was assumed that everyone within the business knew who was a member of the supply chain, as little effort was spent on identifying significant supply chain members with the key processes. This resulted in managers not knowing how to establish a successful alignment due to issues of visibility within the supply chain

(Jüttner et al. 2006). Therefore, the concept of relationship marketing was created to improve alignment. By allowing each node and member of the chain to focus on the business goal and establish communication with the customer side, this increases visibility and emphasises the downstream element in the supply chain (Webster 1992).

Technological progress aided marketing as in the 1980s integration was about vertically aligning operations with strategy through a form of centralisation in order to organise the different product components produced by each node/member of the supply chain (Schoenherr and Swink 2011). The aim of creating headquarter centres was to maximise consumer satisfaction by reducing the response time to demand. According to Frohlich and Westbrook (2001), this required coordination of information technologies to manage the flow of data, hence the development of an EDI system, which helped firms integrate their suppliers and customers to improve performance. There are four dimensions or arcs that are improved with the EDI integration: quality, delivery, flexibility and cost performance (Frohlich and Westbrook 2001).

In the 1990s the focus on alignment included horizontally integrating operations in order to sell products in a variety of markets as the world became more globalised. The proposed integration tactics aimed to coordinate the forward physical flow of activities that suppliers, manufacturers and customers have to undergo by the use of technological tools such as enterprise resource planning (ERP) systems (Chen and Ji 2007). The emergence of ERP was developed by upgrading MRP in the 1970s and 1980s in order to integrate multiple databases and synchronise scheduling and lead-times as it became essential to a company's survival (Hayes 2001). In spite of problems installing the ERP systems due to fears of computer networks handling the change into the new millennium, most large companies had acquired it. This change from MRP to ERP systems improved data availability, capacity and accuracy as it increased the recognition for better planning and integration among logistics components, leading to a new generation of "Advanced Planning and Scheduling" (APS) software. Companies such as Toyota improved their own production system by the initiation of JIT to enable delivery integration that aimed to maximise efficiency, fast product delivery and customisation in product development. The technological improvement of aligning their database to ensure their business operated with high responsiveness, leanness of delivering JIT and reduced waste and cost, resulted in the development of the Toyota Production System (TPS), which became fully integrated into their business framework in the late 1990s (Sugimori et al. 1977). The TPS with JIT was created to stress the importance of delivery integration in terms of implementing fast product delivery and customisation in product development.

Integration Capabilities

The new era of inter-network competition depended on a business's management ability to successfully integrate the company's complex network. By categorising which processes are critical and beneficial to the firm, these processes can be linked across firms and integrated within the firm's internal network (Jayaram et al. 2010b). Management has the ability to accommodate the synergy of intra and inter-company integration by dealing with process excellence in an innovative way to strengthen relationships between nodes such as customer and supplier relationship (Lambert 2000). For example, integration can further be increased if components of the supply chain are added to the operation level.

There are nine management components for a successful integration at the operation level: planning and control, work structure, organisation structure, product flow facility structure, information flow facility structure, management methods, power and leadership structure, risk and reward structure, culture and attitude (Lambert 2000). Das et al. (2006) explore the different mechanisms that are put in place by companies to achieve integration between customers and suppliers, operational integration and technological integration. The former refers to the integration of operational activities such as planning, production, delivery and quality. The latter refers to collaboration techniques aimed at obtaining information sharing or joint decision-making, rather than on the redesign of internal operations (Das et al. 2006). Examples of these techniques are JIT and vendor managed inventory (VMI) that help early supplier involvement and rapid prototyping in designing and developing new products (Cagliano, Caniato and Spina 2004). Furthermore, there is forward physical flow integration requiring a closer relationship between the production systems, customer and the supplier. Additionally there is coordinate integration of backward information and data flows from customers to suppliers. This is a mechanism aimed at leveraging information from counterparts to improve internal activities and operations management (Cagliano, *ibid*). Identifying and integrating the key processes is a key element in achieving alignment between the firm's supply chain and its business strategy. Lambert and Cooper (2000) as well as Ketchen and Hult (2007) stress that with integration, businesses compete as supply chains rather than individual entities, hence firms ensure that every output is specifically tailored to add value to the chain. Therefore, firms face a fundamental decision to select their best-suited suppliers, to ensure coherence and alignment between competitive strategy and functional strategies (Jüttner, Godsell and Christopher 2006).

The adoption of supplier selection criteria has a positive impact on manufacturing performance. There are several categories of supplier selection criteria stated by Cagliano et al. (2004), which align manufacturing performance and competitive priorities. These are cost, quality, delivery and flexibility. In establishing visibility and alignment across the processes, firms must ascertain their business structure by identifying the complexity of their product, availability of raw materials and the suppliers available (Das et al. 2006). They must also identify their supplier members and categorise them into primary and supporting members. A firm can act as primary or as a supporting member to different companies, as a supply chain incorporates all nodes that are linked with an organisation directly or indirectly to establish a flow that connects suppliers and customers from point of origin to point of consumption (Lambert 2000). Primary members are the strategic companies who conduct operational or managerial value-adding activities in order to produce a specific design or product for a certain consumer or market. Supporting members provide resources, knowledge, utilities and assets. A firm must ascertain the dimension of its integration, whether it is horizontal or vertical (Lambert 2000). Added value to the supply chain is achieved when a firm selects the relevant process. However, integrating all processes can be counterproductive if not impossible.

To help companies group their supply chain, Lambert and Cooper (2000), devised a framework with three categories (Fig. 3.1). Firstly, the "Supply Chain Network Structure" consists of the key primary businesses which are external but are crucial to the company's product development. At this level the company identifies its key supplier members, their ability to acquire raw materials and the complexity of

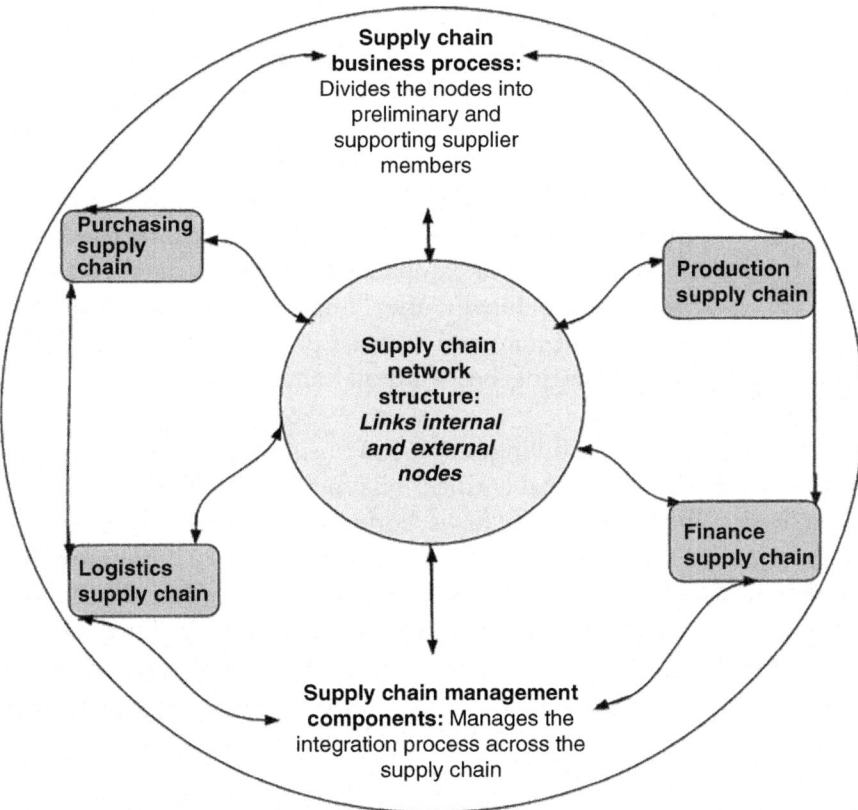

Fig. 3.1 Integrating key decision processes (adapted from Lambert and Cooper 2000)

designing the product. The management responsibility is to divide the supplier members and the task into primary and supporting teams. It is crucial at this stage to establish long-term relationships with supplier members as strong foundations add value to the chain as it mitigates any damage that may be caused by demand volatility (Lambert and Cooper 2000). Secondly, the "Supply Chain Business Process" is referred to as the activities of the primary members to produce specific outputs that add value to the consumer. Integrating customer value can come in the form of services such as warranties for the product or high customer service. Additionally, the company may also review its existing products and their potential in enhancing any features by adding value such as an additional complementary item to be included with the product (Ketchen and Hult 2007). At the "Supply Chain Business Process" level a company identifies which process is relevant to their unique skills and that of their supplier members as these processes will be added to the chain to increase its value to be used as a competitive advantage. This gains the product a unique selling point (USP); for example in highly specialised technical organisations, internal processes are integrated into their framework to be used as a competitive advantage as it is hard to replicate (Webster 1992). Finally the "Supply Chain Management Component" aims to integrate and manage processes across the entire supply chain, thus managing both internal and external supply chain networks.

According to Lee and Billington (1995) businesses compete as supply chains rather than individual entities. The focus in integration has been on activities and information flows both within and across company boundaries in order to foster superior performance. By adapting Lambert and Cooper's frameworks (Lambert and Cooper 2000), the "Supply Chain Network Structure" is further examined to illustrate how each supplier member of the chain acquires their own supply chain in order to offer the best possible service with the lowest cost and highest value, hence illustrating how companies evolved to compete as supply chains. Finch (2004) states that optimising performance adds value to the chain as it ensures that process in every output is specifically tailored to add to the customer's value. To enable a competitive chain with integrated value, the "Supply Chain Network Structure" must be linked together via information flows that revolve around the requirements of the products produced. Figure 3.1 illustrates the levels of integration in the business process whereby entities are divided into preliminary and supporting suppliers and are each linked via information flows. Each entity has the mutual aim to serve the customer's needs while feeding information feedback as it undergoes product development to the "Supply Chain Network Structure", where the responsibility for commercialising the product lies, to ensure that it reaches the end-user. The "Supply Chain Network Structure" unites the internal and external nodes of the chains, which is referred to as integrating and managing the supply chain components (Lambert and Cooper 2000).

Competitive advantage can be enhanced by increasing information flow and developing efficient communication, for example for a company to produce a product efficiently, it will have several entities: integration of business processes, e.g. purchasing of raw materials, production, logistic delivery and a finance department. However, effective communication with these entities and their relevant supply chains must be achieved in order to develop a competitive product. For instance the "Supply Chain Business Process" divides "Purchasing" into a preliminary member while "Production" will be the supporting member. The purchasing entity includes an outsourcing chain of materials that requires consistent communication to ascertain inventory levels with the production entity which includes a chain of second and third party manufacturers. Similarly the logistics entity along with its chain of second and third party distribution centres maintains constant communication with the finance department to ensure the feasibility of the distribution strategy. The finance supply chain entity in some cases can outsource its audits, as firms seek cheaper labour. Figure 3.1 illustrates that the flow of information is constantly communicated with the "Supply Chain Network Structure" with the help of the "supply chain management component" that ensures information which is managed and sent to the relevant supply members, in addition to ensure full integration of processes across the chain.

To further illustrate the importance of sharing information between the nodes in a company, Lambert and Cooper (2000) devised a framework for integrating and managing business processes across the supply chain. The information flows between Tier 1 and Tier 2 suppliers, if applicable, through to manufacturing (which includes the logistics department, purchasing, research and development, finance, marketing and sales), to customers and finally to the end-user (Lambert and Cooper 2000). The manufacturing node indicates that information of product flow is shared between its surrounding nodes. However, there is no indication of information being shared within the inter-nodes. It is clear that the forward movement of product flow shares information with all the key functions across the business supply chain. However, there is uncertainty on how information is distributed within the manufacturing processes from "customer relationship management" to "returns management". The integration between the top intra and bottom inter functions is only superficial, as there is insufficient indication of information flows travelling between the external and the internal functions. Moreover, there is insufficient indication on how the internal supply chain decision making is processed, as authority is not defined with respect to it being a hierarchy process or a bottom-up approach.

Adapting Lambert and Cooper's (Lambert and Cooper 2000) model (Fig. 3.2), the manufacturing department can establish efficient and effective communication with its sectors by establishing a circular information flow network. Once a product has been agreed, it is given to the "Product Development and Commercialisation" sector, which analyses the feasibility of the product. Then to "Demand Management" which looks at the market needs and anticipates possible shifts in taste, while "Manufacturing Flow Management", integrates the supply chain of raw materials with manufacturing while anticipating shifts in consumer taste from the feedback given by "Demand Management". The product's production quantity is then given to the "Order Fulfilment" department which will identify the stock level needed, then inform the "Manufacturing Flow Management" of the right quantity to be manufactured. Next is establishing a strong long-term relationship with the supplier who helped produce the product. Creating strong foundations with suppliers adds value to the chain and increases its survival in a fluctuating market, as suppliers would likely help cost reduction in an economic

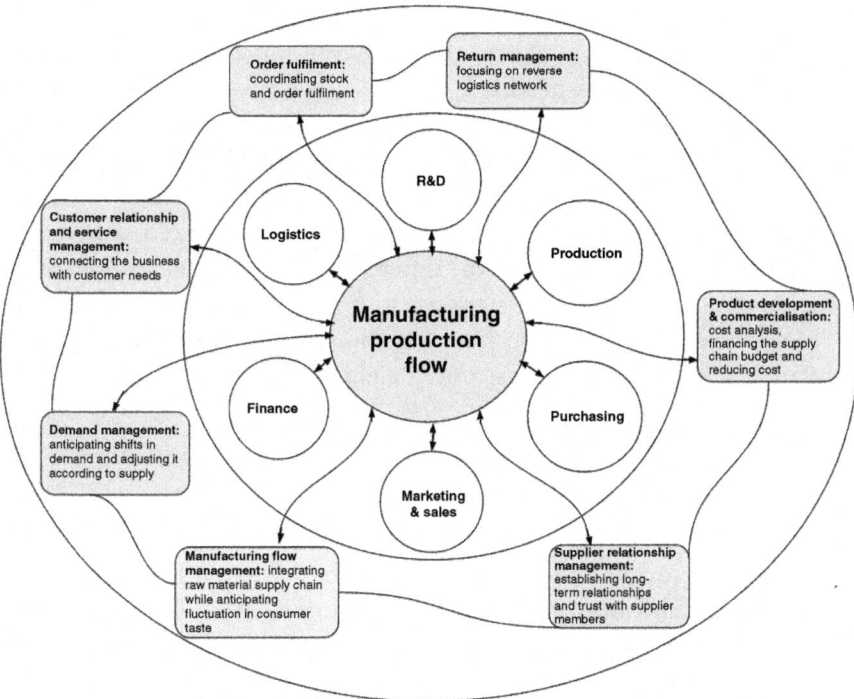

Fig. 3.2 Integrating business processes across the supply chain (adapted from Lambert and Cooper 2000)

downturn for long-term established partners. Creating a foundation with suppliers is achieved by sending information across the chain from manufacturing to Tier 1 and Tier 2 suppliers. Finally, "Customer Service Management" connects the business framework with customer needs to help further establish the product as a brand and to gain loyalty of consumers. During each department's process, the flow of communication with manufacturing remains constant; once the final stage of "Customer Service Management" is complete, "Product Development and Commercialisation" continues with commercialising the product while maintaining links with manufacturing. In the case of faults, the "Returns Management" becomes in charge of errors and reverse logistics. These steps can take place at different times, or altogether according to the company's needs and the product's requirements, and whether it is a new innovative product, or an upgrade to add value to a previous product.

Figure 3.2 illustrates an inner circle where the supply chain main entities are located. The inner circle follows an information flow structure where "Manufacturing Production Flow" acts as a "Supply Chain Network Structure" as it coordinates and links the internal and external nodes of the chain. The outer circle hosts the different sectors that asses the creation of the product. They maintain a consistent flow of information in the form of "Manufacturing Production Flow" as the inner circle, while constantly circulating information amongst their neighbouring sectors.

Integrating the Value Chain

Identifying the supplier members is crucial for firms as it lessens network complexity. Establishing various marketing information flows eases product development and financial transactions. Information flows add value to the chain which in turn increases promotion of the product as it integrates the consumer and the stakeholder with the supply chain (Gibbon 2001). The integration of process into the network structure can take two dimensions, horizontal structure integration and vertical structure integration. It is crucial for a company to integrate processes in both dimensions to ensure competitive advantage is achieved in addition to being essential when integrating the consumer and stakeholder, to maintain investment of trust in the company by analysing the competitive market, managing the supply chain by adding a value chain and ensuring the various dimensions of information flows are organised into an efficient network (Webster 1992).

The traditional basic chain initiated in the creation era was viewed predominantly as a process for moving materials and goods. However, as Era one merged with Era two, technology integrated with supply chains enabling information to integrate with nodes, such as supplier member and processes to form a coherent network. The traditional basic chain advanced through four base-line strategies to enable full integration with

MRP, DRP, EDI and ASP information systems (Kim and Kogut 1996). In addition to undergoing the four base-line integration strategies, the integration of process and information flows between supplier members, the traditional basic chain had to incorporate added value into its structure to increase its competitive advantage. This "added value" enhanced the traditional basic supply chain from merely a means to get products to where they need to be, to a means to strengthen key processes that drive a firm's strategic management and performance (Ketchen and Hult 2007). The evolution to Era two increased the scope of the traditional basic chain from focusing on either speed or cost, to integrating the best attributes of both information technology and added value to cover an array of capabilities such as cost reduction, information sharing, integration of processes to achieve a USP, network integration of supplier members, quality, speed, customer and stakeholder intimacy, prioritisation of long-term relationships and flexibility. This integrated and added value and the enhanced traditional basic supply chain gained popularity as it became embedded in companies' framework as it became known to be a "basic supply chain" that every company primarily acquires (Ketchen and Hult, *ibid*). However as each company needs are different, and with the increase of globalisation, the basic supply chain has branched into six approaches throughout the next three eras to match the market's needs. These approaches were created to fit the product type, whether functional, innovative or innovative functional. These approaches can be categorised under four major strategies (Lean, Agile, Leagile and Basic) that businesses can choose to incorporate based on their specialisation and requirements. The next three eras will explain the increase in globalisation, the need for specialisation and the growth of the competitive specialised global environment for supply chains.

Era Three: Globalisation (1980–2000)

The first successful mass market of the personal computer was incorporated by organisations for software programming to increase productivity in the 1970s. By the early 1980s, further commercialisation led computers being developed for household entertainment, as well as for companies (Leiner et al. 2009). This marked the beginning of global access to new graphical planning and information sharing. Between 1984 and 1988 the installation of major internal computer systems, workstations and PCs at an accelerated rate began, marking the formation of the first internet service provider (ISP) companies. Additionally, in the 1980s the World Wide Web (WWW) theorised that protocols link hypertext documents into a working system, marking the beginning of the modern Internet (Leiner *et al., ibid*). Since the mid-1990s, the Internet has had a revolutionary impact on culture and commerce, including the rise of near-instant communication. This flood of new technology has made the markets globalised and integrated, highlighting the need for improvements in logistics' planning and execution (Hyder et al. 2009). Several research centres have emerged to examine the impact of the new technology on supply chains and to further improve optimisation solutions worldwide. For example, the Production and Distribution Research Centre part of the Georgia Tech Institute, led in combining computerised optimisation models for supply chain design with distribution planning, which led to the development of control technology for automated material handling. The Computational Optimisation Centre at Columbia University developed new optimisation algorithms enabling the solution of scheduling problems. Most of the methodologies developed in these institutes rapidly became integrated with commercial technology and used in the area of logistics and supply chains (Georgia Tech Supply Chain and Logistics Institute 2010).

Global-scale regulations affect the shape and direction of the value chain, due to geographical fragmentation and the continuing evolution of the global economy. Accessing the markets of the developing countries becomes a production network led by firms based in developed countries (Gereffi et al. 2005). Despite globalisation bringing opportunities to those organisations that outgrew their domestic market, there still remains a restriction on global trade. This is seen in the form of tariffs and subsidies. In some cases these barriers are caused by the different technical standards and regulations as countries accept products from other countries (Christopher et al. 2006). In 1946 governments took measures to eliminate trade barriers to free the movement of finance through international agreements such as the General

Agreement on Tariffs and Trade in 1995 and subsequently the World Trade Organisation (WTO). Other barriers are cultural differences and geographical distance, as social norms and values regulate what is regarded as acceptable norms (Hummels et al. 2001). In some countries, the occurrence of corruption provides a barrier, hence firms generally prefer to operate in an environment where the microeconomic systems are stable. Meanwhile, geographical distance leads to transport problems, as the greater the distance between countries, the less they are inclined to trade. However, as technology has advanced, transportation has become cheaper and techniques for carrying fragile products have improved (Hamilton and Webster 2015).

The Capitalist Economy and Global Competition

Since the mid-1990s, the term "supply chain" has been recognised worldwide as an important aspect of business strategy. This has resulted in the CLM changing its name for a second time to the Council of Supply Chain Management Professionals (CSCMP). Thus the relationship between the buyer and supplier has been recognised as important to business strategy and as means to help businesses cooperate (Tan 2001). The increasing trend to separate logistic activities to solve tactical and operational issues from supply chains to solve strategic issues, has led to raw material management integrating with physical distribution and transportation functions as a concept into the business logistics and supply chain strategy (Sheombar 1995). This integration according to Giannoccaro and Pontrandolfo (2001), is accomplished by managing the information flows across geographic locations by the following methods:

1. Operational management: the process of managing all the material and data flows across the supply chain.
2. Organisational management: the process of decision making at different stages of the supply chain depending on the governance policy which determines the relationship between the various supply chain actors.

The focus on globalisation emphasised the need for logistics strategies that are able to deal with complex networks including multiple entities spanning multiple countries with diverse control, as a result of manufacturing globalisation, particularly due to the growth of manufacturing in China (Georgia Tech Supply Chain and Logistics Institute 2010). Thus many global firms such as Toyota noted global market competition and planned to initiate a tactical/operational strategy to enable their logistics and supply chain network to improve manufacturing efficiency and product development cycle time in a crucial environment whereby little inventory is needed to mitigate production and scheduling problems with the aid of JIT systems (Sugimori et al. 1977).

Capitalism Influences on Global Competition

The intense global competition of the 1980s forced multinational organisations to offer low cost yet high quality and reliable products with design flexibility to match consumer needs in any parts of the world (Tan 2001). A global economy and a capitalist society are intertwined as the capitalist system provides constantly expanding wealth and the re-allocation of resources. Economic globalisation can be outlined as a cause for the re-allocation of resources from two different perspectives (Dicken et al. 2001):

1. Economic globalisation gives political purpose providing incentives for the allocation of different capitalism scales.
2. Macroeconomic incentives to extend the competition range for companies to compete at a global level to increase efficiency and to drive prices down.

According to Partridge (2011) there are risks involved in globalised manufacturing, as capitalism does not work without risk. Even though risk in the supply chain is outsourced to distant global mills, factories, dye houses, and farms, the social and environmental opportunities of wealth redistribution under this new regime are not divided fairly. The rapid change in tastes and fashion intensified with globalisation and with it the fierce competition, such as the textile industry (Bruce et al. 2004). This created ethical clothing production such as "Fair Trade" to implement either a Lean or Agile supply chain strategy to be able to survive in a highly competitive market (Porter and Kramer 2006). Meanwhile, Partridge (2011) argues that supply chains have been used as a base for ethical intervention. However, if a company's supply chain is designed with a capitalist rationale or culture, then ethical claims cannot be trusted. Alternatively, to create an ethical supply chain, environmental issues, ethical outsourcing to developing countries as well as economic conditions such as externalities must be accounted for and mitigated. Organisations such as the "Fair Trade" movement, aim to have an in-built supply chain that seeks to tackle the exploitation of workers and ultimately help undeveloped countries by giving aid to the outsourced suppliers to build sufficient infrastructure, improve labour conditions, securing the rights of marginalised producers and building long-term relationships and partnerships (Vieira et al. 2010). This helps the growth of socio-economic environmental certification worldwide in order to create an equitable world, rather than a division of helpers and helpees, as well as achieve better trading conditions and promote sustainability.

Since the late 1990s sustainability concerns have increased with emphasised transparency and concerns for risk from institutional investors as they play an important role in constituting standards due to their direct or indirect involvement in corporate governance through the International Corporate Network (Hawley and Williams 2004). With increased integration of capital markets and growing globalisation, businesses develop a co-operative capitalism structure, as suppliers have a deep interest in global corporate governance standards, resulting in institutions banding their principals together through the International Corporate Network. These standards focus on independence, structure, accountability, transparency and articulating the rights of shareholders and the standards necessary to protect them. Sustainable projects include the reduction of carbon. By reinforcing corporate governance with issues of transparency, accountability and sustainability, this promises to expand a corporation's horizons to attempt a more ethical form of conducting business (Porter and Kramer 2006). This trend also has an impact on public policy as major market actors place pressures on governmental regulators, as corporate obligations move slowly away from the focused notion of profit maximisation to include market risk, social issues and political influences and ethical regulation. Hawley and Williams (2004) conclude that this expansion resulted from the inter-action of financial, market and political pressures to create a more responsible and responsive corporate behaviour. In particular, these trends have the potential to begin a long process of internalisation of negative externalities and fostering of positive ones, as common stan-dards cross market borders.

Benefits of Global Supply Chains

Globalisation creates interconnections between nations, allowing bar-riers (physical, political, economic and cultural) to be removed or reduced in order to liberalise the exchange of goods, services, money and people (Chandak et al. 2014). A global supply chain design model accounts for a variety of cost structures, outsourcing manufacturing, integration of supply chain departments, strategic alignment of the supply chain network and complications of international logistics (Hamilton and Webster 2015).

There are a number of dimensions according to Meixell and Gargeya (2005) that a supply chain will undergo to become global; decision variable, performance measurement, supply chain integration and glo-balisation considerations. Globalisation causes nations and firms to specialise in producing those goods and services at which they are most efficient. Although this allows benefits from economies of scale in production, it may create dependence upon a small variety of commodities, leaving the nation's economy, or the firm vulnerable to external events (Hamilton and Webster 2015). There are on-going emerging issues regarding the global supply chain design. Firstly, firms are increasingly outsourcing to domestic and global markets.

Supply chain managers select the most suited suppliers based on their consumers' needs in terms of quality, quantity, delivery, price and services needed by the firm. The supplier contracts influence the strategic structure such as geographical preferences aim to reduce lead times and cost to a minimum, extend the build-to-order and increase direct sales around the world (Meijboom et al. 2007). Secondly, as firms outsource, they integrate decision processes across the supply chain. This influences the supply chain design as it incorporates the decisions of business processes across multiple organisational structures in different continents, such as integration of VMI and collaborative planning forecasting and replenishment (CPFR). This integration gives the global supply chain the ability to coordinate decisions across multiple supply chain nodes (Meixell and Gargeya 2005). Thirdly, the strategy of supply chain performance varies depending on the products offered to consumers. For example, a global supply chain's aim is to assemble large amounts of commodities in various locations, in order for the buyer-driven supply chain to gain the ability to establish close links with multiple leading firms (Gereffi 1999a). Sourcing globally can improve performance, resulting in benefits (Meixell and Gargeya 2005): improved quality, meeting schedule requirements, assessment of new technologies and supply base broadening, leading firms to find a quick response strategy for improving efficiency, gaining competitiveness, cost reduction and improving performance with the use of the supply chain operations reference (SCOR) model.

The SCOR model developed in 1996, enables users to address, improve and communicate SCM practices within and between all interested nodes/supplier members. According to Irfan (2008), it is a management tool, spanning from the supplier's supplier to the customer's customer and aims to describe the business activities associated with all phases of satisfying a customer's demand. SCOR defines supply chains as the integrated process of Plan, Source, Make and Deliver aligned with operational strategy, material, work and information flows. These integrated processes are explained by Bauhof (2004) as: "Plan", including mapping of demand and supply resources, material requirements, inventory, distribution, production capability and utilising capacity. "Source", including acquisition of infrastructure and raw materials (in-house or outsourcing). "Make", including the execution of production and the relevant elements. "Deliver", is the management of order fulfilment, warehousing, transportation and installation of components. Finally, "Return" is the process to cater for circumstances where reverse-logistics is needed.

There are three levels in the SCOR model. First, scope where the firm analyses the basis of competition, focusing on operation strategy to get products across geographic segments. The second level is "configuration" where the material flow is aligned with information workflow and performance. The third level is "business activity" where the chain is designed in accordance with the other two levels and made flexible to account for changes in the marketplace (Bauhof 2004). The development of the SCOR model in addition to many others has conceptualised economic activities into the supply chain allowing the competition to cross borders and re-define the scopes of trade.

Globalisation and Territorial Borders

Supply chains expanded internationally across national borders, especially with regards to the automobile, computer and fashion industries (Britoa et al. 2008). This expansion imposed challenges upon the managers of the supply chain of new global products. Meixell and Gargeya (2005) reviewed global supply chain designs and their logistics, by identifying that global supply chain definition includes the facilities established at international locations. They pinpointed two forms of design decisions in globalised supply chains:

1. Decentralised – which provides more flexibility as managers are placed at each facility to make decisions based on the local circumstance; and
2. Centralised – decision making where decisions across the facilities are coordinated and reported back to headquarters for the final decision to be made.

Nevertheless, according to Galbraith (1974), information flow helps to reduce environmental uncertainty, especially in the case where a supply chain is clustered across the globe. Meixell and Gargeya (2005) highlighted the on-going issues in global supply chains: geographical distance that increases transportation costs, complicated decisions due to inventory cost trade-offs and increased lead-time. The cultural differences reduce the effectiveness of business processes due to difficulties in demand forecasting and material planning. What affects efficiency of business are infrastructure in developing countries, telecommunications, unskilled labour, technology and quality and availability of supplies. Although global supply chains provide competitive advantage, they carry risks which can influence their performance such as uncertainty in currency exchange rates that affect the price paid for the goods purchased in the supplier's currency, which also influences the timing and volume of purchases and the financial performance of the chain (Meixell and Gargeya, *ibid*). Additionally, economic and political instability affects the value of goods and trade tariffs, as manufacturers set up foreign factories to avoid trade admission fees, hence benefiting from tapping into new markets, with low cost labour, capital subsidies, reduced logistics costs and increased efficiency due to close proximity to their consumers.

A global supply chain allows ideas to cross borders as well as money, commodities and people, challenging the territorial authority of states and their power to regulate what takes place within them, resulting in an imbalance in political economies of scale, whereby economic organisations and political institutions operate on different grounds (Shah 2012). This, according to Hudson (1998), allows for order to be maintained by the use of two dimensions: regulating the scale of accumulated or economic activity and the management of the scale of political regulation. The modern classification of borders is to differentiate state domination in order to regulate the movement of citizens and commodities. Territories are being reconfigured because of the significant reduction in territorial borders due to the changes in organisations' supply chains and the process of globalisation (Cox 2004).

Integrating Global Supply Chains with Value Chain

Conceptualising economic activities into a chain of interconnected elements has been explored in detail by a handful of authors, one of which is Porter (1980) who explored the notion of the value chain in individual firms. Moreover, incorporating the value chain concept within a global economic perspective has also been analysed by Gereffi (1999a) and Gibbon (2001). Both stated that global commodity chains (GCC) provide the means for organisations to study the impact of economic globalisation on their practices. Globalised industries have promoted GCC by establishing two distinct types of international economic networks, "producer-driven" and "buyer-driven" referring to the whole range of activities involved in the GCC design, production and marketing of a product (Gereffi 1999a). According to Dicken et al. (2001), there are four dimensions to GCC which are:

1. An input-output structure: where the value-added chain consists of products, services and resources linked together across a variety of industries.
2. Territoriality: geographical clusters of distribution that can either partly scatter or partly contract.
3. Governance structure: referring to authority and power relationships that assess how the financial and human aspects should be allocated and distributed within a chain.
4. Institutional framework: aims to identify how local national and international institutions influence the globalisation process at each stage of the chain.

While making the traditional basic supply chain global, firms combine their basic chains with their value chains by linking complex information through computerisation and automated process technologies. This simplifies the inter-firm information linkage that reduces the misinterpretation of data (Gibbon 2001).

There are three benefits to linking the information. Firstly, integrating information reduces complexity and helps firms to track outputs and services from their member supplier's base. Secondly, simplifying the allocation of resources, product development and innovation. Thirdly, keeping the member supplier's competence at a consistent level, enhancing the learning process of new technology, increasing capacity and utilisation to benefit from economies of scale (Chandak et al. 2014; Fine 2000). While companies learn new technologies they develop new means of organising and integrating their basic chain with the global value chain, they also establish a uniformed method by coding differentiation of products across the industry that are constantly evolving to enable accuracy, accommodate changes and bundle activities to account for market changes, policy rules and international regulations (Sturgeon 2002). Fully integrating global value chains with the traditional basic chain requires unification of transactions, hence it is crucial to codify transactions, the member supplier's competences and capabilities (Gereffi 1999b). These variables are determined by integrating the upstream end of the value chain that sets the parameters where customers adjust/customise the products, with the downstream end of the value chain, where the product design is determined by innovative research and development to satisfy changes in consumer demand and account for the volatile global market (Gereffi, Humphrey and Sturgeon).

An extensive study by IBM in 2009 of 400 Supply Chain Executives found that the most prominent issues facing companies are visibility, customer demands/intimacy, cost, risk and globalisation. To enable companies to compete in a globalised market, companies must enhance the traditional basic value chain to be smarter. IBM devised three characteristics. Firstly instrumented chains require integration of automation capabilities, such as automated transactions, inventory location, shelf-level replenishment detection and transportation. This enables real-time data collection and transparency that can sense and respond to demand/supply signals. Secondly, the chain must maintain interconnectivity by the use of technological software such as EDI and ERP, to maintain information flows, standardisation of data and processes across its network. Finally, by integrating intelligence into the basic value chain by the use of simulation models to evaluate trade-offs of cost, time, quality, service and carbon emissions, it will be able to mitigate the prominent issues of risk by probability-based risk assessment, those of customer demand/intimacy by simulating predictive analysis and visibility issues by optimised forecasts, in addition to reducing cost by applying efficient networked planning (IBM 2009). With globalisation, the smart basic value supply chain can be a useful strategy amongst firms. However, businesses have realised that specialisation is key to gaining a competitive advantage, as consumers with increased access to information develop a taste for specialised brands and customised goods (Cavinato 1992).

Era Four: Specialisation (1990–2008)

Manufacturers and service providers during the 1990s collaborated with their suppliers to upgrade their management functions which became known as SCM (Lambert and Cooper 2000). As seen from the previous eras, supply chains continued to evolve rapidly. In Era two, integrating supply chain with logistics was taken into account during strategic decision-making (Hale 1999; Houlihan 1988). Furthermore, Era two divided the concept of logistics and supply chains, then integrated their processes in addition to outsourcing, manufacturing and distribution to cater for the emergence of Era three and the influence of globalisation (Tan 2001). Logistics expands further once the entire value chain from suppliers to customers is added. Therefore, it enables channel members to unify and compete as an entity rather than as a purchasing inventory along the value chain (Hale 1999). Era two saw the need to use integration in order to optimise supply chains, hence manufacturers linked their internal processes to external suppliers and customers within the chains to add value to the product being supplied to the consumer across the global market. Wholesalers and retailers integrated their physical distribution therefore offering a competitive advantage that is hard to imitate (Houlihan 1988). In Era three, globalisation occurred and expanded into Era four as in the 1990s after the GCC was introduced, organisations extended their businesses further to incorporate resources to include strategic suppliers and logistics in the value and supply chains (Gereffi 1999a). Efficiency upgraded to include sophistication in managing processes and information, as well as cost and quality consideration. Moreover, to improve the value chain, businesses moved from using only traditional and certified suppliers to embrace the use of highly developed technologies and take risks at product development resulting in a customer focused supply chain whereby each entry in the business is solely focused on consumer marketing (Lambert and Cooper 2000).

During Era three, Lubbers and Koorevaar (1998) saw globalisation as a process in which geographical distance becomes less of a factor as border crossing is no longer considered an obstacle. This resulted in supply chains becoming disordered as companies globalise to meet the global demand. They fail to match the desired production cost while achieving high customer services (Sturgeon 2003). Hence during Eras two and three, the traditional supply chain model developed added value and intelligent capability which labelled it as "Smart Basic Value Chain" (Lubbers and Koorevaar, *ibid*). The fundamental method of operating a supply chain is by using "Push" and "Pull" systems. The "Push" method is commonly used for the Smart Basic Value Chain as it aims to achieve forecast driven, high emphasis on customer service and inventory to buffer fluctuations in demand and lead times (Wright 2010). The use of a "Push" system in the Smart Basic Value Chain is due to its efficiency to cater for functional products which is normally the characteristic of the targeted market. Functional products are necessary goods that consumers require on a regular basis. Therefore, they have a stable forecasted demand with an established stable customer service, indicating controlled lead time as demand is predictable with additional buffer inventories in case of fluctuations (Fisher 1997). The "Pull" method allows supply chains to plan effectively and put aside scheduled resources to meet unpredictable demands. It is best suited for innovative functional products as they require sophisticated integration, efficiency and flexibility (Jüttner et al. 2007). The "Pull" method is characterised by upstream and downstream integration with suppliers and high emphasis on efficiency/flexibility by reduced stock holding and efficient speed in reacting to unpredictable demand (Fisher 1997). The "Pull" concept is most relevant in Agile and

Lean supply chain strategies as they are demand-driven in contrast to the Smart Basic Value Chain which relies on specific long-term forecasting of products. The "Pull" system incorporates the elements needed for supply chains to be Lean or Agile, as it helps companies to organise their supply chains in accordance with functions that enables them to withstand the market-demand-pull (Wright 2010).

In order to analyse the "Pull" method in Lean and Agile strategies, the need for specialisation in the global market needs to be understood. Six processes evolved from the Smart Basic Value Chain which can be divided into four strategies (Lean, Agile, Leagile and Basic Supply Chain (BSC)). Supply chains aim in the short term to increase productivity and reduce inventory and cycle time. In the long term, they aim to enhance strategic planning to increase customer satisfaction, market share and profit for the entire organisation (Lambert and Cooper 2000). This is achieved by suppliers participating in strategy choice from an early stage to ensure cost effectiveness and competitiveness in the global market. If suppliers disagree with a specific design/strategy, manufacturers are able to develop other conceptual solutions (Cavinato 1992). The chain's service focuses on manufacturing, mainly the distribution of raw materials, hence the enhancement of manufacturability is key for both the customer and supplier, requiring the crucial link between the supplier members and the organisation itself (Monczka et al. 1994). In Era three the growth of globalisation and distortion of territorial borders resulted in firms taking either a centralised or decentralised approach. In order to have a distinguished and unique competitive advantage, firms must not only select their management position (centralised or decentralised), but also ensure their supplier's short-term and long-term goals align with their product type (functional, innovative and innovative functional) (Hale 1999). Moreover, their suppliers must be specialised in the product type's market, as the input in designing the chain and choosing the relevant strategy is crucial to the business's competitiveness. Ensuring a coherent, specialised and integrated chain that is aligned with the firm's specialised product type as well as management approach is of crucial importance to survival in a global market, especially since competition is no longer between organisations, but among supply chains (Fisher 1997).

According to Jüttner et al. (2006), due to specialisation and alignment, firms attempt to develop a unique edge for their competitive advantage. They select a suitable management approach, specialised suppliers to deliver their specialised product type and a suitable strategy with relevant characteristics to ensure alignment in their operation. Therefore, the Smart Basic Value Chain branched into six approaches can be categorised into four specialised strategies (Lean, Agile, Leagile and BSC).

Basic Supply Chain Strategy

The first approaches of the Smart Basic Value Chain will be categorised under the strategic category of BSC; similar to the characteristics of the Smart Basic Value Chain, these approaches have a "Push" method and commonly use a centralised management approach to coordinate the chain (Wu et al. 2013). The approaches that fall under the BSC are most suitable for a company that specialises in functional products.

The Progressive Flow Approach

The core feature in a progressive flow approach is that supply and demand are both stable, as it works well for businesses with essential functional products that consumers need daily and products with a short shelf-life. Additionally, it is also suitable for manufacturers of parts or equipment (Alford et al. 2000). This approach typically is for a very mature supply chain with a customer demand profile that has little variation. Hence it fits the "added value" of long-term relationship with supplier members, which is a key characteristic in the Smart Basic Value (Ergen et al. 2007). Moreover, the scheduling needs to ensure a "Smart" steady continuous flow of information that is a key feature in the Smart Basic Value Chain. The production matches demand through a continuous-replenishment method of the "Push" system based on a "make to stock" decoupling point chain. Therefore, the competitive edge is based on offering a continuous-replenishment system to customers in order to assure high service levels and low inventory levels, thus achieving optimisation of costs associated with inventory. Management is centralised and focused on promoting collaboration by using information technology such as EDI and ERP, in order to reduce the order cycle as well as sharing information on sales and inventory to improve visibility, reduce risk, increase customer intimacy by forecasting demand, hence reducing costs. In the most mature stage, collaborative planning with key customers helps to anticipate demand pattern.

The Configuration Approach

This approach is characterised by a degree of configurations determined by the finished product. It allows firms with a functional product to have a competitive positioning to their "Push" system, by offering a unique configuration to the finished product according to the end consumer's needs (Alford et al. 2000). However, this flexibility is limited by technical constraints, as the product is configurable within a limited combination of product specifications, usually by combining parts into a component, usually during an assembly process, according to an individual customer's requirements. However, product configuration may be achieved in other types of processes, such as mixing items, packaging and printing (Mourtzis et al. 2008). The processes prior to product configuration are lengthier than the configuration itself and the downstream processes. Hence, limiting the number of possible finished products resulting from multiple combinations of parts or materials, aids forecasting demand and reduces inaccuracy. Consequently, product configuration and downstream processes are scheduled after receiving the customer's order and to ensure a short order cycle those processes are designed with extra capacity available (Ergen et al. 2007). Due to those factors, this approach employs a "configurable to order" decoupling point on the downstream side, where the processes occurring before configuration are managed under a "progressive-flow" method (Gunasekaran and Ngai 2005). The downstream processes operate to some extent similarly to agile strategy criteria. The customary product configuration decoupling point is at the finished-goods inventory, on the "progressive-flow" downstream side. This approach usually operates under centralised management to reduce complexity in coordinating order cycles and reduce lead times by ensuring the availability of materials and/or parts prior to the configuration process (Alford et al. 2000). Examples of where this approach is applicable is at the assembly of personalised products, such as computers and vehicles, and the paper manufacturing industry, where the decoupling point occurs after the manufacture of the big paper rolls and the products are customised in the cutting and packaging process (Mourtzis et al. 2008).

Agile Supply Chain Strategy

Basic Supply Chain approaches have similar characteristics to the Smart Basic Value Chain, however, as globalisation increases, companies move towards acquiring more flexibility, as observed from the "custom-configured" approach under BSC strategy (Wu et al. 2013). Hence the development of a strategy specialising in being responsive, labelled Agile Supply Chain (ASC) (Macheridis 2014). The principle of being Agile is being market sensitive, as it requires capabilities of reading and responding to real demand by applying three principles: balance, strength and flexibility. However, most firms are forecast driven rather than demand driven. Due to having little direct data, they are forced to generate demand forecasts (Christopher 2000). The Agile strategy is a template suited to products with a short life cycle but high demand uncertainty (Macheridis 2014) such as innovative products which require demand forecasts. The most common problems faced by the Agile strategy are delivery processes, faster responsiveness to the market and ensuring availability of stock in anticipation of consumers' changing taste (Jones et al. 2000).

To mitigate these issues, the Agile strategy integrates information flow between buyers and suppliers thus creating a "virtual" supply chain that accounts for volatility and inventory levels. This virtual chain is linked to "market sensitivity" as it feeds the information through the agile chain to the relevant nodes. The configuration of patterns links the different nodes via "process integration" and feeds the information into a "network base" (Christopher 2000).

It is important that the four processes "virtual, market sensitive, process integration, network based" are intra-linked within the Agile chain via information flows, as businesses do not compete alone as a single entity or as brand, but as supply chains. The expansion of globalisation created the need for a competitive edge, which gave birth to two distinct kinds of specialised competition, "network based" established from market sensitivity and services, catered for by the Agile strategy, and "speed/waste reduction" usually catered for by a Lean strategy. Both strategies cater for cost reduction by utilising economies of scale when possible.

The birth of the two specialised competitors led to the movement from the BSC strategy towards an Agile strategy. Hence, the creation of the two approaches that branched from the Smart Basic Value Chain to be categorised under the Agile strategy. The two approaches created to cater for a "network based competition" have the capability to integrate different structural systems, information flows, logistics process and assimilate a variety of processes (Agarwal et al. 2006). The approaches are based on the Agile Flexible Manufacturing System (FMS) that allows organisations to respond rapidly to changes in demand, making it the perfect model for unpredictable volatility where the requirement for variety and volume is high, making it suitable for companies specialising in innovative products (Christopher 2000). Both approaches can have either a centralised or decentralised management, depending on the firm's capabilities. Additionally, both approaches can use either "Pull" or "Push" systems. However, for an Agile strategy the "Pull" system is commonly applied in companies (Agarwal et al. 2006).

The Agile Approach

The classic agile approach is useful for companies that manufacture products under unique specifications for each customer. This is typically seen in industries that specialise in innovative products as they are characterised by unpredictable demand (Yusuf et al. 2004). They use a "make-to-order" decoupling point, producing the item after receiving the customer's order to ensure low inventory, reduce costs and avoid manufacturing products that have no certainty of future sales (Macheridis 2014). Whether a centralised or decentralised management approach was chosen, the firm must ensure the chain is able to meet unpredictable demand in quantities exceeding the customer's forecast and/or within a shorter lead time than agreed. Management should focus on ensuring agility, which is supported by two main capabilities: excess capacity and integrating processes designed to produce the smallest possible batches (Gunasekaran and Ngai 2005).

For this approach to be successful, the following factors should be in place – reducing lead time, by designing materials on a common platform and ensuring the relevant components are constantly available in inventory (a platform with a group of products that share some key components) (Ergen et al. 2007). Additionally, low-variance designs are marketed with lower prices and lead time, while high variation designs have higher cost and relatively longer lead times (Tang and Tomlin 2008). If extra capacity gradually decreases, the company should invest in additional assets so it can maintain its ability to be flexible. In order to do so, the company may need to switch between "Pull" system of flexibility, to a somewhat "Push" system of efficiency and adjust its value chain to increase visibility of stock levels (Yusuf et al. 2004). To ensure reliable adaptation to the market, collaboration with key customers and supplier members needs to be secured, in order to enable accurate responsiveness to changes in capacity requirements, both in the short term for scheduling purposes and in the long term for asset-investment decisions (Tang and Tomlin 2008).

This approach is commonly employed by manufacturers of intermediary goods that make products for industrial customers in accordance to their specific needs and place a high value on specialised configuration and short lead times. This approach's added value is oriented towards offering products "on demand" and with a high service level, e.g. chemical specialties and machinery services (Garavelli 2003).

The Flexible Approach

This approach is suited to companies that have high demand peaks and long periods of low workload. It is characterised by flexible adaptability and use of a "Pull" system, as it aids the reconfiguration of internal processes in order to meet a customer's specific needs with a definitive "make to order" manufacturing method (Gunasekaran and Ngai 2005). It is typically used by service companies that focus on handling unexpected situations or emergencies. Hence, the focus is not only on the speed of a supplier's response, but also on the ability to tailor solutions to their needs. Consequently, the price becomes largely irrelevant to the customer (Garavelli 2003). The management can be centralised or decentralised, with a focus on ensuring flexibility to support several capabilities: such as extra capacity of critical resources, rapid-response capability, and technical strengths in process, product engineering and an efficient process of information flow that is designed to be quickly reconfigurable (Das and Abdel-Malek 2003). For this approach to be successful, the following factors should be followed: according to Sanchez and Nagi (2001), inventory for only critical resources should be maintained and available on stand-by (e.g. pumps for companies that provide flood recovery services, or metal machining equipment for spare-parts manufacturing). Additionally, establishing strong collaborative relationships with key suppliers is necessary for companies to maintain low to medium capacity to ensure adaptability (Gong 2008). However, having unlimited capacity or a few resources of high capacity is not economically feasible. A typical example of this approach being implemented is in specialised companies that provide metalworking and machining services for the manufacturing of spare parts for industrial customers. This type of company may encounter emergency situations such as the need to immediately replace broken parts. Therefore, they must provide a fast response and sufficient capacity to develop unique parts by configuring and adapting consecutive processes, such as turning, reaming and welding tailored to a specific situation (Kesen et al. 2010).

Lean Supply Chain Strategy

While some companies move towards agile strategies, others find approaches related to Lean strategy more suitable to their needs. The concept of "Lean" was incorporated within the supply chains by Taiichi Ohno (1912–1990), the operations manager of Toyota, due to a supply shortage caused by a fluctuating demand resulting from World War II (Becker 2001). Between the years 1936 and 1956 chief executives of Toyota developed the TPS which incorporated five core systems (5S) (Bullington 2005). These are "sort", a system to classify what is needed and reduce waste; "straighten" which constitutes configuration and setting process in order, including clearly identifying the locations of all items so that anyone can find them and return them once the task is completed; "shine", which includes checking that all processes are set, tasks are completed in accordance to quality control protocols, defects are identified and standards are met; "standardise" which conforms and stabilises the standardisation of processes; and finally "sustain" which directs and improves the 5S operations (Jayaram et al. 2010a). 5S is a tool for systematic organisation of the workplace and applicable to every function within an organisation. For Lean production and systems to become successful requires unwavering commitment, not only from management but also from the personnel within the organisation (Shah and Ward 2003). Applying a Lean supply chain incorporates a decentralised management system that governs five key attributes. These are, "value" defined from the perspective of the customer, "flow" established by understanding the process and clearing any obstacles that do not add value, "perfection" by continuously refining the process to improve efficiency, cycle time, costs and quality in addition to ensuring "responsiveness" and applying a "Pull" system of make-to-order production (Hines 1998). With globalisation, activities such as outsourcing, manufacturing and distribution, this proved problematic with regard to the Lean system of waste reduction as it required a reduction in the numbers of supervisors and quality inspectors as workers are trained to know production standards and requirements and hence have the authority to take action (Sturgeon 2003). This in turn gives the workers identity and loyalty to the firm as they are in charge of its operations and take part in the success of its products. Lean supply chains aim to reduce costs and speed deliveries in the best quality possible (Wright 2010).

The Efficient Approach

This is suitable for industries that are characterised by intense market competition, with several competitors fighting for the same group of customers who may not perceive major differences in their value-added proposals; hence the competition is virtually based solely on offering the best price and speed of order fulfilment. As companies ensure they get the best price for each order, it results in recurrent peaks in demand (Chen and Ji 2007). Consequently, a continuous-replenishment model for inventory management is needed. Production requires a decentralised management in order to increase responsiveness and promote maximum end-to-end efficiency, as well as a "Pull" system based on "make to forecast" scheduling that relies on sales expectations of the product cycle (Heikkilä 2002). This approach ensures high rates of asset utilisation by conducting high overall equipment efficiency in order to reduce cost. This is accomplished by ensuring high levels of forecast accuracy to guarantee product availability and consequently, perfect order fulfilment (Christopher and Gattorna 2005). For this approach to be successful, the following factors should be in place: inventory management should accommodate extra capacity for outbound logistics, to absorb demand peaks without affecting the ability to meet customers' expected receiving dates. Additionally, reducing "high variation, low demand" will reduce costs, inventory levels, variation of configurations and hence complexity in production and service. The product cycle should be forecasted and scheduled to reduce lead time and order fulfilment (Jüttner, Godsell and Christopher 2006). This can be achieved by reducing the amount of time taken for changeovers and consequently the length of the production sequence, as it will be fixed and maintained for long periods of time. This in turn, will increase the manufacturing line's experience for the next cycle (Gunasekaran et al. 2008).

For example, when market demand follows seasonal trends, extra warehousing capacity should be available in anticipation of the need to store additional products during high-demand periods. To improve forecast accuracy, a firm can initiate supplier and customer collaboration, where information is shared on demand variability and scheduling. The purpose is to generate higher levels of customer loyalty and use the information flow to build a continuous-replenishment model. This approach is well suited for businesses with commoditised functional products, such as cement and steel (Jüttner et al. 2007).

The Fast-Prompt Approach

This approach is best for companies that produce trendy products with a short lifecycle, such as innovative products. From the customer's perspective, the main difference among competitors' value proposals is how well they are able to update product portfolios in accordance with the latest trends, for example the fashion and technology industries (Jones and Towill 1998). This focuses competition in the market on manufacturers' ability to continuously develop new products that can be sold at an affordable price. As a result, the main driver of competitiveness is the reduction of market mediation costs, hence understanding market trends and consumers' habits is crucial to maintaining production and distribution cost at an optimal level (Yusuf et al. 2004). Production should be scheduled by sales expectations for the season using a "make to forecast" decoupling point incorporated into a "Pull" system. As the product cycle shortens, production must schedule replenishment before the product goes out of fashion and consumers no longer want to buy it (Bruce et al. 2004). Therefore, having decentralised management helps promote continuous portfolio renewal, supports fast research and development, forecast accuracy to reduce market mediation cost and end-to-end efficiency to ensure affordable costs for customers (Yusuf et al. 2004).

For this approach to be successful, the following factors should be in place. The fast-prompt approach is the most demanding in terms of forecast accuracy, synchronised sales and operations planning, because it has to constantly anticipate market trends. Due to market volatility, it is crucial to develop the ability to produce small batches and purchase raw materials in small quantities (Gunasekaran et al. 2008). Therefore, firms must aim to standardise raw materials by limiting their variety to reduce sourcing complexity. Additionally, establishing collaboration by sharing information and raw materials among several supplier members helps to ensure fast product development and manufacturability (Stratton and Warburton 2003). For companies with high levels of seasonal demand, there must be a pool of suppliers that can provide additional capacity as needed. Although outsourced manufacturing could be more expensive than in-house manufacturing, in the long-term it would be less expensive than unused capacity (Ergen et al. 2007). Examples of companies that benefit from this approach are those that engage in catalogue sales of innovative products. It is also appropriate for retailers that sell trendy products and whose customers tend to visit stores regularly or seasonally. These retailers rely on the loyalty of their customers by ensuring they see a new product each visit (Stratton and Warburton 2003).

The Lean strategy can be applied to innovative functional products such as automobiles and is used extensively by Toyota. To increase the speed and efficiency of their "Pull" system they developed the JIT technique into their production line at the "make to order" decoupling point (Alford et al. 2000). The JIT concept aims for materials to flow from the supplier to production. Finally, the partly finished goods arrive at the manufacturing stage to be personalised by the customer leading to few raw materials and buffer stocks in warehouses, as no output stock of finished goods is released without being demanded, due to the "make to order" system (Womack and Jones 1994). JIT aims to keep the scheduling of activities and resources aligned exactly within the requirements of no "safety stock", generating minimal waste and reducing error, allowing JIT the ability to identify potential problems of demand and waste (Melton 2005). However, in order for this model to be fully effective, a company requires efficient communication with its suppliers and the relationship between the supply chain entities must be based on trust and reliability (Kilpatrick 2003). Therefore, it aims to facilitate their elimination and drive the continuous improvement of the production

Fig. 3.3 Lean automotive model (adapted from James-Moore and Gibbons 1997)

system (Naslund 2008). To implement a full Lean strategy with a JIT concept, certain elements need to be applied (James-et al. 1997) (Fig. 3.3).

Elimination of Waste

Each stage of the Lean strategy aims at reducing excess inventory; this is achieved by EPR and JIT. The common processes taken to reduce waste are to identify the areas in which waste occurs and its cause (Ketikidis et al. 2008). Additionally, the reduction of lead time requires several stages to deliver a commodity that consists of many sub-processes such as: order entry, assembly, inspection, packaging and shipping. In order to reduce lead time, a firm must reduce non-value-added activities, which include the time taken to change-over, set-up, inspect and waiting for approval. This can be reduced by the use of quick response manufacturing (QRM) (Ketikidis *et al.*, ibid).

Process Control

Aims to create smooth operation flow with reduced bottlenecks by limiting the number of components, to reduce production capacity particularly when resources are not utilised efficiently. The balance between the work stations and the process times requires vigorous maintenance; hence the buffer of inventory will naturally be maintained (Kilpatrick 2003).

Optimisation and People

For the supply chain to gain a high level of efficiency and thorough attention to detail, maintenance is required in all aspects of manufacturing in order to maximise overall equipment effectiveness and utilisation (Li et al. 2006). The aim of quality assurance is to remove the cause of bad quality. To achieve the highest quality possible with minimum cost is considered the essence of a lean supply chain. In order to acquire quality assurance, the supply chain must focus on the prevention of failures and sustain improvement of processes by documenting the standard operation procedures (Shah and Ward 2003). This can be implemented by the use of Total Quality Management (TQM), by implementing the 5S of Total Product Maintenance (TPM), which allows operators to be trained to maintain their own charged products, therefore developing a self-help culture where workers are welcomed to improve the overall quality of machinery and operations (Bullington 2005). This creates a peoples' culture that embeds loyalty to the firm, team work, employee contribution, learning and respect.

Flexibility

Given the competition to retain customers is between supply chains rather than competing brands, flexibility has become ever more crucial. Firms need to increase performance, apply flexible facilities, coordinate supplies with customer orders, establish fast process setups and reduce research and development lead times (Womack and Jones 1994). Additionally, value-adding activities should be maintained to allow the supply chain to progress as an innovative model. This is achieved by incorporating "Lean enterprise", which aims to group individuals, functions and operationally synchronise them into a coherent framework (James-Moore and Gibbons 1997).

Some firms choose to specialise their supply chain by operating under either BSC, Agile or Lean strategies, others require a hybrid strategy that has both characteristics of Lean and Agile. This supply chain strategy is called Leagile and combines the "Flexible" approach from the Agile strategy and the "efficient" approach from the Lean strategy. The Leagile strategy along with its relevant approaches will be explored further in Era five.

Era Five: Specialised Globalisation (2008–2016 and Onwards)

Era five is an extension of Era four as it continues to explore the rise of the global economy and the need for specialisation in order for firms to gain a unique competitive advantage. Supply chains depend on coordinating the performance of others within the supply chain as the global economy increases the expectations of consumers with regard to cost and services resulting in supply chain re-engineering (Cagliano et al. 2004). Era five deals with the challenging economic climate and increasing competitive pressures, leading businesses to constantly change their operating methods by breaking down their intra- and inter-organisational barriers to reduce uncertainty and increase control over the supply chain (Jones and Towill 1998). Thus cross-functional integration allows individual organisations to incorporate different channels of supply participants. Challenges exist in the integration of the customers and suppliers during the re-engineering processes (Changchien and Shen 2002). These issues include, working with different engrained cultures based on past relationships, establishing trust in how benefits will be realised, coordinating resources across multiple companies, determining project leaders and resources, sharing funding and fearing loss of competitive information (Done 2011).

Leagile Supply Chain Strategy

Era five explores the Leagile strategy, which is a hybrid model that combines "Lean" and "Agile" to optimise SCM. Hence, it combines the strength of both, and reduces all types of waste (inventory, unused capacity, poor quality, obsolete items, etc.) in order to minimise costs, and virtually integrate the supply chain components to create a better response system (Bruce et al. 2004).

There is a substantial difference between the performance of lean and agile supply chains. As mentioned previously, lean supply chains are efficient for functional or innovative functional products, while the agile supply chain shifts towards products and services that are innovative and volatile (Slack 2005). According to Naylor et al. (1999), agility is using marketing knowledge and virtual corporation to exploit profit opportunities in a volatile market. On the contrary, lean uses strategies to eliminate losses, such as time and ensures quality control. Christopher and Towill (2001) state that in order for a supply chain to qualify in the market and to win orders, it must identify specific aspects that act as indicators to determine the level of performance (e.g. quality, cost, response time and service). A Leagile supply chain is sensitive to the market and is ready to respond to real demand with a logistics goal including short response, feasible deadlines, ability to change the volume and the mix of production (Christiansen et al. 2007). Leagile strategies utilise the unique characteristics of both "agile" and "lean" (e.g. Agile manufacturing) and can be considered an alternative to leanness, or as the second stage after leanness is achieved. Agility stands for using the market knowledge and virtual network of communication to exploit the profitable opportunities found in the volatile market environment (Naylor et al. 1999). This can be considered the second stage after developing a lean supply chain which aims to eliminate waste and create a value stream to ensure the accuracy of scheduling.

Both models of lean and agile can be combined in a single strategy by the use of the de-coupling point (Jones et al. 2000). Agility is different from lean which focuses on doing more for less to obtain a "zero inventory". However, agile supply chains also focus on waste elimination which reduces buffer stock levels, though with a different strategic approach from lean supply chains. Moreover, agile supply chains focus on high responsiveness, high quality assurance and efficiency, all of which is shared with the lean supply chain within the smooth operation flow concept (Wright 2010). Therefore a Leagile supply chain strategy has several key characteristics that combine an approach from each lean and agile strategy (Wright, *ibid*). Leagile strategy combines the "flexible" approach from the agile strategy and the "efficient" approach from the lean strategy. Some of these combined key characteristic of both approaches are the following.

Flexibility and Efficiency: Similar to the lean/agile strategy, it aims to fulfil quality and volume of various demands. This can be achieved by reducing product specification, thus reducing complexity by standardising the products to maximise mass customisation (Ergen et al. 2007).

Postponement: As used by the lean strategy it allows the supply chain to manufacture semi-finished goods that are not completely assembled until the final stage where customisation takes place when the market requirements and the customer is known (Jayaram et al. 2010a). The stage where the semi-finished goods are stocked is referred to as the "de-coupling" point within the downstream lean supply chain (Pagh 1998). The Postponement stage offers the supply chain operational, economic and market advantages, as it allows the lean supply chain to respond quickly to customise consumer demand with minimum waste as inventory levels are kept low (Wright 2010).

Virtual network: As used by the Agile strategy it enables the supply chains to make use of the Internet and allows technology to share data flows and information between customers, buyers, suppliers, manufacturers and distributors. This can be achieved through the use of CPFR (Ketikidis et al. 2008).

Market Sensitivity: Similar to agile strategy, the supply chain is capable of responding to demand with fast adaption to customer requirements. This can be achieved by the use of the efficient consumer response (ECR) and the customer relationship management (CRM) systems (Hayes 2001) in addition to the use of information systems as stated by Ketikidis et al. (2008) for logistics and supply chain integration of

ERP systems to improve visibility of resources and aggregation of data. The link is information flow co-ordination, which can be incorporated into the supply chain design in order to reduce uncertainty in a high "clock–speed" industry by applying product platforms (Fine 2000). These platforms are a collection of assets that are shared by a set of products to increase product efficiency during manufacturing, development and reduce lead-time (Meijboom et al. 2007). According to Robertson (1998) these product platform assets can be divided into five categories:

1. Components: consist of the relevant tools needed to designs a product, using fixtures, circuit designs and software programs.
2. Processes: the equipment used to make or assemble components.
3. Products: the final design and production process, including the equipment used to make and assemble components.
4. Knowledge: includes the design know-how, technology applications and limitations, production techniques, mathematical models and testing methods.
5. People and relationships: consist of teams, building long-term relationships between the team and the larger organisation including building relations with a network of suppliers.

Figure 3.4 illustrates how the supply chain can excel by identifying the ways in which the "market winners" can be highly competitive in the "market qualifiers" metrics (Jones et al. 2000). As each supply chain

• Quality • Price • Lead time	• Service level
• Quality • Lead time • Service level	• Price
Market qualifiers	Market winners

Fig. 3.4 "Market qualifiers" matrix (adapted from Jones et al. 2000)

(lean/agile) responds to different markets, they require different strategies. However, to establish an optimum strategy the matrix helps firms create a system-induced process which combines both lean/agile models to battle uncertainty and hence reduce the bullwhip effect depending on the commodity and market demand in question (Jones and Towill 1998).

The "Market Qualifiers" metrics by Jones et al. (2000) is adapted in Era six to create the MDM that is divided into four quarters, each designated to a supply chain strategy, its approaches and characteristics (Agile, Lean, Leagile, BSC). In order to help to choose the most suitable strategy, firms can identify the two most significant factors in the MDM, the "Cost" of the supply chain and tolerated lead-time "JIT Lean". Once these factors are identified among other variables, the firm can decide where its supply chain is located in the market and where it needs to be. However, to be able to incorporate the MDM effectively, the firm must be able to undergo a re-engineering process, significantly changing their current business processes, job definitions, organisational structure, business policies and culture (Bevilacqua et al. 2009). In essence, after incorporating the MDM and diagnosing the best-suited strategy, a firm will create a new business model based on the MDM that increases the impact on performance, which according to Changchien and Shen (2002), will either be caused by a change in technological upgrade or an increase in profit margins. The sector that most firms re-engineer is the organisational element (e.g. customer service, logistics and purchasing), with the process involving external customers and/or suppliers, otherwise it is just an internal project masquerading as supply chain re-engineering (Agarwal et al. 2006). Therefore, re-engineering decisions are generally based on either qualitative or simulation analysis, with detailed simulation on how their chosen diagnosed strategy by the MDM is considered the best option, as it customises and builds models that are tested in accordance with the simulation tools (Swaminathan et al. 1998).

Era six, focuses upon designing a hybrid MDM model to unify all the previous models in past eras, in order to help firms establish a pathway most suited to their market and commodity.

Era Six: Hybridisation (2011–2016 and Onwards)

Eras five and six reflect a disturbed economic climate that began in December 2007 then took a sharp downward turn in September 2008. This economic recession caused many systems to imbalance such as the financial, maritime and oil sectors with its domino effect remaining in Europe to around 2015 and subsequently further exacerbated by disturbances including the economic and political impact of the UK planning to leave the European Union (Borok, Soloviev, Intriligator and Winberg 2008). The main feature of Era six is to unite all the previous supply chain models to create an MDM model adapted from the "Market Qualifiers" metrics by Jones et al. (2000), where the MDM helps a company to decide under which quarter (Agile, Lean, Leagile or BSC) its business strategy falls. Moreover, it allows a firm to create its own hybrid strategy tailored to its specific needs. Changchien and Shen (2002) suggest that a firm can diagnose the most suitable quarter in the MDM by understanding the needs of the consumer and the capabilities needed for the company to operate in a certain market. To enable complete and consistent application of the diagnosed strategy from the MDM, perfect alignment must be achieved with the aid of supply chain re-engineering. Each firm is unique and therefore requires different standards of re-engineering. However, firms must analyse the fundamentals that drive their chain re-engineering processes, internal and external resources, availability of automation process and level of employee empowerment. The most challenging factor facing manufacturers during the re-engineering process is the integration of the upstream of outsourcing functions and the downstream of delivery functions with regard to product design manufacturing. This integration facilitates the value creation transferring it from the supplier to the end customer (Changchien and Shen 2002). The major drive for integration is sophisticated and advanced information technology (IT) which allows companies to grow through vertical integration as perceived in the agile supply chain model. However, with integration comes the search for new markets as companies seek to become integrated global enterprises by merging their access to data, costs, personnel, stocks, sales, inventory and profit files. This requires absolute trust and advanced (IT) which not only combines the strength of EDI but also ERP and APS systems (Hayes 2001). Additionally, global enterprises aim to reduce costs to a minimum by reducing inventory which is implemented by the use of JIT purchasing, scheduling and distribution. This waste reduction is what the lean supply chain is renowned for, and as previously mentioned, it leads to more frequent monitoring of specific components, deliveries quality and precise scheduling to the end consumer (Walker 2008).

Era six maps the creation of the hybrid MDM supply chain model that unifies all the previous approaches and strategies in past eras. It is here that we begin to look to the future and how the development of supply chains over the previous five eras can be used to direct future development of a practical system of supply chain strategy selection by the industry.

The Multi-dimensional Matrix

In Eras four and five the Smart Basic Value Chain was branched into six approaches categorised into four supply chain strategies. The first is the BSC, which caters for functional products and is forecast driven, has high emphasis on customer service and includes an inventory with buffers to account for fluctuations in demand and lead times. Secondly, the agile strategy with its approaches focusing on innovation and innovative functional products. Therefore, its logistics operations ensure flexibility between inputting supply within and between companies, as it focuses on maximising the response to a customer's demand. Thirdly, the lean strategy with approaches targeting functional and innovative functional products, hence its logistics aim to eliminate losses and focus on speed. Finally, the Leagile strategy is mainly used for products that are innovative or innovative functional. However, with the increase in customisation, personalisation in the global market, the Leagile strategy can be used for functional products with configuration

Table 3.1 The four strategies and six approaches of supply chains

Basic supply chain (BSC)	Agile supply chain (Agile)	Lean supply chain (Lean)	Leagile supply chain (Leagile)
1. Progressive flow approach	3. Agile approach	5. Fast – prompt approach	From lean: *The efficient approach*
2. Configuration approach	4. Flexible approach	6. Efficient approach	From agile: *Flexible approach*

demand, for example personal computers (Table 3.1) (Banomyong and Supatn 2004).

The specialised four strategies, their characteristics and approaches are inadequate to provide sufficient decisive measurements for firms to establish the needs of their supply chain to improve or be re-engineered. Using an MDM model, this study aims to clarify and expand the variables that enable firms to diagnose the nature of their supply chain and what they require to improve it. In order to develop this, several measuring variables need to be identified to clarify the choice of relevant strategies by helping firms establish the parameters under which their business strategy operates and help lead them towards the strategy that is most relevant for their business framework. These measuring variables will be identified through a review of existing literature and data collection from the industry. A conceptual framework will be developed illustrating how these variables will be identified and used to create the MDM model. Additionally, a preliminary conceptual framework of the MDM will be outlined to illustrate the mechanism of how the MDM will be designed and used. This section will also examine the first two measuring variables that are needed to create the preliminary MDM, which will provide the basis of the initial data collection.

Conceptual Frameworks

Here we begin to identify the measuring variables needed to aid companies' decision making to be incorporated in the MDM model. The conceptual framework (Fig. 3.5) outlines the pathway the study will take in the following chapters.

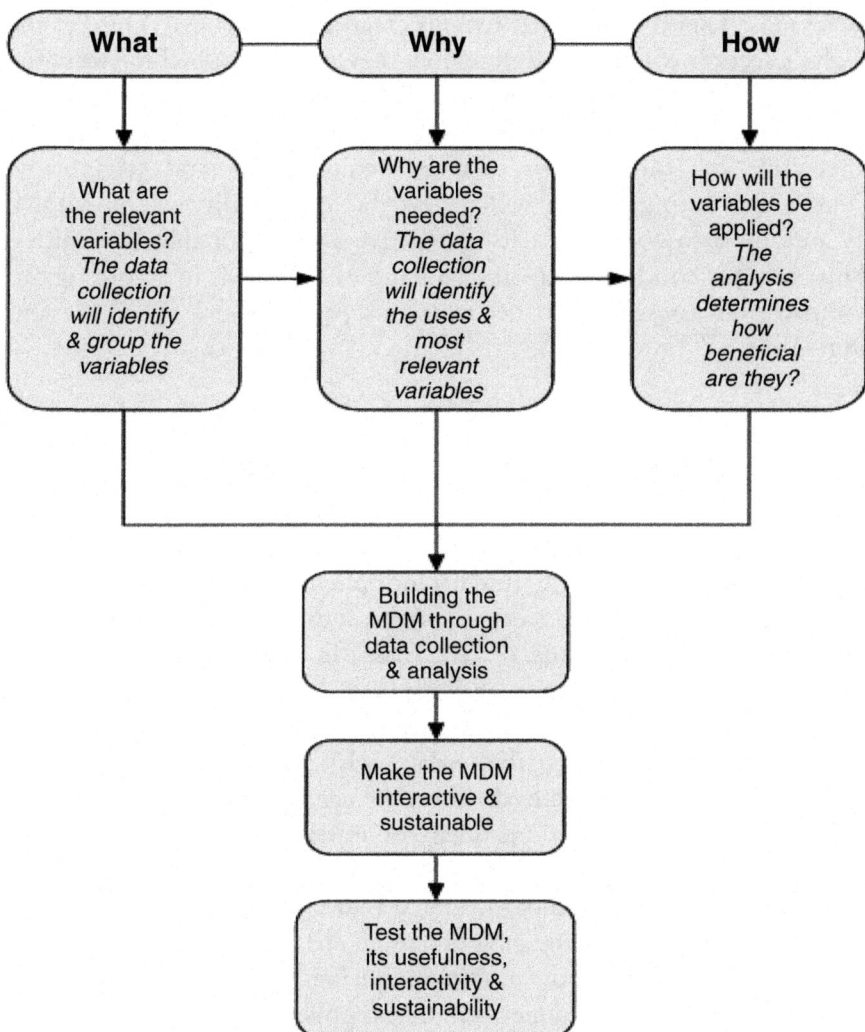

Fig. 3.5   Conceptual framework of the study

Firstly the preliminary MDM with the first two identified variables will be analysed through data collection, to identify the remaining relevant variables. Secondly, once they are collected and categorised into groups, the data collection will confirm the value of these variables, those most relevant and their uses in creating the MDM. Thirdly, the analysis section will then examine how they will be applied to create the MDM and how beneficial they will be to the companies using them. Focus will also be on how the MDM can be made sustainable and interactive to suit modern business requirements and technology. Finally, the testing section will review the applicability of the MDM, its usefulness to companies, its interactive and sustainable capabilities. This will be conducted by introducing the MDM to a prestigious company for assessment to determine its potential use for SMEs and large firms.

Conceptual Framework for the MDM

According to Kandasamy et al. (2007), fuzzy modelling has been used by applied mathematicians to understand phenomena in social science including by doctors, engineers, scientists, industrialists and statisticians to represent the uncertainty or "fuzziness" in a real system or process. This can be seen in examples of work including Roubens (1997), who points out recent advances in using fuzzy modelling in multiple attribute decision-making methods that deals with ill-defined information. He used fuzzy ranking methods to review aggregation problems in procedures, choice issues and treatment of interactive models. Moreover, fuzzy methods have been used by Kok et al. (2000) in creating decision-support systems in the field of integrated water management from a social science perspective, as many environmental changes are human-induced. Due to the ambiguity in combining qualitative social concepts in a quantitative modelling framework they applied fuzzy set theory and fuzzy modelling maps to integrate qualitative scenarios with quantitative, hence integrating models to establish a decisive decision-support system for the coastal city of Ujung Pandang, Indonesia. Fuzzy methods have also been used in logic-driven approaches to understand system behaviour, as Gobi and Pedrycz (2007) have applied fuzzy modelling to design a two-phase optimisation process using adaptive fuzzy logic, leading to creating an effective learning mechanisms structure that achieves high accuracy, interpretability and transparency, through the use of "Fuzzy Rules" in digital systems.

The use of fuzzy methods has become more common in social science according to Kandasamy et al. (2007) leading to the development of "Fuzzy Matrix" modelling, highly applicable for the development of the MDM model outlined in the following chapters. The structure and parameters of the "Fuzzy Matrix" will be created using the basic fuzzy principles of (If-Then) which are statements used to set fuzzy conditions (Jin 2000). For example, IF a statement gives the desired intelligence to a "Fuzzy rule" formula, THEN the condition is found to be TRUE, hence returning a predefined value. However, if the condition is FALSE, it returns a different predefined value (Carlsson and Fuller 2001). The growth of fuzzy theory resulted in an increase of the applications of fuzzy sets in social research (Bezdek 1993).

According to Swaminathan et al. (1998) the practice of supply modelling in research is achieved through comparison or translation of different strategies to define a single dimension or describe a single model through multiple dimensions, through the basis of case evidence or theoretical perspective. However, Carlsson and Fuller (2001) concluded that supply strategies are characterised by multiple dimensions, hence to obtain a holistic perspective, a study would be required to analyse the relative different strategies through several dimensions.

The creation of the MDM is based on the "Market Qualifiers" metrics by Jones et al. (2000), therefore it will be shaped into a matrix with four quarters in order to ease the process for companies to allocate their business strategy, commodity and market. A quarter will be designated to the lean strategy and its relevant approaches which target relatively stable demand to minimise losses and maximise profit by reducing fixed costs. A quarter will be designated to the agile concept and its relevant approaches with the capabilities to react to market demand in an extremely volatile environment. This quarter is suited for firms who adopt a virtual integration to unite all their information flows to battle any changing turbulence in demand (Christopher and Towill 2001). The Leagile strategy quarter is designed to incorporate different key characteristics of lean and agile, which are opposing models; however, once combined they can enable the supply chain to develop fast market knowledge and enhance their information provided the decoupling point has been accurately identified between each intersection from each lean/agile model. Finally the BSC strategy quarter has approaches designed for functional products. It has the characteristics to integrate added value and information technology to align the different processes in the chain in order to create a reliable and cost competitive based business structure (Cagliano et al. 2004).

To help ease the selection procedure for companies, several measurement variables will provide guidelines to help them determine the best strategy and under which quarter their supply chain lies in relation to their market. The company can then evaluate this strategy and establish the options it has, tailoring its needs and identifying the level of re-engineering it may require. These measurement variables will be established through data collection; however, a preliminary framework of the MDM must be established with introductory variables to initiate the data collection process.

From the earlier discussion focusing on the supply chain literature there are several key measurement variables that companies compete on, for example lead times, cost, added value such as speciality services and customisation. Lean, agile and BSC have "cost" as one of the core competitive characteristics and lean strategy has waste reduction (including lead times) as its primary competitive advantage with the use of JIT. Meanwhile, Leagile combines both lean/agile by having some of its competitive advantage based on cost and lead time (Cagliano et al. 2004). Hence "cost" and "lead times" are two reliable introductory measurement variables that can be used as a basis for the preliminary MDM framework to initiate data collection for the other relevant measurement variables.

The definition of "cost" in this study includes the production process, its logistics distribution and delivery to the end customer, including the cost of lead times during that process. The end customer can vary from end consumer to retailer to end warehousing. The specific definition of the end customer will depend on the company's classification of the term. The definition in this study for "lead times", is the more time is lost the greater the waste, as time is a resource. Therefore, leanness means developing a value stream to eliminate all waste, including time and to ensure a sophisticated level of scheduling by the use of JIT. Hence, the more a supply chain strategy moves towards eliminating "lead times" by using JIT, the leaner it becomes (Cagliano et al. 2004). Therefore, "lead times" are measured by the JIT system, hence the term is "JIT lean". Using these two measuring variables "cost" and "JIT lean", firms can classify under which quarter their business lies.

Using the "Market Qualifiers" metrics by Jones et al. (2000) as a basis noted earlier (Fig. 3.4), the matrix divides the market into two, "Market Qualifiers" and "Market Winners", by which a firm can identify under which market it belongs. The "Market Qualifiers" indicates the base line for companies to enter in a competitive market arena, while the "Market Winners" analyses the specific capabilities a firm has in order for it to fill the demand. These two markets cater for three different product types, functional, innovative and innovative functional. The two upper quartiles often cater for innovative and innovative functional, with the "Market Winners" competing on service level such as availability, flexibility, responsiveness and customisation, while "Market Qualifiers" compete on quality, lead time and price, as their commodities tend to be costly. The lower two quartiles often cater for functional and innovative functional, with the "Market Winner" competing on commodity and product prices, while "Market Qualifiers" compete on quality, lead time and services.

As price and lead times are self-clarified variables, in contrast to quality and service level that consist of several functions, we will consider price as "cost" and lead time as "JIT lean" to be the introductory measurement variables on which the MDM will be built. These two variables will be placed on the axis of the MDM. The vertical axis represents "JIT lean", as the more a company achieves leanness by reducing lead time the higher it is located on the vertical axis (Fig. 3.6). The horizontal axis represents "cost"; the higher a company's costs are, the further down the horizontal axis they will be. Once companies examine the level of leanness and their costs, the axis will help them determine which quarter is most relative to them. Based on the matrix by Jones et al. (2000), the MDM adapts the upper left quarter as lean strategy, due to its competing category in high leanness, low costs due to reduced inventory levels and high quality control due to trained personnel. The upper right quarter is adapted as Leagile in the

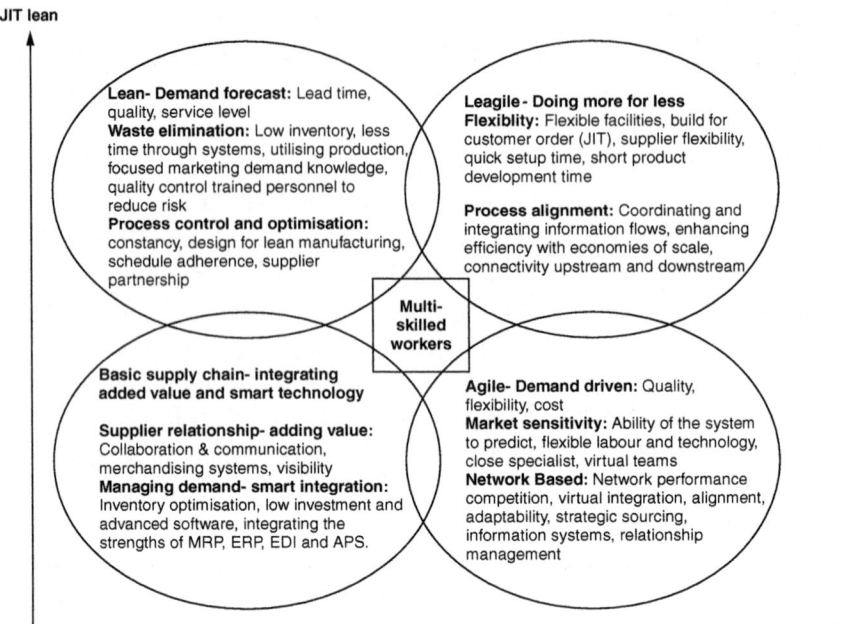

JIT lean

Lean- Demand forecast: Lead time, quality, service level
Waste elimination: Low inventory, less time through systems, utilising production, focused marketing demand knowledge, quality control trained personnel to reduce risk
Process control and optimisation: constancy, design for lean manufacturing, schedule adherence, supplier partnership

Leagile- Doing more for less
Flexiblity: Flexible facilities, build for customer order (JIT), supplier flexibility, quick setup time, short product development time
Process alignment: Coordinating and integrating information flows, enhancing efficiency with economies of scale, connectivity upstream and downstream

Multi-skilled workers

Basic supply chain- integrating added value and smart technology
Supplier relationship- adding value: Collaboration & communication, merchandising systems, visibility
Managing demand- smart integration: Inventory optimisation, low investment and advanced software, integrating the strengths of MRP, ERP, EDI and APS.

Agile- Demand driven: Quality, flexibility, cost
Market sensitivity: Ability of the system to predict, flexible labour and technology, close specialist, virtual teams
Network Based: Network performance competition, virtual integration, alignment, adaptability, strategic sourcing, information systems, relationship management

Cost

Fig. 3.6   Conceptual framework for the multi-dimensional matrix

MDM, as it acts as a hybrid strategy with high leanness that ensures high service level that are often associated with high cost. The lower left quarter is defined as BSC as it competes on relatively high quality, service level and predictable demand scheduling, hence fairly low lead times and low cost due to economies of scale. The lower right quarter is defined as agile strategy, as it competes on relatively high leanness due to its responsiveness which is associated with higher cost competition for delivery to the end consumer.

The MDM conceptual framework indicates these four quarters cross-over as some characteristics show similarity, hence they integrate across strategies. These cross-over areas are termed "fuzzy" and are the basis for the MDM to be developed as a "Fuzzy Matrix" model (Jin 2000). The interpretability of the "Fuzzy Matrix" is achieved through data collection and deductive reasoning, which will allow the MDM to diagnose the company's position, generate recommended strategies as well as provide options that companies can use to tailor their own strategy. The "Fuzzy Matrix" is generated by simplifying the fuzziness of the four strategies in the MDM, providing an interpretation to the fuzziness and testing the fuzziness of the data.

To re-emphasise, the MDM four quarters take the shape of a matrix, with the first upper left quarter designated for the approaches of lean supply strategy, with the characteristic features of eliminating waste while maintaining quality. The lean system is an operational technique focused on resource productivity (Sanchez and Nagi 2001). The lower left quarter is for BSC approaches enhanced by economies of scale, and smart processes to increase visibility, connecting information flows to enable flexibility of supplier arrangements. It has the characteristics to connect the upstream and downstream of the supply chain to add value by coordinating and integrating the information flows internally within the company and its suppliers (Lee et al. 2007). The lower right quarter is designated for agile approaches which share the characteristics that focus on vertically integrating information and services with regard to market sensitivity. Agility is a collection of inclusive strategies focused on exploring volatility to gain a competitive edge (Stratton and Warburton 2003). Agile's characteristic of "flexibility" has the ability to adapt with minimum time waste and cost. This is shared by the upper right quarter with Leagile strategy, as it combines the shared characteristics of Lean/Agile strategies indicating that these two lean/agile strategies can exchange characteristics via the "fuzzy area". The Leagile unique capability is switching between decoupling points at the production phase from lean manufacturing to agile strategy and agile manufacturing to lean strategy. The decoupling point is divided into three categories: craft production mainly for innovative products, mass production mainly for innovative functional and lean production mainly for functional products (Hormozi 2001). This decoupling point where both strategies intersect is challenging to identify for firms, resulting in complexity in identifying how to combine leanness with agility.

Therefore, the "fuzzy area" in the MDM framework provides hybrid capabilities, to give companies the option to select the characteristics that cross between these strategies to create their own tailored supply chain. The integrated segments of the matrix allow firms to create their tailored hybrid strategy. However, the disintegrated segments of the matrix allow firms to pick one of the traditional supply chain strategies in accordance with their market and commodity. For example, the middle square that intersects with all four quarters in Fig. 3.6 is a "fuzzy area" that illustrates an example of a shared characteristic between all four strategies. This characteristic is the use of multi-skilled works in the supply chain to provide a unique advantage to the company so it can compete globally with the help of close supervision by specialists (Done 2011). This requires a method shared by all four strategies to integrate information flows, people's skills and virtual teams to process the information given from the demand of the market and relate it to the product development.

In the following chapters, this study will build a fuzzy matrix based on the MDM conceptual framework. The data collection will identify the relevant measurement variables and the option available in the "fuzzy area" that companies can use to create their own hybrid strategy tailored to their needs. The aim is for the MDM to help firms diagnose their supply chain and strategy they require for their market, in addition to allowing companies the option to create their own tailored strategy.

In the next era, the MDM will be made interactive in order to survive in the technological world. Rapid developments in computer and data networks have resulted in a third revolution of technology. Along with the challenging economic climate and the increasing competitive pressures, the MDM urgently needs to incorporate advances in technology as firms require fast and reliable communication among different nodes, resulting in a cyber-network that links the whole supply chain together as well as calculates or compares the firm's supply chain with its competitors. This requires full automation of processes and nodes along the entire supply chain. To achieve complete automation is complex as Era seven will indicate.

Era Seven: Interactivity and Automation (2016 to Future)

Era seven is a continuation of Era six, as it incorporates the advances in information technology to enable fast and reliable communication among different nodes creating a cyber-network that links the whole supply chain together as well as comparing the firms' supply chain with its competitors. A major constraint is the willingness of these nodes to communicate with other nodes in the chain, mostly because of data sensitivity issues (Min and Bjornsson 2004). Communication is very important in supply chains as it enables integrating knowledge that is spread across each of the nodes to facilitate smooth flow of materials from start to finish, as examined by Kumar et al. (2008) in a study of transition in the B2B e-Marketplace. To enable full integration of communication, standardisation of information technology must be facilitated across all sectors of the chain (Carlsson and Fuller 2001). This requires automation of supply chain capabilities to ensure full alignment between processes. Once that is completed, the supply chain can accomplish full automation and integration of information (Alford et al. 2000). However, there are several problems that require the supply chain process to be automated. They include shortages, excessive finished goods inventories, under-utilised plant capacity, unnecessary warehousing costs and inefficient transportation. There are several pathways to automate a supply chain including gathering all companies into an e-marketplace, where negotiations on goods and services can take place (Kumar et al. 2008). However, automating business dealing processes into one e-marketplace fosters centralisation which does not facilitate crucial aspects of the supply chain such as collaboration, alliance and long-term relationships, but rather increases rivalry as companies aim to dominate one another in their pursuit of the best suppliers (Huhns et al. 2002).

To enable more flexibility in an automated system, two properties must exist:

1. Disintermediation: creating direct association between users and their software without the use of an intermediary body. This provides participants with the ability to interact and gather remote information on applications and human resources.
2. Error tolerance and exploitation: due to systems being extremely complex, errors occur, thus a system should have room to manoeuvre and anticipate such conduct if it occurs allowing its

components to interact in time and mitigate these errors and pro-
hibit them from reoccurring by following systematic protocols
(Huhns et al. 2002).

For firms to establish a fully automated system, these two properties
are combined in a new tool that develops and uses computer agent
software. This software facilitates information and service by exchanging
them with other programs, thus collaborating to solve complex problems
(Huhns et al. 2002; Min and Bjornsson 2004). By using the WWW, an
"agent" is an information gathering program that strategically forms and
re-forms coalitions, creating dynamic business partnerships without the
user's immediate presence. The agent helps increase sales through
matching the end user's needs with product offerings, as well as reduce
transaction costs by using the automated business process. Each agent
communicates with other agents over the Internet exchanging information dynamically such as inventory level, sales data, sales forecast and
production or delivery schedule to mitigate the bullwhip effect
(Sturgeon 2003). An agent gathers and shares schedule data, instead
of sales data and sales forecast; this is sent to a supplier and the sub-
supplier agent. On the basis of this information, the production schedule is updated and modified to meet changes in demand (Min and
Bjornsson 2004).

Era seven looks at updating the MDM to be interactive to accommodate the rise in technology and automation. However, incorporating an agent system within the interactive MDM is complex.
Nevertheless, the interactive MDM can be enhanced to include the
agent system by the firm if it wished to further enhance the model.
Development of the MDM to be an efficient interactive model will
require adherence to the two properties we noted earlier that will allow
it to be a flexible integral tool that can be incorporated in an automated
business structure – "disintermediation" and "error tolerance", and for
these qualities to be built into its system. This can be achieved by
future model users as they require (Huhns, Stephens and Ivezic
2002). Each firm has its own unique attributes and adding relevant
variables into the MDM will make it exclusive to the firm. This can
be a single or regular procedure to keep the MDM up to date and

mitigate any errors (Roubens 1997). The programming can be done by qualified IT staff.

When a company decides to implement the MDM, it must first establish its market (functional, innovative or innovative functional). It must then determine its level of leanness and cost of its supply chain. Additionally, classifying its production strategy is important, whether it is designed-to-order, make-to-order or make-to-stock as these three categories cause problems associated with sudden change in product design, raw material inventory shortages and lead-time respectively (Li et al. 2006). According to Min and Bjornsson (2004) the construction materials and categorisation of production strategy divides suppliers according to their production capacity into four categories: "stock supplier", "build-to-order supplier", "mass producer" and "capacitated supplier". The stock supplier and the mass producer need accurate demand forecast as they have a short lead-time to reduce inventory and transportation costs; the build-to-order and a capacitated suppliers require accurate data on the end-users' actual construction progress and demand forecasting. Once these factors are established, the firm can use the interactive MDM which will generate the most suitable strategy for a firm as well as provide options for the firm to choose from (Min and Bjornsson, *ibid*). The recommendation given by the MDM may cause the firm to undergo a re-engineering process. However, supply chain strategy re-engineering has the potential to significantly impact performance in the future, hence it is essential for the firm to perform a detailed risk analysis before adopting a new process (Swaminathan et al. 1998).

The "error tolerance" system can be further enhanced by the firm based on the automated supply chain configurer (ASCC) model established by Piramuthu (2005). This model is linked to the agent system as it resides at every node in the supply chain. Each of the sectors represents an agent that makes decisions based on the information they have about the nodes in the next stage upstream to them, and the prior information that comes from a stage downstream from them. For example, the "sampler" agent in ASCC filters the information to extract necessary training examples that are used as input in the next "learning" phase. The learning agent learns the patterns that exist in the training examples, to formulate an algorithm to solve complex problems in the supply chain. These algorithms and patterns are then stored in a "knowledge base" where they are examined and tested. If an element is found to be incomplete the problem is rectified through incremental learning using the "performance element" agent. The knowledge base agent gathers and sorts the information, patterns and algorithms that pass the performance test and allows them to proceed to the "dispatcher" agent. There the best choice is identified and given back to the (upstream) stage. This automated process repeats itself continually until all errors are identified, resolved and all orders are dispatched (Piramuthu 2005).

The ASCC software is something to consider for future model development. It provides firms with an opportunity to enhance and incorporate the interactive MDM within their automated structure. According to Piramuthu (2005), ASCC is ideal for specialised automated production, i.e. cars, oil, aerospace and cloths. Their supply chain would benefit from the cyber software and gain production speed by incorporating a cyborg production chain for fast assembling components. Although this is present in many current industries (cars, oil and aerospace) it is not present as a means to link the entire supply chain into a single unit (Alford et al. 2000).

Preliminary Interactive Multi-dimensional Matrix Outline

Here we will use the basic principles of fuzzy theory to create a fuzzy matrix that will have "disintermediation" and "error tolerance" capabilities. Additional measurement variables will be identified and incorporated into the MDM. For more clarification, the measurement variables will be divided into "logistics strategies" and "supply chain strategies". The MDM will then be made interactive and established as a website by the use of "Fuzzy rules-If/Then" programming. This will enable the MDM to adapt to technological advances in the business world. Furthermore, the interactive feature will enable the MDM to be more user-friendly and easy for firms to enhance or edit the model to accommodate their specification and preferences.

Once the measurement variables are identified and grouped into "logistics" and "supply chain" strategies the results will be translated into fuzzy rule statements that will be used to create the interactive programming for the MDM. The website will feature the MDM as an interactive matrix that companies can use to diagnose their supply chain in relation to their market as well as to choose the best strategy for their business structure. The interactive MDM for each group, "logistics strategies" and "supply chain strategies", will feature a dropdown box where the most relevant measurement variables can be accessed and selected (Fig. 3.7). Once the scale is chosen from the measurement variable boxes, the interactive MDM will generate a recommended strategy based on these premises along with a choice of option for the company to use if it wished to create a tailored strategy. The website will ensure disintermediation, as any member of staff can efficiently use the website and the interactive MDM model. Additionally, the error tolerance element is included in the interactive MDM, as a company can easily incorporate additional variables as fuzzy rules and program them to establish the MDM as "exclusive" to the company.

According to Carlsson and Fuller (2001) research contributions generally investigate supply chain strategies one dimension at a time. However, by discussing a multiple strategy in the form of multi-dimensions, a broader perspective can be provided to evaluate the impact on manufacturing performance. For example, if a company's strategy moves towards leanness then by definition it will move towards adopting a leaner manufacturing model resulting in lower costs, higher quality, higher speed and reliability. Similarly, if a company moves towards agility, its manufacturing will acquire flexibility while ensuring the needed quality level. If a company moved towards Leagile, its manufacturing will adopt both aspects, high quality, higher speed, reliability and flexibility. Meanwhile, if a company moves towards BSC, its manufacturing would acquire cost reduction, and planned inventory to suit a predictable demand (Cagliano et al. 2004). Although firms can tailor their own unique strategies by adding extra measurement variables to the

Fig. 3.7 Interactive multi-dimensional matrix

MDM, the variables that form a supply strategy would not necessarily present constant patterns of relationships between each other. The company can choose to add additional measurement variables in the form of different combinations that align with the goals and supply chain structure of the company (Lee 2002). This in turn helps companies select the best strategy that could cope with the challenges of globalisation, such as visibility, cost, risk and customer intimacy (Cavinato 1992). The next chapter will explore the different methodological approaches that are of relevance to this study. Once a suitable method is identified, it will be used to meet the aim of this study, which is to create the interactive MDM.

References

Agarwal, A., Shankar, R., & Tiwari, M. (2006). Modelling the metrics of lean, agile and leagile supply chain: An ANP-based approach. *European Journal of Operational Research, 173*(3), 211–225.

Alford, D., Sackett, P., & Nelder, G. (2000). Mass customisation: an automotive perspective. *International Journal of Production Economics, 65*(3), 99–110.

Banomyong, R., & Supatn, N. (2004). Comparing lean and agile logistics strategies: a case study. *Thammasat Business School, Thailand, 12*(3), 3–19.

Bauhof, N. (2004). SCOR model: Supply chain operations reference model. *Beverage Industry, 1*(1), 1–3.

Becker, R. M. (2001). Lean manufacturing and the Toyota production system. *Automotive Manufacturing and Production, 113*(6), 64–65.

Bevilacqua, M., Ciarapica, F., & Giacchetta, G. (2009). Business process re-engineering of a supply chain and a traceability system: A case study. *Journal of Food Engineering, 93*(1), 13–22.

Bezdek, J. (1993). Fuzzy models – what are they and why?. *IEEE Transactions on Fuzzy System, 1*(1), 1–5.

Borok, V., Soloviev, A., Intriligator, M., & Winberg, F. (2008). Pattern of macroeconomic indicators preceding the end of an American economic recession. *Journal of Pattern Recognition Research, 1*(1), 40–53.

Britoa, M., Carboneb, A., & Blanquartd, C. (2008). Towards a sustainable fashion retail supply chain in Europe: Organisation and performance. *International Journal of Production Economics, 114*(1), 534–553.

Bruce, M., Daly, L., & Towers, N. (2004). Lean or agile: A solution for supply chain management in the textiles and clothing industry?. *International Journal of Operations and Production Management, 24*(2), 151–170.

Bullington, K. (2005). Lean supply strategies: Applying 5S tools to supply chain management. *International Supply Management, 90*(1), 1–5.

Cagliano, R., Caniato, F., & Spina, G. (2004). Lean, Agile and traditional supply: How do they impact manufacturing performance?. *Journal of Purchasing and Supply Management, 10*(4), 151–164.

Carlsson, C., & Fuller, R. (2001). Optimization under fuzzy if–then rules. *Fuzzy Sets and Systems, 119*(1), 111–120.

Cavinato, J. (1992). A total cost/value model for supply chain competitiveness. *Journal of Business Logistics, 13*(2), 285–301.

Chandak, S., Chandak, A., & Sharma, A. (2014). Globalisation of supply chain management for an automotive industry-future perspective. *International Review of Applied Engineering Research, 4*(2), 155–164.

Changchien, S., & Shen, H. (2002). Supply chain re-engineering using a core process analysis matrix and object-oriented simulation. *International and Management, 39*(5), 345–358.

Chen, K., & Ji, P. (2007). A mixed integer programming model for advanced planning and scheduling (APS). *European Journal of Operational Research, 181*(5), 515–522.

Chiu, M., & Lin, G. (2004). Collaborative supply chain planning using the artificial neural network approach. *Journal of Manufacturing Technology Management, 15*(8), 787–796.

Christiansen, P. E., Kotzab, H., & Mikkola, J. H. (2007). Coordination and sharing logistic information in leagile supply chains. *International Journal of Procurement Management, 1*(2), 79–96.

Christopher, M. G. (1992). *Logistics: the strategic issue*. London: Chapman and Hall. 62–75.

Christopher, M. G. (2000). The agile supply chain: Competing in volatile markets. *Cranfield School of Management, 1*(1), 1–10.

Christopher, M. G., & Gattorna, J. (2005). Supply chain cost management and value-based pricing. *Industrial Marketing Management, 34*(2), 115–121.

Christopher, M. G., Peck, H., & Towill, D. R. (2006). A taxonomy for selecting global supply chain strategies. *The International Journal of Logistic Management, 17*(2), 277–287.

Christopher, M. G., & Towill, D. R. (2001). An integrated model for the design of agile supply chain. A practitioner perspective. *European Journal of Purchasing and Supply Chain Management, 6*(1), 117–127.

Cox, L. (2004). Border lines: Globalisation, de-territorialisation and the reconfiguring of national boundaries. *Macquarie University, Sydney, Australia, 1*(1), 1–17.

Croom, S., Romano, P., & Giannakis, M. (2000). Supply chain management: An analytical framework for critical literature review. *European Journal of Purchasing and Supply Management, 6*(1), 67–83.

Crowley, M. (2003). An introduction to the WTO and GATT. *Economic Perspectives, 1*(1), 42–54.

Das, S., & Abdel-Malek, L. (2003). Modelling the flexibility of order quantities and lead-times in supply chains. *International Journal of Production Economics, 85*(3), 171–181.

Das, A., Narasimhan, R., & Talluri, S. (2006). Supplier integration: Finding an optimal configuration. *Journal of Operations Management, 24*(5), 563–582.

Dicken, P., Kelly, P., Olds, K., & Yeung, H. (2001). Chains and networks, territories and scales: Towards a relational framework for analysing the global economy. *Global Network, 1*(2), 89–112.

Done, A. (2011). *Supply-Chain Evolution: Knowledge-Based Perspectives.* IESE Business School, University of Navarra, Spain. 1 (1), pp. 1-26.

Ergen, E., Akinci, B., & Sacks, R. (2007). Life-cycle data management of engineered-to-order components using radio frequency identification. *Advanced Engineering Informatics, 21*(3), 356–366.

Finch, P. (2004). Supply chain risk management. *Supply Chain Management: An International Journal, 9*(2), 183–196.

Fine, C. H. (2000). Clock-speed-based strategies for supply design. *Production and Operations Management, 9*(3), 213–221.

Fisher, M. (1997). What is the right supply chain for your product?. *Harvard Business Review, 1*(3), 105–116.

Forrester, J. W. (1958). Industrial dynamics: A major breakthrough for decision makers. *Harvard Business Review, 38*, (4 July-August), 37 and 50-69.

Frohlich, M., & Westbrook, R. (2001). Arcs of integration: An international study of supply chain strategies. *Journal of Operations Management, 19*(1), 185–200.

Galbraith, J. R. (1974). Organization design: An information processing view. *European Institute for Advanced Studies, 4*(3), 28–36.

Garavelli, A. (2003). Flexibility configurations for the supply chain management. *International Journal of Production Economics, 83*(4), 141–153.

Georgia Tech Supply Chain and Logistics Institute. (2010). The Evolution of the Supply Chain and Logistics. http://www.scl.gatech.edu/scl-evolution.php.

Gereffi, G. (1999a). Commodity chains framework for analysing global industries. *Review of International Political Economy, 6*(1), 1–7.

Gereffi, G. (1999b). International trade and industrial upgrading in the apparel commodity chain. *Journal of International Economics, 48*(1), 37–70.

Gereffi, G., Humphrey, J., & Sturgeon, T. (2005). The governance of global value chains. *Review of International Political Economy, 12*(1), 78–104.

Giannoccaro, I., & Pontrandolfo, P. (2001).Coordination mechanisms for supply chain management, *Proceedings of the 8th International Annual Conference of EurOMA*, Bath, UK. 2 (2), pp. 550-63.

Gibbon, P. (2001). Upgrading primary production: A global commodity chain approach. *World Development, 29*(2), 345–363.

Gobi, A., & Pedrycz, W. (2007). Fuzzy modelling through logic optimization. *International Journal of Approximate Reasoning, 45*(4), 488–510.

Gong, Z. (2008). An economic evaluation model of supply chain flexibility. *European Journal of Operational Research, 148*(6), 745–758.

Gunasekaran, A., Lai, K., & Cheng, T. (2008). Responsive supply chain: A competitive strategy in a networked economy. *OMEGA: The International Journal of Management Science, 36*(5), 549–564.

Gunasekaran, A., & Ngai, E. (2005). Build-to-order supply chain management: A literature review and framework for development. *Journal of Operations Management, 23*(5), 423–451.

Hale, B. J. (1999). Logistics perspectives for the new millennium. *Journal of Business Logistics, 20*(1), 5–7.

Hamilton, L., & Webster, P. (2015). *The international business environment.* 3rd. ed. London: Oxford University Press. 4–260.

Harland, C. M., & Lamming, R. C. (1999). Developing the concept of supply strategy. *International Journal of Operations and Production Management, 19*(7), 650–673.

Hawley, J., & Williams, A. (2004). Shifting ground: Emerging global corporate governance standards and the rise of fiduciary capitalism. *School of Economics and Business Administration*, Saint Mary's College of California, Moraga CA, *1*(1), 1–43.

Hayes, D. (2001). Market reaction to ERP implementation announcement. *Journal of Information Systems, 15*(1), 3–18.

Heikkilä, J. (2002). From supply to demand chain management: Efficiency and customer satisfaction. *Journal of Operations Management, 20*(6), 747–767.

Hines, P. (1998). Benchmarking Toyota's supply chain: Japan vs. U.K. *Long Range Planning, 31*(6), 911–918.

Hormozi, M. (2001). Agile manufacturing: The next logical step. *Benchmarking: An International Journal, 8*(2), 132–143.

Houlihan, J. B. (1988). International supply chains: A new approach. Management decision. *Quarterly Review of Management Technology, 26*(3), 13–19.

Hudson, A. (1998). Beyond the borders: Globalisation, sovereignty and extra-Territoriality. *Geopolitics, 3*(1), 89–105.

Huhns, M., Stephens, L., & Ivezic, N. (2002). Automating supply-chain management. *Association for Computing Machinery, 1*(1), 1017–1024.

Hummels, D., Ishii, J., & Yi, K. (2001). The nature and growth of vertical specialization in world trade. *Journal of International Economics, 54*(3), 75–96.

Hyder, E., Heston, K., Paulk, M., & Hefley, B. (2009). *eSourcing capability model for service provider- eSCM-SP.* Zaltbommel: Van Haren Publishing. 1–8.

IBM. (2009). The smarter supply chain of the future. *Global Chief Supply Chain Officer Study*, *1*(1), 2–50.

Imenda, S. (2014). Is there a conceptual difference between theoretical and conceptual frameworks?. *Journal of Social Science*, *38*(2), 185–195.

Irfan, D. (2008). A SCOR reference model of the supply chain management system in an enterprise. *The International Arab Journal of Information Technology*, *5*(3), 288–295.

James-Moore, S. M., & Gibbons, A. (1997). Is lean manufacture universally relevant? An investigative methodology. *International Journal of Operations and Production Management*, *17*(9), 899–911.

Jayaram, J., Das, A., & Nicolae, M. (2010a). Looking beyond the obvious: Unravelling the Toyota production system. *International Journal of Production Economics*, *128*(3), 280–291.

Jayaram, J., Tan, K.-C., & Nachiappan, S. P. (2010b). Examining the inter-relationships between supply chain integration scope and supply chain management efforts. *International Journal of Production Research*, *48*(22), 6837–6857.

Jin, Y. (2000). Fuzzy modelling of high-dimensional systems: Complexity reduction and interpretability improvement. *IEEE Transactions on Fuzzy Systems*, *8*(2), 212–221.

Jones, R., Naylor, B., & Towill, D. (2000). Lean, agile or leagile? Matching your supply chain to the marketplace. *International Journal of Production Research*, *38*(17), 4061–4070.

Jones, R., & Towill, D. (1998). Shrinking the supply chain uncertainty cycle. *International Journal of Operations Management*, *24*(7), 17–22.

Jüttner, U., Christopher, M., & Baker, S. (2007). Demand chain management-integrating marketing and supply chain management. *Industrial Marketing Management*, *36*(4), 377–392.

Jüttner, U., Godsell, J., & Christopher, M. (2006). Demand chain alignment competence: Delivering value through product life cycle management. *Industrial Marketing Management*, *35*(9), 989–1001.

Kandasamy, W., Smarandache, F., & Ilanthenral, K. (2007). *Elementary fuzzy matrix theory and fuzzy models for social scientists*. Michigan: ProQuest Information and Learning. 7–47.

Kesen, S., Kanchanapiboon, A., & Das, S. (2010). Evaluating supply chain flexibility with order quantity constraints and lost sales. *International Journal of Production Economics*, *126*(4), 181–188.

Ketchen, D., & Hult, T. (2007). Bridging organization theory and supply chain management: The case of best value supply chains. *Journal of Operations Management, 25*(7), 573–580.

Ketikidis, P., Koh, S., Dimitriadis, N., Gunasekaran, A., & Kehajova, M. (2008). The use of information systems for logistics and supply chain management in South East Europe: Current status and future direction. *Omega: The International Journal of Management Science, 36*(5), 592–599.

Kilpatrick, J. (2003). Lean principles. *Utah Manufacturing Extension Partnership, 1*(1), 1–5.

Kim, D., & Kogut, B. (1996). Technological platforms and diversification. *Institute for Operations Research and Management Sciences, 7*(3), 283–301.

Kok, J., Titus, M., & Wind, H. (2000). Application of fuzzy sets and cognitive maps to incorporate social science scenarios in integrated assessment models. A case study of urbanization in Ujung Pandang, Indonesia. *Integrated Assessment, 1*(1), 177–188.

Kumar, V., Lavassani, K., & Movahedi, B. (2008). Transition to B2B e-marketplace enabled supply chain: Readiness assessment and success factors. *International Journal of Technology, 5*(3), 75–88.

La Londe, B. J., & Masters, J. M. (1994). Emerging logistics strategies: Blueprints for the next century. *International Journal for Physical Distribution and Logistics Management, 24*(7), 35–47.

Lambert, D. M. (2000). Supply chain management. *The Ohio State University, 1*(1), 1–29.

Lambert, D. M., & Cooper, M. (2000). Issues in supply chain management. *Industrial Marketing Management, 29*(1), 65–83.

Lambert, D. M., Stock, J. R., & Ellram, L. M. (1998). *Fundamentals of logistics management.* London: Irwin/McGraw-Hill. 9–328.

Lee, H. L. (2002). Aligning supply chain strategies with product uncertainties. *California Management Review, 44*(3), 105–119.

Lee, H. L., & Billington, C. (1995). The evolution of supply chain management models and practice at Hewlett-Packard. *Interfaces, 25*(5), 42–63.

Lee, H. L., Park, N., & Lee, S. (2007). Analysis of the manufacturing lead time in a production system with non-renewal batch input, threshold policy and post-operation. *Applied Mathematical Modelling, 31*(1), 2160–2171.

Leiner, B., Cerf, V., Clark, D., Kahn, R., Kleinrock, L., Lynch, D., Postel, J., Roberts, L., & Wolff, S. (2009). A brief history of the internet. *Computer Communication Review, 39*(5), 22–31.

Li, S., Nathan, B., Nathan, T., & Rao, S. (2006). The impact of supply chain management practices on competitive advantage and organizational performance. *The International Journal of Management Science, 34*(4), 107–124.

Lubbers, R., & Koorevaar, J. (1998). The Dynamic of Globalization. http://koorevaa.home.xs4all.nl/html/dynamic.html.

Macheridis, N. (2014). Managing projects: A template for an agile approach. *Lund Institute of Economics Research, 2*(1), 6–14.

Meijboom, B., Voordijk, H., & Akkermans, H. (2007). The effect of industry clock-speed on supply chain co-ordination. *Business Process Management, 13*(4), 553–571.

Meixell, M., & Gargeya, V. (2005). Global supply chain: A literature review and critique. *Transportation Research, 41*(E), 531–550.

Melton, T. (2005). The benefits of lean manufacturing: What lean thinking has to offer the process industries. *Chemical Engineering Research and Design, 83*(6), 662–673.

Min, J., & Bjornsson, H. (2004). Agent-based supply chain management automation. *Stanford University, Centre for Integrated Faculty Engineering, 1*(1), 1–6.

Monczka, R. M., Trent, R. J., & Callahan, T. J. (1994). Supply base strategies to maximize supplier performance. *International Journal of Physical Distribution and Logistics, 23*(4), 42–54.

Mourtzis, D., Papakostas, N., Makris, S., Xanthakis, V., & Chryssolouris, G. (2008). Supply chain modelling and control for producing highly customized products. *Manufacturing Technology, 57*(5), 451–454.

Naslund, D. (2008). Lean, six sigma and lean sigma: Fads or real process improvement methods?. *Business Process Management Journal, 14*(3), 269–287.

Naylor, J. B., Naim, M., & Berry, D. (1999). Leagility: Integration the lean and agile manufacturing paradigms in the total supply chain. *International Journal of Production Economics, 62*, 107–108.

Pagh, J. (1998). Supply chain postponement and speculation strategies: How to choose the right strategy. *Journal of Business Logistics, 19*(2), 13–33.

Partridge, D. (2011). Activist capitalism and supply-chain citizenship: Producing ethical regimes and ready-to-wear clothes. *Current Anthropology, 52*(3), 105–106.

Persson, J. (1997). *A Conceptual and Empirical Examination of the Management Concept Supply Chain Management*. Licentiate Thesis, Lulea University of Technology, Lulea. Sweden. pp. 42-48

Piramuthu, S. (2005). Knowledge-based framework for automated dynamic supply chain configuration. *European Journal of Operational Research, 65*(3), 219–230.

Porter, M. (1980). *Competitive strategy techniques for analysing industries and competitors.* New York: Simon and Schuster Inc. 5–340.

Porter, M., & Kramer, M. (2006). The link between competitive advantage and corporate social responsibility. *Harvard Business Review, 78*(1), 1–13.

Robertson, D. (1998). Platform product development. *University of Pennsylvania, 1*(1), 1–33.

Roubens, M. (1997). Fuzzy sets and decision analysis. *Fuzzy Sets and System, 90*(4), 199–206.

Sanchez, L., & Nagi, R. (2001). A review of agile manufacturing systems. *International Journal of Production Research, 39*(16), 3561–3600.

Schoenherr, T., & Swink, M. (2011). Revisiting the arcs of integration: Cross-validation and extensions. *Journal of Operations Management, 1*(1), 1–17.

Shah, N. (2012). The territorial trap of the territorial trap: Global transformation and the problem of the state's two territories. *International Political Sociology, 1*(1), 1–20.

Shah, R., & Ward, P. (2003). Lean manufacturing: Context, practice bundles and performance. *Journal of Operations Management, 21*(3), 129–149.

Sheombar, H. S. (1995). *Understanding logistics coordination: A foundation for using EDI in operational (re) design of dyadical, value adding partnerships.* Den Bosch: UTN Publishers. 50–120.

Shukla, K. R., Garg, D., & Agarwal, A. (2011). Understanding of supply chain: A literature review. *International Journal of Engineering Science and Technology, 3*(3), 2059–2072.

Slack, N. (2005). The flexibility of manufacturing systems. *International Journal of Operations and Production Management, 25*(12), 1190–1200.

Stevens, G. (1989). Integrating the supply chain. *International Journal of Physical Distribution and Materials Management, 19*(8), 3–8.

Stratton, R., & Warburton, R. (2003). The strategic integration of agile and lean supply. *International Journal of Production Economics, 85*(4), 183–198.

Sturgeon, T. (2002). Modular production networks: A new American model of industrial organization. *Industrial and Corporate Change, 11*(3), 451–496.

Sturgeon, T. (2003). What really goes on in silicon valley? Spatial clustering and dispersal in modular production networks. *Journal of Economic Geography, 3*(1), 1–36.

Sugimori, Y., Kusunoki, K., Cho, F., & Uchikawa, S. (1977). Toyota production system and Kanban system materialization of just-in-time and respect-for human system. *International Journal of Production Research, 15*(6), 553–564.

Swaminathan, J., Smith, S., & Sadeh, M. (1998). Modelling supply chain dynamics: A multiagent approach. *Decision Sciences, 29*(3), 607–631.

Tan, K. C. (2001). A framework of supply chain management literature. *European Journal of Purchasing and Supply Management, 7*(2), 39–48.

Tang, C., & Tomlin, B. (2008). The power of flexibility for mitigating supply chain risks. *International Journal of Production Economics, 116*(1), 12–27.

Vieira, L., Aguiar, L., & Barcellos, M. (2010). Understanding the coordination mechanisms in a fair trade fruit supply chain. *Journal of Operations and Supply Chain Management, 3*(2), 13–25.

Walker, K. (2008). SOX, ERP and BPM. Business performance. *Strategic Finance, 1*(1), 47–53.

Webster, F. E. (1992). The changing role of marketing in corporation. *Journal of Marketing, 56*(4), 1–17.

Womack, J. P., & Jones, D. T. (1994). From lean production to the lean enterprise. *Harvard Business Review, 72*(2), 93–103.

Wright, N. (2010). Lean and agile supply chain. *Scandinavian Brewers' Review*, Auckland University of Technology, New Zealand, *67*(4), 1–6.

Wu, G., Liao, S., Chiu, C., & Chang, K. (2013). New product development projects selection for Taiwanese Century-old businesses. *Journal of Life Science, 10*(3), 1152–1161.

Yusuf, Y., Gunasekaran, A., Adeleye, E., & Sivayoganathan, K. (2004). Agile supply chain capabilities: Determinants of competitive objectives. *European Journal of Operational Research, 159*, 379–392.

4

A Methodology for the Strategic Supply Chain Model

Application of the Chosen Methodology

The knowledge to be acquired for the development of the MDM model is through mixed methods and the qualitative approach is conducted via several rounds of questionnaire using the Delphi method. However, to avoid any ambiguity with the panel's opinions, these questions contain basic fuzzy elements using "truth functions" that can then be analysed via SPSS and Excel-in turn forming the quantitative approach. It is rational for mixed methods that no single approach can view the entire picture but rather a mixture of approaches can provide more information than a single approach (Franklin and Hart 2007). In order to translate this into the decision making MDM, a "top-down" deductive approach is taken to derive the essence from the recommendations which will then be tested to formulate conclusions (Table 4.1).

Implementation of Selected Approaches

The theoretical framework contained several models in order to achieve the objective of this study. The adopted supply chain models improve upon

© The Author(s) 2017
S. Sindi, M. Roe, *Strategic Supply Chain Management*,
DOI 10.1007/978-3-319-54843-2_4

Table 4.1 The chosen methodological approaches and their application

	Research philosophy	Research paradigm	Research angle
Logic	*Epistemology* Focuses on practical applied research, integrating different perspectives to help interpret the data	*Pragmatism* Understands that there are different ways to interpret data and there is no single concept that reflects the entire picture	*Deductive* When the conclusion is logically presented from a set of premises that are true, the conclusion is also true
Data method	Mixed data method of quantitative and qualitative	Mixed data method of quantitative and qualitative. The use of relevant methods to create truth functions for the Fuzzy Delphi	Deductively analyses the mixed methods
Use of data method in this study	Uses previous knowledge to develop parameters that help understand how the problem happened, and how can it be solved by developing truth functions for a Fuzzy Delphi and analysing it via SPSS to build a model that achieves the aim and objective of the research	Application of relevant mixed methods to analyse Fuzzy Delphi using SPSS and Excel to create the MDM model	Using deductive reasoning to interpret the answers of the Fuzzy Delphi and to test the MDM via semi-structured interviews

previous models and are created using a Soft Systems Methodology (SSM) modelling technique used for tackling real-world problematic situations that lack a formal definition (Zimmer 2010). In applying the "pragmatic" paradigm to achieve the aim of this project, the conceptual framework for the MDM model is created using SSMs to provide a framework for users to help them deal with the unstructured problems of supply chains (Checkland and Poulter 2006). Once a conceptual framework for the MDM has been created, Unified Modelling Language (UML) will be used to make the MDM interactive as a web-based model. UML was selected because it is a generic modelling system that helps develop models to provide a standard way to design a visualised system. It is widely used for software modelling as it is highly adaptable to different purposes and usages (Gu et al. 2012). The UML takes conceptual models from a variety of objectives and creates a web-based syntax. According to Hiremath and Skibniewski (2004), the UML is used in building interactive models for automated construction processes and vendor management as well as supply chain and logistics modelling.

Using the "epistemological" approach, data will be gathered through a Delphi study that is combined with fuzzy principles to ensure that the MDM can accommodate fuzziness in expert opinion. The Delphi technique is a structured communication originally developed as a systematic study, based on an interactive forecasting method which relies on a panel of experts (Skulmoski et al. 2007), while fuzzy principles verify statements with degrees of belief meaning that once each statement is proven to be either true or false, it is given a degree of truthfulness and a degree of falsehood (Trochim and Donnelly 2006).

The analysis uses a "deductive" approach, which looks at the issue in general terms and then increasingly specifically. This approach initially finds the relevant theories that help businesses identify the best applicable supply chain for their commodity and market (El Hussein et al. 2014). The answers from the fuzzy Delphi are analysed through SPSS and Excel. Using deductive reasoning, the results will expand the experts' reasoning to generate scatter diagrams and "truth functions" that will be incorporated in building the interactive MDM as a web-based model.

The methodological stages of this study will be conducted in two parts (Table 4.2).

A summary of the advantages and disadvantages of Fuzzy Delphi is illustrated in Table 4.3.

The Fuzzy Delphi method is a technique of mixed method data collection as it uses crisp numbers that can be analysed to establish the mean and median to evaluate research criteria. In order to deal with the fuzziness of human participants, Lshikawa (1993) combined fuzzy set theory proposed by Zadeh (1965) to improve the convergence of the uncertainty in experts' options and present them in meaningful crisp numbers. However, due to the

Table 4.2 Methodological stages of the research

Methodology	Part one: Fuzzy Delphi qualitative method	Part two: Analysis and testing quantitative method
	Applied to group decision making to clarify fuzziness in concepts and understand experts' opinion (Hsu et al. 2010).	The analysis and testing affirm whether the MDM and its interactive capability is applicable.
	1. Statements are created for a pilot Delphi with two variables called "Membership Functions". The feedback creates the bases for the MDM and establishes what the experts require in order for them to answer the next rounds with complete and relevant information. The pilot study also establishes the fuzziness which then initiates the first round of Fuzzy Delphi	1. The results of the Fuzzy Delphi are analysed via SPSS and Excel to find the frequency of opinions, the mean and determine the consensus.
	2. The first round of Fuzzy Delphi uses the amendments from the pilot study to add relevant variables to create statements that use experts' opinion to build the MDM.	2. Through deductive reasoning the analysis is translated into scatter diagrams and fuzzy rules which are then incorporated via UML into the MDM to be displayed on a website as an interactive model able to diagnose the best supply chain strategy for companies to choose from according to their market and commodity.
	3. The final round is created from the amendments of the previous rounds in order to assess if the experts have established a consensus.	3. The testing is a qualitative method of semi-structured interviews by a panel of experts, to determine the applicability of the MDM model. Deductive reasoning is used to draw conclusions from the experts' answers.

need to study different supply chain strategies the problem of uncertainty will be overcome by using different statistical tools such as SPSS and Excel, while the evaluation of the results will be presented using deductive reasoning to create a decision-making matrix.

Fuzzy Delphi has been increasingly applied in a variety of disciplines including decision analysis, organisational management and forecasting (Burney and Mahmood 2006; Edwards and Akroyd 1999). Fuzzy Logic

Table 4.3 Advantages and disadvantages of fuzzy Delphi

Advantages of fuzzy Delphi	Disadvantages of fuzzy Delphi
1. It is a well-formalised method as it forces people to think about the future. If structured correctly it can allow for longer-term thinking.	1. There is a danger of regarding results as facts.
2. It gives participants the opportunity to think in more depth as they gather further information between the rounds.	2. A poorly designed Delphi will provoke opposed views and elicit poor quality information. It may fuel criticisms of the overall objective and the future foresight of the research. Therefore, a great deal of attention must be given to the choice of participants, the preparation of the questionnaire and it must be thoroughly tested to avoid ambiguity.
3. It highlights clearly whether there is consensus on an issue or not.	3. Single opinions that might be of special value are excluded and normally ignored. The accumulated results are published to ensure anonymity. It is difficult to find contradictions in answers later on because of this.
4. It provides a psychological and communication effect as it is a tool which helps expressing ideas in a clear and concise manner.	4. Care has to be taken to prevent group effects. For example, in all panels or expert groups, the opinions will reflect the set of participants involved: a narrow set of participants may lead to unrepresentative views or a smaller scale of important knowledge.
5. The judgements gathered from the Delphi study allows for the analyses to rank and prioritise ideas.	5. Some participants drop out during the process, especially after the first round. Additionally, further qualitative assessment of the Delphi study may produce useful information; however, this step is often not carried out due to lack of time.
6. The output of the Delphi study is in a form which can aid operational change for example in policy-making research.	6. It is often difficult to convince people to answer a questionnaire more than once and incentives may be needed (i.e. make available to the experts the results) as the dropout rate increases after the second or third round.

(*continued*)

Table 4.3 (continued)

Advantages of fuzzy Delphi	Disadvantages of fuzzy Delphi
7. A Delphi study is actually always a mix of methods because a research question needs several tools to prove the hypotheses put forward. The Fuzzy Delphi method was applied to select the competence of managers because it not only solved the disadvantages resulting from the conventional Delphi Method, but also because its results would not easily be affected by extreme opinions.	7. It is not applicable in all fields or cases because the statements have to be formulated relatively quickly. Even when it is applicable, this short formulation reduces the statements from being formed with close to complete information.

has also been used by Boissonnade (1984) for pattern recognition in the evaluation of seismic intensity and damage forecasting in the development of models that estimate earthquake insurance rates and strategies. Furthermore, Zhao (1996) used Fuzzy Logic to address the issue of maritime collision prevention and liability. This shows that fuzzy principals can be applied confidently within Delphi in the field of social science to identify any patterns in the study and determine any skewness of experts' opinions (Edwards and Akroyd 1999). These patterns will be incorporated into the supply chain MDM model to avoid conflict between the experts' opinions and the implementation of the model.

The next chapters will expand on the method of data collection and the use of Fuzzy Delphi to create the MDM model which will then be analysed and tested. Further explanation will be made regarding choosing the panel of experts and using their recommendations to amend the Delphi rounds. Furthermore, the methods of minimising non-response in Delphi will be examined as well as the ethical implications.

References

Boissonnade, A. C. (1984). *Earthquake damage and insurance risk*. Ph.D. Thesis. Stanford University. pp. 40-80.

Burney, S., & Mahmood, N. (2006). A brief history of mathematical logic and applications of logic in CS/IT. Karachi University, Pakistan. *Journal of Science, 34*(1), 61–75.

Checkland, P. B., & Poulter, J. (2006). *Learning for action: A short definitive account of soft systems methodology and its use for practitioners, teachers and students*. Chichester: John Wiley and Sons Ltd. 50–150.

Edwards, J., & Akroyd, R. (1999). Modelling rhetorical legal "logic" a double syllogism. *International Journal Human-Computer Studies, 51*(1), 1173–1188.

El Hussein, M., Hirst, S., Salyers, V., & Osuji, J. (2014). Using grounded theory as a method of inquiry: advantages and disadvantages. *The Qualitative Report, 19*(13), 1–15.

Franklin, K., & Hart, J. (2007). Idea generation and exploration: Benefits and limitations of the policy Delphi research method. *Innovation in Higher Education, 31*(2), 237–246.

Gu, V., Cao, Q., & Duan, W. (2012). Unified modelling language (UML) IT adoption - A holistic model of organizational capabilities perspective. *Decision Support Systems, 54*(1), 257–269.

Hiremath, H., & Skibniewski, M. (2004). Object-oriented modelling of construction processes by unified modelling language. *Automation in Construction, 13*(4), 447–468.

Hsu, Y., Lee, C., & Kreng, V. (2010). The application of fuzzy Delphi method and fuzzy AHP in lubricant regenerative technology selection. *Expert Systems with Applications, 37*(4), 419–425.

Lshikawa, A. (1993). The new fuzzy Delphi methods: Economization of GDS (Group decision support). *IEEE: System Sciences, 4*(4), 255–264.

Skulmoski, G., Hartman, F., & Krahn, J. (2007). The Delphi method for graduate research. *Journal of Information Technology Education, 6*(1), 1–21.

Trochim, W., & Donnelly, J. (2006). *Research methods knowledge base*. London: Cengage Learning. 70–300.

Zadeh, L. A. (1965). Fuzzy sets. *Information and Control, 8*, 338–353.

Zhao, J. (1996). *Maritime collision and liability*. Ph.D. Thesis. University of Southampton, U.K. pp. 50-120.

Zimmer, C. (2010). *Network theory*: A key to unraveling how nature works. http://e360.yale.edu/feature/network_theory_a_key_to_unraveling_how_nature_works/2233/.

5

Data Collection for Strategic Supply Chain Modelling

The Delphi technique is designed as a group communication process that aims to conduct detailed examinations and discussions of a specific issue for the purpose of goal setting, policy investigation or predicting the occurrence of future events. It was developed by Dalkey and Helmer (1962) as part of the Rand Corporation Air Force project, and has since become a widely used and accepted method for achieving convergence of opinion from experts, within their domain of expertise, concerning real-world issues from various topic areas. Delphi is unique amongst surveys as instead of trying to identify "what is", it addresses "what could/should be" (Hsu and Sandford 2007). Additionally it is well suited as a method for consensus-building by using a series of questions repeated multiple times to collect accurate data from a panel. These questionnaires are developed and refined during the sequential stages until consensus is achieved (European Commission 2008). This study will take advantage of one of the strengths of the Delphi method which is the ability to gather opinions from experts from different backgrounds and use it to get a selected set of indicators from a broader available set.

The choice of participants for the panel, time frames for conducting and completing a study, the possibility of low response rates and

© The Author(s) 2017
S. Sindi, M. Roe, *Strategic Supply Chain Management*,
DOI 10.1007/978-3-319-54843-2_5

questionnaire amendments based on the feedback from the respondent group are all areas which should be considered when designing and implementing a Delphi study (Davidson 2013). The Delphi process has been used in various fields of study such as programming, management, organisational strategy planning, policy assessment and resource utilisation to develop a full range of alternatives, explore or expose underlying assumptions, as well as correlate judgments on a topic spanning a wide range of disciplines (Hsu and Sandford 2007). Here, the selection of participants has been conducted through establishing contacts with academic and industrial experts via email and social media.

The time frame to complete the Delphi for this study was limited to a maximum of 3–4 months. The feedback loops are a unique and crucial element in the Delphi technique for establishing consensus as it is a structured group interaction process that is organised over several rounds for the purpose of collecting opinions and feedback from the participants that result in amendments to the statements. Opinion collection in Delphi is achieved by conducting a series of surveys using questionnaires. The survey is then sent out to be answered and feedback is sent back from the participants. This feedback determines if a consensus has been achieved or whether further amendments are to be made to the statements. Once any amendments have been made the survey is sent back to the participants until consensus has been established. Figure 5.1 illustrates the feedback loop process in the Delphi technique.

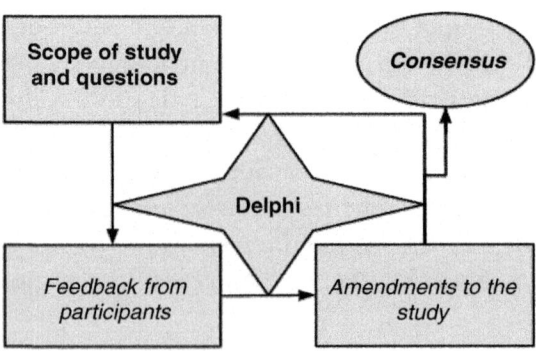

Fig. 5.1   Delphi study feedback loops

Rationale for Adopting Delphi

Turoff and Linstone (2002) suggested that Delphi is a unique technique that encourages participants to voice their opinion without fear of peer-pressure. This encourages experts to remain honest and consistent and to retain independent thinking alongside gradual formulation of reliable judgments as it is free from personality influence and individual dominance (Delbecq et al. 1975). Therefore, the key advantage of the approach is that it avoids direct confrontation of experts, resulting in specialising in generating consensus or identifying divergence of opinions among groups opposing or differing from each other (Kalaian and Kasim 2012). Furthermore, it focuses and retains attention directly on the issue while allowing the sharing of information and reasoning among participants.

Hsu and Sandford (2007) specifically indicate the unique ability for the Delphi technique to achieve the following objectives: determine or develop a range of possible program alternatives; explore or expose underlying assumptions or information leading to different judgments; seek out information which may generate a consensus on the part of the respondent group; correlate informed judgments on a topic spanning a wide range of disciplines; and educate the respondent group to the diverse and interrelated aspects of the topic.

The advantages of Delphi led it to be a popular tool for researchers to use in subsequent studies, in addition to enabling managers to make decisions based on information gathered using group consensus. The definition commonly used to describe Delphi is as a method for structuring a group communication process, and is effective in allowing a group of individuals deal with a complex problem to accomplish structured communication, to assemble feedback from individuals, to assess group judgment and to provide opportunity for views to be revised with some degree of anonymity (Okoli and Pawlowski 2004).

The Delphi technique like any other has disadvantages, such as information coming from a selected group of people may not be representative. However, it can be argued that experts represent the opinion of many; hence there is little need for a large sample (Kalaian and Kasim 2012). Delphi does not depend on a statistical sample that attempts to be representative of any population as it is a group decision requiring qualified experts who have deep understanding of the issues. Hence, one of the most critical requirements is the selection of qualified experts. Another disadvantage is that Delphi is more time-consuming than group process methods as it requires skill in written communication and participant commitment (European Commission 2008).

It has been applied to a wide variety of situations as a tool for expert problem solving. Some of these methods are tailored to specific problem types and outcome goals, leading to the widespread use of the "ranking and multiple choice-type" Delphi as it develops a tailored understanding by grouping options aimed at achieving a consensus about the relative importance of an issue or its effect on the topic of a question (Okoli and Pawlowski 2004). Here, the Delphi technique will be based on a multiple choice type questionnaire that will aim to achieve the following:

1. Incorporate experts' opinion about definitions and characteristics of the various indicators of supply chain strategy,
2. Identify feedback on the processes in each round and with amendments made accordingly and
3. Reach a consensus regarding the best suited supply chain strategy for each variable indicator.

Choosing Expert Participants

The expert panellists who participated in the Delphi were academic and industrial specialists in the areas of supply chain, logistics consultation and senior management positions. Based on the panel selection procedures put forward by Okoli and Pawlowski (2004) an international selection of experts was made to give the study more depth and verity. This provides a broad range of views, in accordance with two criteria, the expert's profile and the Delphi's needs, resulting in the final list of experts shown in Appendix 2 including details of institution or job title and field of expertise. Names are not provided to protect participants' anonymity.

The choice of experts met the following requirements:

- Technical knowledge and professional experience in the area of supply chains and logistics
- Willingness and ability to participate during the time of the survey
- To be neutral in their assessment and to choose the product, good or commodity in a market suitable to their expertise while answering the Delphi questions.

The number of experts used in a Delphi study is determined by the number required to constitute a representative pooling of judgments and the information processing capability of the research team (Hsu and Sandford 2007). However, what constitutes an optimal number of participants has never been formally defined. This is due to the variable number of Delphi iterations depending largely on the subject being investigated and the degree of consensus sought by the investigators, hence it can vary considerably. Nevertheless, Delbecq et al. (1975) recommend that researchers should use the minimum sufficient number of participants and then seek to verify the results through follow-up explorations. They further suggest that 10–15 experts can be sufficient if the background of the Delphi subjects and the knowledge of the experts are homogeneous. Ludwig (1997) states the approximate size of a Delphi panel is generally under 50 and usually between 15 and 20 experts if the participants come from various backgrounds. Hsu and Sandford (2007) further explain that if the sample size of a Delphi study is too small, the study may not be considered as having provided a representative pooling of opinions. If the sample size is too large, the drawbacks from the Delphi technique such as potentially low response rates from experts pulling-out, conflict of opinions and extension of time to achieve consensus may skew the results (Stata Press 2013).

However, this study's mixed methodology requires the use of statistical analysis of the Delphi survey–a key component in designing the study and choosing the sample size of the panel. The sample size determines the time invested and the likelihood of successful achievement of a study's objective (Stata Press 2013). The tool used for statistical analysis in this study is SPSS which requires a complex sample to enable an accurate result of the issues in question. Complex samples are clarified by Hanafin (2004) as usually large due to the nature of different viewpoints included, as experts are required to choose their own markets to answer the questions. It has been suggested previously that a Delphi panel varies depending on the issues examined. The key aspect for participants involved in Delphi is to have "willingness" and "ability" to make a valid contribution to the issues in question (Hanafin, *ibid*). Therefore, to attain an adequate sample size that remains within both boundaries of Delphi and the requirements of statistical analysis, this study generated a panel size between 50 and 100 experts. A sample below 50 would be too small for statistical analysis while above 100 although in some ways ideal, would be too large within the time constraint to reach a consensus and would lead to a possible reduction of responses from the panel (Stata Press 2013).

Delphi Rounds

The adoption of a "multiple choice-type" approach (Hanafin 2004) allows for the use of measures of dispersion (e.g. standard deviation, mean, median, maximum, minimum, frequencies and percentages) crucial in identifying reliable consensus. The purpose of Delphi is to establish agreement that can be measured and is usually determined through statistical variance in responses across rounds. Less variance in the rounds indicates a greater consensus, although according to Rowe and Wright (1999), respondents with more extreme views were more likely to drop out of the study than participants with more moderate views, resulting in the decrease in variance as a consequence of decrease in participants rather than consensus.

According to Hsu and Sandford (2007) the number of rounds is determined by the level of consensus that is considered suitable for the study. However most changes as a result from feedback occur in the transition from the first to the second round. Similar to the number of participants in the Delphi panel, there are no set numbers of rounds to be conducted in order to achieve a consensus (Kalaian and Kasim 2012). The Delphi technique may require as few as two rounds if panellists have been provided with sufficient explanation leading to an early group consensus (Hanafin 2004). Furthermore, Black et al. (1999) clarify that two or three rounds are likely to result in some convergence of individual judgements, while more than three rounds are likely to have little impact on the level of agreement and to have adverse effects on the response rate. Other examples of Delphi have required up to four rounds, which resulted in lower response rates between each iteration (Hanafin 2004). According to Kalaian and Kasim (2012) most Delphi examples suggested that comparing the averages or percentages of responses for each question from any two consecutive rounds will determine if another round is required. Additionally, once feedback from participants ceases, it is an indication that no further amendments are needed; hence further rounds will not aid the establishment of a consensus. Using both approaches of ceased feedbacks from the last round and statistical comparison of mean, frequencies and percentages between two consecutive rounds, the Delphi generates the data required to conclude if no additional round for administering the Delphi survey is needed. To date, this method is typically used for analysing the collected Delphi survey data.

Iteration is a key feature of the Delphi technique and feedback on the questionnaire is provided by participants at each round for amendments to be completed for the next round. Feedback has been defined as the means by which information is passed between panellists so that individual judgement may be improved and debiasing achieved (Rowe and Wright 1999). Feedback from participants varies and may be provided in a number of different ways such as an attachment to the questionnaire or via email. The purpose of feedback is to improve the Delphi and allow each expert to revise his/her own judgement via the amendments made in light of the judgement of others (Turoff and Linstone 2002).

The analysis of Delphi has two purposes (Munier and Rondé 2001). Firstly, to illustrate the feedback and amendments between rounds and secondly, to identify when consensus has been reached. However, there is little agreement about the best method of identifying consensus; whether it is mathematical aggregation, statistical analysis or deductive qualitative reasoning. Rowe and Wright (1999) suggest that a number of different descriptive statistics combined with deductive reasoning should be used to determine a consensus. Statistical analysis can include median, mode, frequencies, percentages, ranks, upper and lower quartile ranges, regression weights or induced (If-Then) rules, combined with deductive reasoning to examine the reasons behind expert decisions in order to establish a coherent consensus. Here the selection was multiple choice Delphi integrated with (If-Then) rules. Therefore the methods proposed by Rowe and Wright (1999) in using deductive reasoning combined with statistical analysis of frequency and percentages were most suitable for this study to determine the degree and type of consensus. The (If-then) rules were integrated with Delphi to create a better understanding of the "reasons" behind the expert's feedbacks and decisions.

Creation of Rounds

Using a hybrid research design characterised by statistical analysis and deductive reasoning in the Delphi enabled the assessment of experts' judgments more accurately, captured the areas of collective knowledge held by the experts which is not often verbalised or explored, and focused on emerging new ideas about the issue in question (Franklin and Hart 2007). Both Rowe and Wright (1999) have compared hybrid iterations with statistical analysis of consensus based on deductive reasoning; with iteration analysis based on standard statistics without deductive reasoning. Their findings indicated the former has greatly improved the accuracy of understanding the consensus. Moreover, combining the "multiple choice" Delphi with (If-Then) rules for the statements provides accurate results as it allows the experts to provide a rationale for the choice of what they believe is most suitable for the (If-Then) statement. This allows for the statistical analysis to be conducted using frequency and percentages on the "multiple choice options" and a detailed deductive explanation of the reasons from the experts based on the (If-Then) statements. Furthermore, Rowe and Wright (1999) state that analysing a multiple choice type Delphi with (If-Then) rules using statistical models without reason will not give an authentic measurement of the consensus. Applying deductive reasoning with statistical analysis, however, will enable a holistic view of the experts' judgment, suggesting a significantly greater degree of accuracy.

The Delphi study will begin by creating a pilot test to ensure participants understand the requirements and provide "deductive reason" feedback for the variables, measurements and scope that is relevant in achieving the objective of identifying the best suitable supply chain strategy. The pilot Delphi study is created using the hybrid method of a multiple choice Delphi and (If-Then) statement which includes three options for the experts to select. The feedback is analysed using deductive reasoning and amendments will be applied for the first round to commence. The Delphi in this research relies on the knowledge and expertise of the participants to use deductive reasoning in giving clear and accurate indicators on the improvements needed for each round. Once feedback ceases, the Delphi study will be analysed using the hybrid method of statistical frequency and percentages as well as deductive "reasoning" to evaluate the type of consensus achieved.

Delphi Types

The main purpose of adopting a Delphi technique for decision making is to provide a structured approach to collecting data in situations where obtaining a consistent sample is difficult and complex to achieve. The aim of employing a Delphi technique is to achieve consensus through a process of iteration. There are various types of Delphi, each suited to different studies (Table 5.1) and largely determined by the objectives of the study.

Clearly different Delphi studies vary in their difficulty to plan and conduct. They are generally fairly time-consuming and labour intensive and require (external) expert preparation and, therefore, can be relatively expensive. Different Delphi studies require various formalisations of methodology, amount of data, number of experts involved, different knowledge from experts and different combinations of interviews and questionnaires. However, Delphi's ability to accommodate diverse

Table 5.1 Types of Delphi techniques

Delphi Type	Explanation
Classical (Original) Delphi	Evolved by Dalkey and Helmer (1962). Anonymity decision-making consensus.
Modified Delphi	Face-to-face interviews or a focus group for the first round. The number of rounds also varies; however, this form of Delphi technique uses a more quantitative method of analysis. The critical unified factors remain the use of an expert panel and the anonymity of the panel members. While focus groups and group interviews have taken place in the first round, the responses after are anonymous (Davidson 2013).
Policy Delphi	Differs from other Delphi techniques in the formation of its expert panel and the overall goal of the research issues as the aim is not for making a decision or achieving consensus but rather to clarify an understanding of different plurality standpoints. It also has various number of rounds and ensures anonymity within the panel (Rauch 1979).
Decision Delphi	Aims to bring a group of decision makers together to make decisions about future developments in contrast with the policy Delphi that aims to understand social situations. Whereas the classical Delphi deals with facts, a policy Delphi deals with ideas. The decision Delphi is not used as a tool for obtaining a group opinion about forecast statement (as in the case of the classical Delphi) but as a means to analyse decisions (Rauch 1979).
Real-Time Delphi	Real-time Delphi varies in its structure and is sometimes referred to as a consensus conference. Its aim is to ensure expert availability in order to reduce the drop-out rates and increase the efficiency of the processes. This is done by ensuring that participants are provided with a hyperlink to a welcome page where they read the details of the study, what is required and access the initial questionnaire. The process uses a refined interface, and the authors argue the outcomes (Gnatzy et al. 2011).
e-Delphi	Similar to real-time Delphi, e-Delphi replicates the process of classical Delphi, but the questionnaire, feedback and participation of the expert panel is all done via email or online surveys. It can be argued that this approach is categorised under modified Delphi (Gnatzy et al. 2011).
Technological Delphi	Technological Delphi has similarities to real-time Delphi yet there are differences. The key one is that technological Delphi uses handheld devices to respond

Table 5.1 (continued)

Delphi Type	Explanation
	immediately to the questions. For example voting can take place in real time and this process tends to have a more quantitative approach as it is more difficult to ask and explore open-ended questions (Davidson 2013).
Disaggregative Delphi	Disaggregative Delphi is critical of the classical Delphi. Consensus is formed when panellists are asked to give estimates of probable and preferable futures. The method uses cluster analysis to disaggregate responses to key variables, which is considered more accurate. This study uses two rounds. In the first, quantitative questions are asked, while the second is qualitative and involves interviews with panel members (Davidson 2013).
Fuzzy Delphi	Fuzzy Delphi is mostly utilised to generate a professional consensus for complex topics (Wu et al. 2013). The advantage of fuzzy Delphi is that every expert opinion can be considered and integrated to achieve consensus for group decisions. Moreover, it reduces the time of investigation and the consumption of cost and time. Additionally, the advantage of fuzzy Delphi method is its simplicity. All expert opinions can be encompassed in one investigation. Hence, this method can create more effective criteria selection. However, the number of rounds varies and anonymity must remain. Fuzzy Delphi is a traditional forecasting approach that does not require large samples. However, once combined with quantitative questions and statistical analysis, the study moves towards larger samples to ensure accuracy.

opinions makes it popular and credible for various fields of study (Turoff and Linstone 2002). The common advantage in the various types of Delphi is guaranteed anonymity which encourages opinions that are free of influences from others and, therefore, more likely to be honest. It also has the capacity to capture a wide range of inter-related variables and multi-dimensional features from across a geographically dispersed panel of experts.

Amongst all Delphi types there are common disadvantages; for example a consensus can represent the lowest common denominator. However, according to Hanafin (2004), it could be argued that all approaches gaining consensus run this risk. Another common disadvantage is time, which when extended may threaten the credibility of the study. However this can be mitigated by ensuring the commitment and expertise of the panel, reducing the number of rounds and achieving consensus.

From Tables 5.1 and 5.2 it is clear that although there are differences between the various techniques, a number of characteristics are common. These include creation of statements to acquire opinions from experts, anonymity, iterations, controlled feedback and amendments, and qualitative and/or quantitative statistical analysis of the group responses. While there are no required number of rounds, the most common number of iterative rounds appears to be two to three.

Table 5.2 Advantages and disadvantages of various Delphi techniques

Advantages and disadvantages of Delphi	
Advantages	Disadvantages
As with other well-formalised methods, it forces people to think about the future.	A Delphi survey is actually always a mix of methods because a topic generation procedure is needed.
It gives participants the opportunity to think in more depth and gather further information between the rounds (psychological effect).	However, there is a danger of regarding results as facts.
It highlights clearly whether there is consensus on an issue or not.	Single opinions that might be of special value are also pooled and normally ignored. Only the accumulated results are published to preserve anonymity. It is difficult to find out reasons for dissenting answers later on, as this anonymity has to be respected.
There is a psychological and a communication effect in being forced to express ideas in a clear and concise way.	A poorly designed Delphi will provoke antagonism and elicit poor quality information. It may fuel criticisms of the overall foresight activity with which it is associated. Therefore, a great deal of attention must be given to the choice of participants; the questionnaire must be meticulously prepared and thoroughly tested to avoid ambiguity.

Table 5.2 (continued)

Advantages and disadvantages of Delphi	
Advantages	Disadvantages
The judgements allows for analyses, rankings and priority-settings.	Care has to be taken over group effects. As in all panels or expert groups, the opinions will reflect the set of participants involved: a narrow set of criteria for these may lead to unrepresentative views or miss out important sources of knowledge.
The output is in a form which is operational for many actors including policy makers.	Some participants drop out during the process (especially after the first round). In addition, although further qualitative assessment of Delphi inquiry may produce useful information, this step is often not carried out due to lack of time.
Even oriented towards action, Delphi surveys allow for longer-term thinking.	It is often difficult to convince people to answer a questionnaire twice or more and incentives may be needed (e.g. that the experts receive the results). The dropout-rate increases after the second or third round, so most current studies are limited to preparation and two rounds.

Choosing a Hybrid Fuzzy Delphi

The Delphi method developed by Helmer and his associates has been widely used as one of the long-term forecasting methods (Dalkey and Helmer 1962). The disadvantages of the traditional Delphi method include low consistency of expert opinions, high enforcement cost and modification of experts' individual opinions in order to reach consistent overall opinions (Chung and Chiang 2011). One of the weaknesses of Delphi is that it requires repetitive surveys of the experts – usually more than twice – to allow accuracy of the forecasted values to converge. However, with repetition comes cost and lower response rate, particularly for a complicated survey.

To overcome these difficulties, the Fuzzy Delphi method proposed by Murray et al. (1985) aims to integrate the Delphi method and fuzzy theory. They added the membership function found in fuzzy theory to establish fuzzy rules in the form of statements to be given to each participant. Ishikawa (Ishikawa 1993) associated membership functions with "the extent of expertise". This allowed for a tailored expert panel that is specialised in the understanding of the specific membership functions that are given the questionnaire in the form of fuzzy rule statements. Therefore it is important that accurate fuzziness is incorporated in the findings of the Delphi study which can be analysed statistically using max-min and fuzzy integration algorithms. The integration of experts' opinions with fuzzy numbers is based on the concepts of cumulative frequency distribution and fuzzy integral, enabling a well-formed linguistic and systematic structure of rounds, resulting in a reduction of iterations (Ishikawa, *ibid*).

Hsu et al. (2010) further acknowledge the following advantages of Fuzzy Delphi compared to other Delphi methods:

1. It reduces investigation time and costs.
2. Individual experts' opinions can be clearly expressed without distortion due to the membership functions being integrated by fuzzy rule sets.
3. This creates a semantic structure that helps opinions to be clearly expressed.
4. The fuzziness in the issues being studied are investigated and addressed during the process.
5. The Fuzzy Delphi is simple to create and conduct; its analysis process is simple and can statistically address issues such as multi-level, multi-attribute and multi-scheme decision-making problems under uncertainty (Hsu et al. 2010; Murray et al. 1985).

Shapiro and Koissi (2013) modified Fuzzy Delphi to include the Analytic Hierarchy Process (AHP) which is a theory of measurement through pair-wise comparisons that relies on judgment to derive priority scales. The implementation of AHP required the construction of hierarchies, allowing the study to make judgments or perform measurements on pairs of elements with respect to a criterion, deriving preference scales, which are then synthesised throughout the structure to select the preferred alternative (Shapiro and Koissi, *ibid*). AHP has been incorporated in a study by Hsu et al. (2010), applying a triangular fuzzy number into the Fuzzy Delphi to encompass experts' opinions and establish the value of the triangular fuzzy number of each alternate factor given by the experts. This allows the significant triangular fuzzy number of the alternate factors to be calculated using maximum and minimum values of expert opinions as two terminal points of triangular fuzzy numbers and the geometric mean is taken as the membership degree of triangular fuzzy numbers to derive an accurate statistical value for the experts' opinion and hence provides an unbiased effect whilst avoiding the impact of extreme values. This according to Hsu et al. (2010) will counter the disadvantage found in other Delphi methods such as experts' judgments which cannot be properly reflected in quantitative terms, in addition to ambiguity in the outcome due to the differences in the meanings and interpretations of expert opinions. AHP can be applied to risk assessment and decision making as it eliminates ambiguities such as incomplete or unreliable data, and vague or subjective information due to expert human error in the communication of linguistic variables. As AHP has proved to be a reliable tool in Fuzzy Delphi, there has been considerable further research of its value (Shapiro and Koissi 2013).

This has led to the widespread use of Fuzzy Delphi in various fields for index selection. For example Ma et al. (2011) adopted it to quantify experts' attitudes towards road safety. Kuo and Chen (2008) applied it to create key performance indexes when offering mobile services, while Chang et al. (2009) applied Fuzzy Delphi with AHP for decision-making issues tackling uncertainty and imprecision of service evaluation during pre-negotiation stages where the expert's comparison judgments are represented as fuzzy triangular numbers. Furthermore Liu (2013) applied Fuzzy Delphi and fuzzy AHP to evaluate the important indicators of managerial competences. Fuzzy Delphi is useful as it is effective in establishing accurate outcomes. It aids human thinking and perceptions by reducing ambiguity as it is equipped to represent uncertainties and deal with problems in a vague environment. It has the ability to transform crisp linguistic variables into fuzzy sets, as their values are not numbers but words or sentences in a natural or artificial language. The concept is very useful in situations that are complicated or difficult to be appropriately described by traditional quantitative expressions (Chen 2014).

Creating a Hybrid Fuzzy Delphi

Here Fuzzy Delphi will incorporate different characteristics found in other Delphi studies in order to make it reliable and tailored to specific needs. The panel is constructed of decision-making experts as characterised by decision Delphi. Questionnaires will be sent to the participants via a hyperlink to a welcoming page with details of the study and access to the questionnaire online via Qualtrics, hence combining the elements of both real time and e-Delphi. Testing the Fuzzy Delphi will be conducted using semi-structured interviews to ensure the accuracy of the results and statistical analysis, hence combining the elements of modified and disaggregative Delphi.

The Fuzzy Delphi will include multiple choice questions to help produce the most accurate results. Additionally, multiple choice questions are most suited to the Fuzzy Delphi as this gives the experts options and room to account for any uncertainty or "fuzziness" (Wu 2011). Each question will be given with an objective to measure a membership function, also known as "variable function". The questions will be asked in a format of (If-Then) statements. This will ensure more accurate results in addition to being the most suitable method for writing statements that can be translated into fuzzy rules (Murray et al. 1985). Each membership "variable function" will be expressed in a statement where experts will have three to four options to choose from. The results will be statistically analysed and contain deductive reasoning in order to further understand the expert's decision, while testing will be conducted via semi-structured interviews. Deductive reasoning plays an important part in analysis and provides accurate understanding of the issues being studied.

In adding fuzzy principals into Delphi feedback loops, the Fuzzy Delphi can be illustrated as an integrated system between Delphi study and fuzzy controller system (Fig. 5.2). The purpose of fuzzy control as defined by Terano et al. (1994) is to influence the behaviour of a system by changing inputs to that system according to a rule or set of rules (If/Then statements) that model how the system operates, in the case of this study, the interactive MDM. The fuzzy controller is used to define a relationship that transforms the desired and observed state of the system into an input or inputs that will alter its future state (Terano *et al., ibid*). The input value is based on the difference between two values (defuzzification and fuzzification) (Fig. 5.2), where the output of the fuzzy system establishes the desired state of the system (Yager and Zadeh 1992).

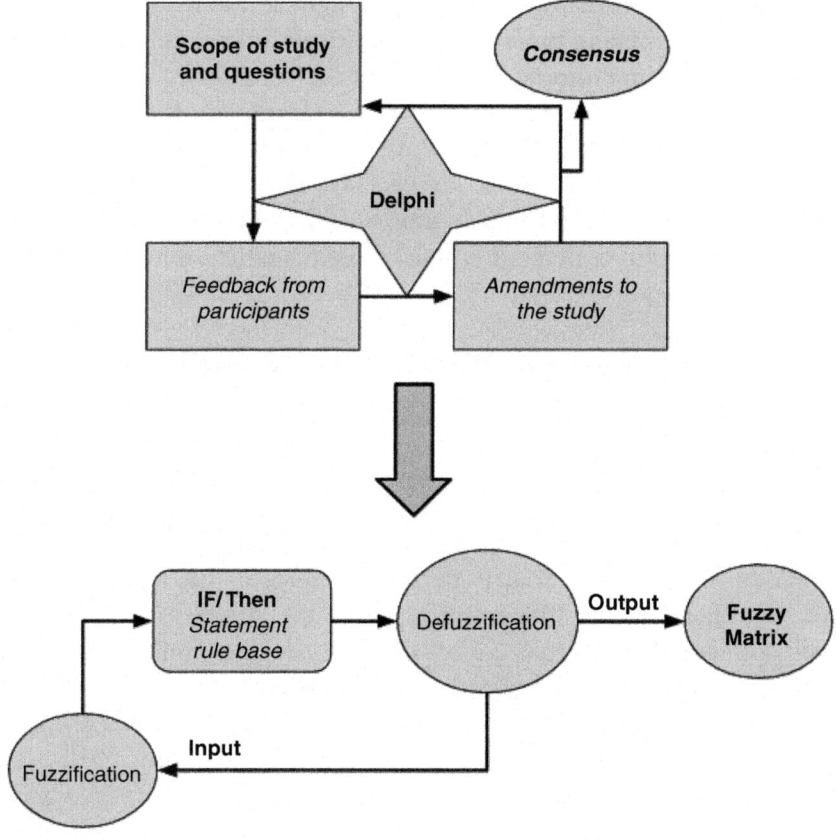

Fig. 5.2 Combining Delphi and fuzzy controller into Fuzzy Delphi

Fuzzy Delphi is based on combining both the Delphi feedback loop process and the fuzzy controller system in order to defuzzify the expert's opinions and create fuzzy rules that build the interactive MDM. The first stage is creating the (If-Then) statements which are the inputs to be sent. This stage is similar to the Delphi process as it defines the scope of study and sets the questions. Next the statements are sent to the panel to be defuzzified and feedback is given. The feedback amends the statements which become the fuzzy input to be re-written as (If-Then) statements to be sent again. Once a consensus is achieved it becomes the output that creates the fuzzy rules that build the fuzzy matrices called the interactive MDM.

The drawback of the fuzzy controller system is that it usually assumes that the system is being modelled in is linear or at least behaves in some fashion that is a monotonic function. As the complexity of the system increases it becomes increasingly difficult to formulate the desired outcome as the fuzzy controller can only describe a small section of the whole system (Driankov et al. 1996). The next chapters will further illustrate how the membership functions – (If-Then) statements – will result in the fuzzy rule that will be added to create the interactive MDM.

Minimising Non-response in Data Collection

In all data collection, the issue of non-response is critical. If a small number of the invited participants chose not to respond at any stage of the data collection, the quality of the information generated will be downgraded. In order to mitigate the effects of non-response, asking recognised experts, potential leaders in the project field and verifying those who have first-hand relationship with the targeted issue can help. A recommended individual can also help through a preliminary introduction of both the researcher and the targeted panel especially in a society where personal relationships are of vital importance, such influence and assistance are extremely useful (Kalaian and Kasim 2012). It is equally important to illustrate why the experts are chosen for the Delphi study as well as why that specific topic is necessary and important. If the participants are unwilling to participate in the Delphi study they can inform the statement sender of their decision during the initial contact. Additionally, even if experts chose to participate they can become unavailable during different stages of the study (e.g. due to clash of holiday schedules). To deal with this issue there are several reminder strategies; for example, providing incentives, setting deadlines, use of telephones, post cards or e-mail (Turoff and Linstone 2002).

Minimising non-response was managed though establishing face-to-face contact with some of the panel members via conferences and university associations. Additionally, contacts were established via personalised emails sharing interest in the issues addressed. The panellists were given a reason to participate in this research as well as an incentive to be updated with the results and informed of the outcome of this study. Panellists were notified of their important role in partaking in the Fuzzy Delphi study and the crucial effects their withdrawal would have on the results. Hence, they understood the impact of their commitment to the study. Although there is no binding contract to the Delphi, participants who withdrew were reminded via e-mail of the significance of their input in the creation of the interactive multi-dimensional model to aid companies identify the best suited supply chain strategy for their market. All panellists were ensured of anonymity and confidentiality through the study.

To ensure suitable ethical compliance, participants were informed about the purpose of the study, the procedures to be followed, the anticipated time commitment and contact details if they wish to ask any questions. They were free to withdraw at any time. Other ethical issues revolved around consent, privacy, anonymity and confidentiality. All individual names, contact details and positions were held securely throughout the Delphi process and questionnaire feedback and by a single researcher. Participants were informed that although their names and contact details will remain confidential, for research purposes their institution and position title or expertise should be listed to clarify their authenticity. The majority of participants gave their consent and provided full details while others wished for anonymity. A restricted list of panellists' data can be found in Appendix 2. During the Fuzzy Delphi process, assurance of confidentiality was given to all participants via a code number generated by Qualtrics, which also complies with participant confidentiality by making the completion of the contact detail fields non-mandatory. Therefore, completed questionnaires were identifiable only by their code number and the participants' institution and position title or expertise.

References

Black, N., Murphy, M., Lamping, D., McKee, M., Sanderson, C., Askham, J., & Marteau, T. (1999). Consensus development methods: A review of best practice in creating clinical guidelines. *Journal of Health Services Research and Policy, 4*(4), 236–248.

Chang, C., Wu, C., & Lin, H. (2009). Applying fuzzy hierarchy multiple attributes to construct an expert decision making process. *Journal of Expert Systems with Applications, 36*(4), 7363–7368.

Chen, H. (2014). Applying fuzzy multiple criteria decision-making method and service failure index to evaluate restaurants' performance. *Journal of Management and Strategy, 5*(4), 14–25.

Chung, C., & Chiang, C. (2011). The critical factors: An evaluation of schedule reliability in liner shipping. *International Journal of Operations Research, 8*(4), 3–9.

Dalkey, N., & Helmer, O. (1962). An experimental application of the Delphi method to the use of experts. *U.S. Air Force Project Rand., 1*(1), 12–27.

Davidson, P. (2013). The Delphi technique in doctoral research: Considerations and rationale. *Review of Higher Education and Self-Learning, 6*(22), 53–65.

Delbecq, A. L., Van De Ven, A. H., & Gustafson, D. H. (1975). *Group techniques for program planning: A guide to nominal group and Delphi processes.* Glenview, IL: Scott: Foresman and Company.

Driankov, D., Hellendoorn, H., & Reinfrank, M. (1996). *An introduction to Fuzzy control.* 2nd. ed. Heidelberg: Springer-Verlag. 2–74.

European Commission. (2008). *Final report of Delphi study E3M project – European Indicators and ranking methodology for University* 3rd. *Mission.* European Commission: Brussels. 3599/001–001. pp. 4-33.

Franklin, K., & Hart, J. (2007). Idea generation and exploration: Benefits and limitations of the policy Delphi research method. *University of Arkansas for Medical Sciences, 31*(2), 237–246.

Gnatzy, T., Warth, J., Gracht, H., & Darkow, I. (2011). Validating an innovative real-time Delphi approach – A methodological comparison between real-time and conventional Delphi studies. *Technological Forecasting and Social Change, 78*(3), 1681–1694.

Hanafin, S. (2004). Review of literature on the Delphi technique. *Royal College of Surgeons Ireland, 2*(1), 5–40.

Hsu, C., & Sandford, B. (2007). The Delphi technique: Making sense of consensus. *Practical Assessment Research and Evaluation, 12*(10), 1–5.

Hsu, Y., Lee, C., & Kreng, V. (2010). The application of Fuzzy Delphi method and Fuzzy AHP in lubricant regenerative technology selection. *Expert Systems with Applications, 37*(4), 419–425.

Kalaian, S., & Kasim, R. (2012). Terminating sequential Delphi survey data collection. *Practical Assessment Research and Evaluation, 17*(5), 2–9.

Ishikawa, A. (1993) The new Fuzzy Delphi methods: Economization of GDS (Group Decision Support). *IEEE: System Sciences, 4*(4), 255–264.

Kuo, Y., & Chen, P. (2008). Constructing performance appraisal indicators for mobility of the service industries using Fuzzy Delphi method. *Expert Systems with Applications, 35*(3), 1930–1939.

Liu, W. (2013). Application of the Fuzzy Delphi method and the Fuzzy analytic hierarchy process for the managerial competence of multinational corporation executives. *International Journal of E-Education, E-Business, E-Management and E-Learning, 3*(4), 313–317.

Ludwig, B. (1997). Predicting the future: Have you considered using the Delphi methodology? *Journal of Extension, 35*(5), 1–4.

Ma, Z., Shao, C., Ma, S., & Ye, Z. (2011). Constructing road safety performance indicators using Fuzzy Delphi method and grey Delphi method. *Expert Systems with Applications, 38*(3), 1509–1514.

Munier, F., & Rondé, P. (2001). The role of knowledge codification in the emergence of consensus under uncertainty: Empirical analysis and policy implications. *Journal of Research Policy, 30*(1), 1537–1551.

Murray, T., Pipino, L., Van, G., & John, P. (1985). A pilot study of fuzzy set modification of Delphi. *Human Systems Management, 5*(1), 76–80.

Okoli, C., & Pawlowski, S. (2004). The Delphi method as a research tool: An example, design considerations and applications. *Information and Management, 42*(1), 15–29.

Press, S. (2013). Stata power and sample-size reference manual release. *Texas Stata Press, Version, 13*, 1–50.

Rauch, W. (1979). The decision Delphi. *Technological Forecasting and Social Change, 15*(1), 159–169.

Rowe, G., & Wright, G. (1999). The Delphi technique as a forecasting tool: Issues and analysis. *International Journal of Forecasting, 15*(3), 353–375.

Shapiro, A., & Koissi, M. (2013). Fuzzy logic modifications of the analytic hierarchy process some preliminary observations. *Society of Actuaries, 1*, (ARCH 2014.1 Proceedings), 1–18.

Terano, T., Asai, K., & Sugeno, M. (1994). *Applied Fuzzy systems*. London: Academic Press Limited. 9–161.

Turoff, M., & Linstone, H. (2002). *The Delphi method techniques and applications*. Portland OR: Portland State University and New Jersey Institute of Technology. 3–100.

Wu, C., Hsieh, C., & Chang, K. (2013). A hybrid multiple criteria decision making model for supplier selection. *Journal of Mathematical Problems in Engineering, 13*(ID 324283), 1–8.

Wu, K. (2011). Applying the Fuzzy Delphi method to analyse the evaluation Indexes for service quality after railway re-opening – Using the old mountain line railway. As an example. *Recent Researches in System Science, 1*, 474–479.

Yager, R., & Zadeh, L. (1992). *An introduction to Fuzzy logic applications in intelligent systems*. New York: Springer. 45–100.

6

The Application of Fuzzy Delphi to Strategic Supply Chain Modelling

Due to the nature of conducting a questionnaire that relies on experts choosing their own products and customers in order to select a valid option, the Delphi study requires flexibility in designing its statements to take into account this variability. This suggests a degree of fuzziness to create a generic model accounting for different perspectives that can also be tailored to a company's needs. Fuzzy Delphi's characteristics were considered most suitable to accomplish this collection of data.

Collection Process

The selection of experts and accurately specifying the appropriate issue are the most important steps in the entire process of a Delphi study as they directly relate to the quality of the results generated.

Selection of the panel was conducted by researching a considerable number of worldwide experts in the field of supply chains and contacting them via email, Linkedin and conferences. The panel should be highly trained and competent within the specialised area of knowledge related to the target issue, to enable them to answer the statements with experienced

© The Author(s) 2017
S. Sindi, M. Roe, *Strategic Supply Chain Management*,
DOI 10.1007/978-3-319-54843-2_6

judgment (Davidson 2013). Senior academics, policy-makers and consultants and managers from supply chain and/or logistics industries were chosen. A letter was emailed to each expert, explaining the terms and the importance of experts completing all the rounds. Some 90 experts were found to establish a panel within a variety of supply chain and logistics disciplines worldwide.

Pilot Delphi

The pilot Delphi study was created focusing on the "Cost" and the "JIT Lean" of a supply chain as a crisp set (Fig. 6.1) in order to determine the fuzziness which initiates the Fuzzy Delphi parameters. The statements were designed using "If" and "Then", to enable accurate fuzzy answers to the Delphi.

A crisp set according to Terano et al. (1994) indicates a group which has clear characteristics such as {0,1} and computing language which operates under crisp logic. The foundations of crisp logic are that it has two defined values such as "yes" or "no" and "true" or "false" as

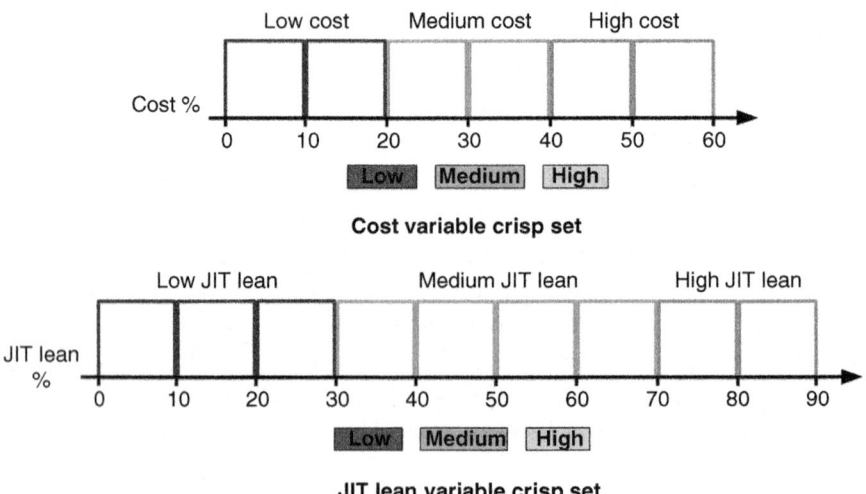

Fig. 6.1 Cost and JIT variable Crisp Sets

commonly found in a standard Delphi study. However, the opposite of that would be fuzzy set and fuzzy logic. The crisp set and fuzzy set are linked, as the latter is an extended concept that includes the concept of the former (Terano *et al.*, *ibid*). To gain an understanding of the fuzziness, this study commenced with a crisp set in the pilot Delphi to determine experts' perception of a fuzzy set that will be used for the actual Fuzzy Delphi iterations.

The pilot Delphi was initiated by giving the panel the (If-Then) Cost and JIT Lean statements based on the following:

SME's [50–250 Employees, ≤ £10 m–50 m turnover, ≤ £10 m–43 m balance sheet total] and multinational corporation (MNC) which manufactures products or sources commodities domestically or internationally to be sold at a local or international market, excluding service providers.

The pilot Delphi was conducted with crisp set percentages for Cost and JIT Lean; 0–60% for Cost and 0–90% for JIT Lean. The selection of Cost range from 0% to 60% rather than 100% was because the cost of a product from manufacturing to end customer cannot exceed 50% of production and distribution cost. For example, using the 0–60% maximum range of this study, if production and distribution of a product is 12%, this will include the cost of materials, the cost of operating the equipment to make the product, the cost of storage and distribution to the end customer; the remaining 48% would be labour, equipment repair, rental of premises or warehouses, cost of resources and materials, cost of outsourcing to any third party company, taxation, customs, marketing and net profit. Therefore the cost of a product cannot be 60% or the company would make a loss. To avoid ambiguity, this study plotted the range of a product cost to be maximum from 0% to 60%. Similarly the JIT Lean was plotted to be 0–90% maximum initially, as it is impossible to achieve 100% leanness as companies cannot eliminate all waste. For example, Herzog and Tonchia (2014) used a case study of 72 medium- and large-sized Slovenian manufacturing companies and found that all firms have a degree of waste although a very few companies can achieve >90% leanness. Although the pilot study starts with a crisp set of 0–90% JIT Lean, it looks at identifying whether the leanness range can increase throughout the pilot Delphi and Fuzzy Delphi rounds, and to determine its maximum range.

The experts were given a crisp set of the Cost range (Fig. 6.1). The expected outcome would be for the "Low cost" range to be between 0% and 20%, the "Medium cost" to be between 21% and 40% and for the "High cost" to be between 41% and 60%.

Moreover, the experts were given a crisp set for the JIT Lean range (Fig. 6.1). The expected outcome would be for the "Low JIT Lean" range to be between 0% and 30%, the "Medium JIT Lean" to be between 31% and 70% and for the "High JIT Lean" to be between 71% and 90%.

Furthermore, the pilot panel was asked to react to the statements with regard to the four dimensions of supply chain strategies (Agile, Lean, Leagile and BSC). Each dimension was assigned using the theoretical framework noted earlier to its relative quarter in the matrix. The Basic Supply Chain (BSC) strategy was placed in the lower left quarter of the matrix with low cost and relatively low JIT Lean. Meanwhile, the Lean supply chain strategy was allocated in the upper left quarter with low cost and high JIT Lean. The Leagile supply chain strategy took the upper right quarter with high cost and high JIT lean while the Agile strategy was allocated to the bottom right quarter with high cost and relatively lower JIT Lean. The experts were asked to rank "Cost" and "JIT Lean" according to what they deemed "High", "Medium" or "Low" with regard to the four main strategies of supply chains, Agile, Basic, Lean and Leagile. This process was conducted for both "Lean JIT" and "Cost" of a supply chain.

For the "Cost function", the experts were presented with six statements coinciding with the "Cost range" (0–60%). For example the first statement presented to the experts was "If a company's supply chain cost is 0–10% of the revenue then it is: Low cost, medium cost or high cost". The multiple choice statement allows experts to think rationally before choosing what they believe is the best suited option for their selected commodity or product. This results in experts exercising careful judgment and giving a well-thought response, which gives a preliminary indication of what the consensus might be (Munier and Rondé 2001). Moreover, with the "JIT Lean function", experts were presented with nine statements coinciding with the "JIT Lean range" (0–90%). For example, the first statement was "If a company's supply chain is 0–10% JIT then it is: low lean, medium lean or high lean". Experts then consider which choice best suits the percentage of JIT Lean in order for deliveries to be on time. This means that if a company's supply chain is 10% JIT Lean, then there is a 80% lead time, hence the majority of experts have considered the most appropriate choice is "Low lean", indicating it is not a favourable position for the company.

Moreover the answers from the pilot Delphi not only created a fuzzy area but also established a slightly changed range for the Cost and JIT Lean percentage (e.g. Cost percentage = 0–9%, 10–19, 20–29, and JIT Lean percentage range = 0–9%, 10–19%, 20–29%) (Fig. 6.1).

For the Cost percentage the "Low" range became from 0% to 19% where an intersection occurs between sets as some experts opinions differed in classifying 9–10% as medium, although the majority consensus agreed it is "Low cost". Moreover, a fuzzy area appeared as the majority of experts started choosing >19% as "Medium" range. Although there is a fuzzy area between 29–30% and 39–40% as some experts ranked it as "High", the consensus remained "Medium" until

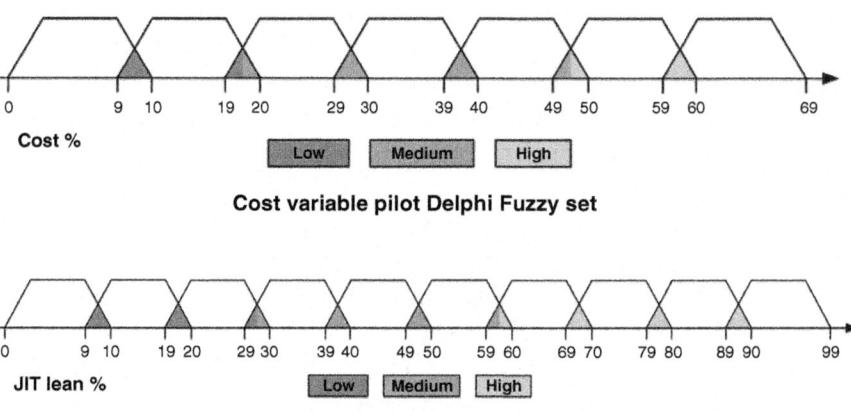

Fig. 6.2   Cost and lean variable pilot Delphi Fuzzy sets

49% where the fuzzy area shows the majority of experts started choosing "High" Cost (Fig. 6.2).

For the JIT Lean percentage the "Low" range became 0–29% where a fuzzy area appeared as experts started switching to "Medium" range. Although there are intersections between 9–10% and 19–20% due to some experts ranking the ranges as "Medium" the majority consensus remained "Low". At 59–60%, another prominent fuzzy area became clear as experts started choosing "High" JIT Lean (Fig. 6.2). Similarly, the intersection between 39–40% and 49–50% was due to some experts ranking it as "High", though the consensus remained "Medium" JIT Lean. The intersections between 69–70%, 79–80% and 89–90% show an area where a number of experts ranked these ranges as either "Low" or "Medium", although the consensus remained "High". However, although the answers for the cost didn't show experts exceeding 60%, with the JIT Lean, several experts stated that only >90% is considered "High" JIT Lean. This was taken into consideration in the amendments to the Fuzzy Delphi.

In order for the statements to be translated into fuzzy rules they must allow a degree of fuzziness. Therefore by having multiple choices, the supply chain and logistics variables measurements can be ranked into "Low, Medium and High", with "Medium" as the fuzzy area. These three perimeters allow the fuzzy principles to create the variables that account for a grey area which is the fuzziness in the experts' answers. This provides more accuracy as it allows for medium flexibility for decision–making rather than the traditional "yes" or "no" answers, giving managers room to manoeuvre around decision-making, allowing for creative judgment based on intuition and experience.

The preliminary consensus from the pilot study created the range for the fuzzy area by identifying the medium percentages for both "Cost" and "JIT Lean". From the experts' answers (Fig. 6.2) the fuzzy area can be identified as "Medium Cost" between 20% and 49% and "Medium JIT Lean" between 30% and 59%. The experts' answers indicate that some companies may find themselves in the fuzzy area illustrated in Fig. 6.3 if they catered for a high-end product but it is not considered a favourable position. The preliminary results from the pilot study

Lean JIT		Cost →						
High lean	90–99%	Lean						Leagile
High lean	80–89%							
High lean	70–79%							
High lean	60–69%							
Medium lean	50–59%							
Medium lean	40–49%							
Medium lean	30–39%							
Low lean	20–29%							
Low lean	10–19%							
Low lean	0–9%	BSC						Agile
Cost		0–9%	10–19%	20–29%	30–39%	40–49%	50–59%	60–69%
		Low cost	Low cost	Medium cost	Medium cost	Medium cost	High cost	High cost

Fig. 6.3 Preliminary MDM

indicate that experts recommend a company to be in the "Low Cost" range between 0% and 19% and in the "High JIT Lean" range between 60% and 99%. The experts considered the "High Cost" range and "Low lean" range to be a dangerous position for the company which should be avoided.

The four dimensions of supply chain strategies (Agile, Lean, Leagile and BSC) are designated into quarters due to their different "Cost" and "JIT Lean" requirements. However, all four dimensions share characteristics; hence they merge together within the fuzzy area. For example, the Agile strategy is commonly used for innovative products, which require higher cost and accounts for flexible lead-times that are above the medium JIT Lean, hence a company adopting this strategy may be allocated in the medium fuzzy area (Jüttner et al. 2006). The experts' answers conclude that Agile strategy should have a maximum cost up to "20–<29% cost" and a minimum lead-time of ">59% JIT Lean" (Fig. 6.3). The fuzzy area between BSC and Lean is due to both strategies being most suited to a functional product, hence when a company uses a BSC strategy it would commonly require low cost and scheduled and predictable lead-times preferably above the medium JIT Lean, while companies implementing a Lean strategy would naturally tailor their systems to reduce waste with minimal lead-times and cost (Hines 1998). The experts' statements suggest that a BSC strategy shares a fuzzy area with regard to having a minimum lead-time of "50–59%", companies with a BSC strategy should aim to be above that percentage. Lastly the Leagile strategy is commonly most suited to an innovative functional product that commonly requires higher cost and minimal lead-times; hence companies who adopt a Leagile strategy could be allocated at the lower end of the medium cost fuzzy area and aim to be above the fuzzy area of medium JIT Lean.

The amendments from the pilot study suggested that the scope of the variable functions were insufficient in determining the most suitable strategy for the supply chains. The experts requested definitions of what constitutes the "Cost" and "JIT Lean" variable functions. Therefore for the final Fuzzy Delphi, extra definitions and variable functions were added in order to establish a more accurate representation of the experts' judgment.

The pilot study was conducted using Google surveys linked to Google spreadsheet (Excel) in order to automatically generate the preliminary MDM as the questionnaire was being answered in real time. The formulas used were "date" to initiate the timestamp, "chart" for the Excel sheets", "array formulae", "count if" and "If-Then", to link the survey with the Excel sheet in order to interactively build the preliminary MDM. Each participant has a time stamp as they answer the pilot study, in addition to the Excel sheets interactively linked to generate the preliminary MDM. For the final Fuzzy Delphi rounds the survey tool used was Qualtrics, as it provided advanced tools that help import the data directly into SPSS and Excel which eases the analysis process. The interactive MDM would be a web-based tool created via HTML and JavaScript, while the interlinked Google Survey method was deemed unnecessary for the final Fuzzy Delphi study.

Fuzzy Delphi Rounds and Responses

The amendments from the pilot study were made for the first round of Fuzzy Delphi, with added variable functions. These included logistics based variable functions entitled "delivery strategies" that consisted of delivery to request, commit date and order fill lead time, in addition to "distribution strategies" that consist of strategic, tactical and operational distribution. Additionally there are customer order path, manufacturing lead time, shipping errors and customer service. The supply chain based variable functions include innovative, innovative functional and functional product. Additionally it includes a group of "product strategy" variables such as high-end product and push system. It also includes a "customisation" group variables consisting of self-customisation, collaborative customisation, adaptive customisation, cosmetic customiser and transparent customiser. The "life cycle" variable function looks at the different strategies for the innovative and functional product.

The amendments to the variable functions included different parameters. In addition to choosing between "Low, Medium or High", the experts choose which supply chain strategy (Agile, Lean, Leagile or Basic) is most suitable for each of the variable functions. The fuzzy aspect of these parameters is the rating of which strategy is recommended to be most favourable and which becomes an option therefore giving managers a range to choose what best suits their need, in addition to their recommendation.

The amendments regarding the definition of "Cost" and "JIT Lean" were made to identify the "Cost" from the stage of manufacturing (cost of production) to end-customer. The definition of end-customer varies between different companies from end-retail customer, distribution centres or end-wholesaler. Therefore, when experts answer the statement, they not only chose their own products but also who they considered as an end-customer.

Hence, the supply chain "Cost" definition consists of producing a product, logistics distribution and delivery to the end-customer, including the cost of lead-times during that process.

The definition of JIT Lean is the assumption that time is lean; the more time is lost the greater the waste, as time is a resource. Leanness means developing a value stream to eliminate all waste, including time, and to ensure a sophisticated level of scheduling (Mason-Jones et al. 2000). Therefore, the more a supply chain strategy moves towards leanness by eliminating waste and reducing lead-time, the more lean it becomes as defined by the JIT system. Hence, the definition: time equals leanness measured by the JIT system.

The "Cost" and "JIT Lean" definitions were added to the new variable function to construct the Fuzzy Delphi to be sent for its first round. Hence, the experts would be required to choose a product, commodity or good, determine their end-customer, then begin the Fuzzy Delphi study by answering the statements for each added variable function based on the "Cost" and "JIT Lean" definition provided. Bearing in mind their chosen factors and the percentages they selected for the "Cost" and "JIT Lean", the experts were asked to choose the best supply chain strategies (Agile, Lean, Leagile and BSC) for each variable function based on their chosen conditions. The purpose of allowing the experts to choose their own product, commodity or good and to determine whom is their end customer, is to allow the Fuzzy Delphi study to gain a variety of opinions that would enable it to create the MDM model that accounts for various circumstances. This would be difficult to underline and account for otherwise, without the experts setting their own conditions and answering the Fuzzy Delphi statements based on their experience. This ensures that experts' answers have undergone a process of decision-making that will help in the creation of the multi-dimensional model for companies to use in identifying or diagnosing the supply chain strategy that best suits them. The statements in the Fuzzy Delphi are considered a hybrid between a multi-choice and ranked type Delphi. Although experts are asked to choose one option of a supply chain strategy (Agile, Lean, Leagile and BSC), the results indicate a ranking between the strategies that is most favoured and the ones considered an option. This ranking is essential in creating the (If-Then) fuzzy rule statements that require options that the interactive MDM can recommend based on the selected criteria, and the company can select the options most suited to its requirements.

Round One: Processing Data

After the amendments from the pilot Delphi were made, the fuzzy parameters were created along with the amended statements which initiated the first round of the Fuzzy Delphi. The responses from the first round slightly altered the range for the Cost and JIT Lean fuzzy set percentages, illustrated in Fig. 6.4.

The matrix indicates a fuzzy area between 29–69% JIT Lean and 19–39% Cost. Some firms may find themselves in this area due to their

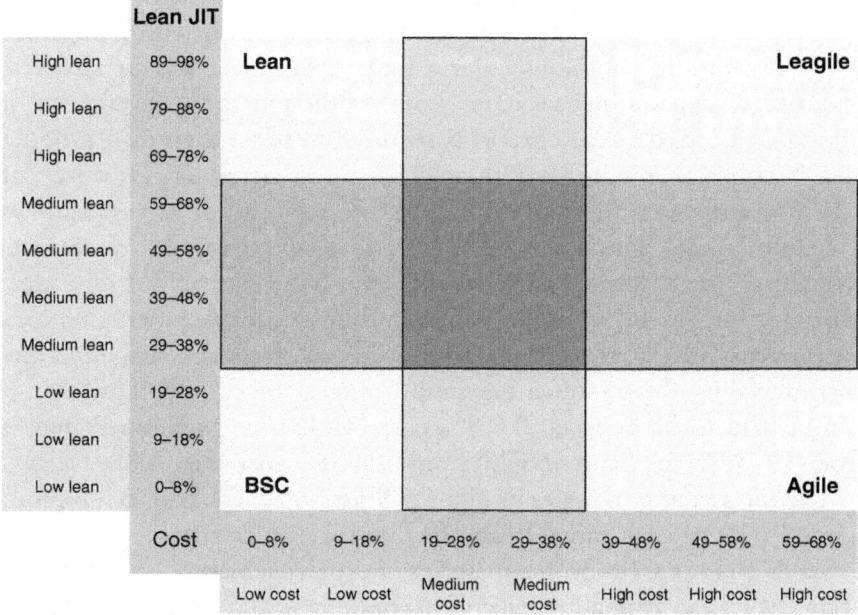

Fig. 6.4 Fuzzy Delphi round one MDM

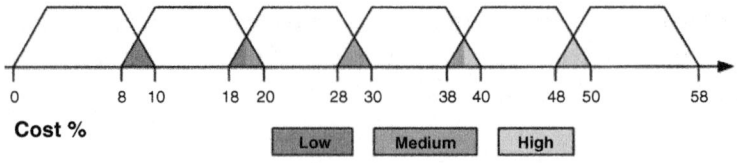

Cost variable round one Fuzzy Delphi

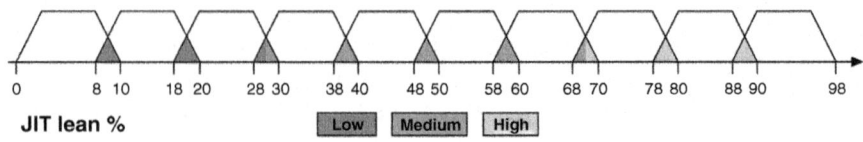

JIT lean variable round one Fuzzy Delphi

Fig. 6.5   Cost and JIT lean variable round one Fuzzy Delphi

type of product. However, the favourable position as indicated by the consensus is >59–68% JIT Lean and below 19–28% Cost.

The intersections in the first diagram are between the cost percentage sets where experts' opinions enter a fuzzy area. From 8% to 10% the majority of experts believe it is "Low", although some divergence of opinions occurred as each expert is required to select their own product and distribution method for their chosen end customer. However, at 18–20% a distinct difference occurs as the majority of experts shift to "Medium" cost. Between 28–30% the majority consensus remains as "Medium" with some difference in opinion, creating a fuzzy area. However, at 38–40% another distinct shift occurs as expert opinions go towards "High" cost. None of the experts' feedback suggested any cost exceeding the 58–60% maximum range. Hence, the "Low" range can be said to be between 0–18% cost, while the "Medium" range is from 19–39% cost, and "High" from 40–60% cost (Fig. 6.5).

The intersecting triangles in Fig. 6.5 illustrate where experts' opinions crossed over as each range (fuzzy set) intersected creating a fuzzy area. From 8–10% and 18–20% a majority of experts achieved a consensus of "Low" JIT Lean with a few exceptions ranking it as "Medium" although at 28–30% JIT Lean expert opinions shifted with the majority ranking it as "Medium". This can be seen throughout with a few exceptions in the fuzzy triangle area until 68–70%, where another shift occurs with the majority of experts choosing "High". The amendments from the pilot study accounted for a range >90% JIT Lean, therefore the intersections between 78–80% and 88–90% are due to some experts rating it as medium, through opinions began to shift to "High" JIT Lean up until >90%. Hence, 0–28% can be categorised as "Low", while 29–68% JIT Lean is "Medium", and finally from 69% to >90% JIT Lean is "High" (Fig. 6.5).

These ranges for the "Cost" and JIT Lean" were taken into consideration for the second round of Fuzzy Delphi, in addition to the amendments given by the panel's feedback.

Further Amendments

The experts reached a partial consensus on some of the variable functions yet differed on others. The amendments they advised towards establishing a majority consensus were to further explain each variable function with a clear and simple definition in addition to clarifying the scope and definition of a supply chain for this study and to further explain the definitions for the strategies within the study (Agile, Lean, Leagile and BSC).

The function variables were given a more comprehensive and detailed definition and the statements related to them were further clarified. Hence, when the Fuzzy Delphi was sent for the second round further explanation was added. For example the "delivery strategies" group variable functions was written as: "there are three types of deliveries according to Gunasekaran et al. (2001), delivery to request, delivery to commit date and order fill lead time".

The statements were as follows:

"If" supply chain delivery cost is calculated by "Delivery to Request", "Then" the supply chain is operating under: Lean, Agile, Leagile, Basic supply chain strategies.

"If" supply chain delivery cost is calculated by "Delivery to Commit Date", "Then" the supply chain is operating under: Lean, Agile, Leagile, Basic supply chain strategies.

"If" the supply chain delivery cost is calculated by "Order Fill Lead Time", "Then" the supply chain is operating under: Lean, Agile, Leagile, Basic supply chain strategies".

The amendments to the second round for the "Delivery strategies" group included the following clarification:

"Distribution strategy consists of various cost elements to develop the appropriate trade-offs in the delivery system that can be applied as a basis for planning a supply chain end delivery strategy from manufacturing to customer, in addition to re-assessing the distribution system, so that overall cost effectiveness can be achieved (Beamon 1999). There are three types of deliveries according to Gunasekaran et al. (2001), delivery to request, delivery to commit date and order fill lead time".

The (If-Then) statements remained the same with slight clarification:

"To classify the response time between order and corresponding delivery":

If the supply chain delivery cost is calculated by "Delivery to Request"/ "Delivery to Commit Date"/"Order Fill Lead Time". Then the supply chain is operating under: Lean, Agile, Leagile, Basic supply chain strategies".

Additionally, the experts required the supply chain and the four strategies to be clarified and defined within the scope of this study. Furthermore, due to the slight change in the "Cost" range, extra clarification was added, though the definition for "JIT Lean" remained the same. Therefore, the second round of Fuzzy Delphi included the following:

"This research aims at helping companies identify the best supply chain strategy for their commodity and market. There are four strategies:

Lean:	Lean focuses on the elimination of waste with a bias towards "pulling" goods through the system based on demand.
Agile:	Focus is on flexible, efficient response to fluctuations and unique customer demand.
Leagile:	A hybrid of Lean and Agile: Using make-to-stock/lean strategies for high volume, stable demand products, and make-to-order/agile for customised, innovative and innovative functional products. Has flexible production capacity to meet surges in demand or unexpected requirements. Uses postponement strategies, where "platform" products are made to forecast, and then final assembly and configuration to complete the final customer order.

Basic supply
chain (BSC):   Basic or daily products that require a reliable chain to plan, source, make and deliver (from in-house manufacturing or outsourcing to retail)"

Cost: is calculated from the stage of manufacturing (cost of production) to end-customer. The end-customer varies between different companies from end-retail customer, distribution centres or end-wholesaler. Please choose the supply chain of your own products and what you considered as an end-customer.

The supply chain "Cost" consists of producing a product (raw materials, equipment or machinery operations at the manufacturing node), logistics distribution (from resource or component plants to manufacturing and the overall supply chain) and delivery to the end-customer (delivering the commodity from plant to warehouse, retailer, wholesaler or consumer), including the cost of lead-times during that process. The cost excludes overall gain from gross profit, labour, premises or equipment hire; it is only the estimated cost being invested in creating the product, its supply chain and logistics

JIT Lean: the more a supply chain strategy moves towards leanness by eliminated waste and reducing lead-time, the more lean it becomes as defined by the JIT system, as time equals leanness measured by the JIT system.

Moreover, as requested by the experts, the supply chain definition and scope was included and explained in the second round:

According to Fisher (1997), the supply chain converts raw materials into parts, components and eventually finished goods, then transports all of them from one point of the supply chain to the next. The specific supply chain point analysed in this study is from manufacturing to retail. This study focuses on the retail industry (e.g. textile and automobiles), excluding food, jewellery, pharmaceutical, telecommunication services electronic devices, watches and white goods.

For further clarification and to help the experts avoid ambiguity, the Fuzzy Delphi was divided into two parts. Part one included the questions regarding "Cost" and "JIT Lean" with the following explanation:

Part One

"This part of the questionnaire requires a generic answer regarding what constitutes 'high cost' for a company that wishes to transfer its goods from the 'Manufacturing' node to the 'Retail' node as well as what constitutes 'high lean', which is the minimal delays in shipment and product delivery to the customer".

Further explanation of the "JIT lean" was added to avoid ambiguity – "Just in Time" (JIT), is a Japanese production strategy created by Toyota that strives to improve a business's return on investment by reducing inventory and associated carrying costs (Hines 1998). JIT relies on signals or "Kanban" between different points, which tell production when to make the next part (Kootanaee et al. 2013). In this study, Leanness is measured by "JIT Lean", for example: "If a company is 20% "JIT Lean" (20% Leanness), then there are 80% delays".

Meanwhile, the second part of the Fuzzy Delphi study was divided into three sections to aid the experts' thinking process.

Part Two

"This second stage requires a general answer regarding retail consumable goods, where the main focus of the supply chain is between manufacturing and retail outlet. In this study only delivery, distribution, manufacturing, product demand and output are measured and used as an example to formulate the multi-dimensional matrix. The output in this research is measured by customer satisfaction. Specific attention will be placed on high-end products due to their unpredictable nature and extreme fluctuating demand (e.g. high-end mountain bikes, men suits, women's ball gowns and wedding dresses)".

Further explanations were added to each of the three sections in part two. These sections were, "Measuring resource performance" which included "Delivery strategy", "Manufacturing cost of innovative, functional and innovative functional product" and "Distribution strategies". Secondly, "Measuring output" by customer satisfaction which included, "Customer order path", "Manufacturing lead-time", "Shipping errors" and "Customer service". Thirdly, "Measuring product demand" by the life cycle of "Innovative", "Functional" and "High-end product", as well as identifying the best supply chain strategy for a high-end product. The third section provided a definition of customisation to help experts identify the most suitable supply chain strategy for each type of customisation; this included "Self-customisation", "Collaborative customisation", "Adaptive customisation", "Cosmetic customiser" and "Transparent customiser". Additionally, this section also contained a definition on the statement of the "Push" system in order for the study to differentiate and identify cohesively the best supply chain strategy for both the Lean "Pull" strategy and the "Push" system.

With these amendments to help the experts avoid ambiguity, the Fuzzy Delphi was sent again for the second round in an attempt to reach consensus. Once a consensus is established, the answers from the (If-Then) statements would create the fuzzy rules to build the interactive MDM model.

Round Two: Establishing Consensus

The second round was completed with positive feedback and no further amendments, indicating that all panel members answered the statements with ease and reached a unified agreement. The Fuzzy Delphi was conducted using a questionnaire tool (Qualtrics) which eased the process of clarifying the amendments from round one and helped detect if a consensus has been established from the second round. Qualtrics also aids the analysis process as it allows the data to be directly downloaded into an SPSS and Excel file.

From the second round of Fuzzy Delphi, the added clarification for "Cost" from round one did not present a change in the maximum 0–60% scope, as the majority of experts classified above 40% Cost as high, and no feedback was given to alter the maximum scope for the cost percentage. However, the range sets for "Cost" and "JIT Lean" was slightly altered again. The intersections nearly disappeared with consensus reducing the fuzzy area and creating a different range for each set.

The "Cost" percentage developed a range from 0% to 10%, 11% to 20%, 21% to 30%, etc. The "Low Cost" range from the second Fuzzy Delphi changed slightly with the fuzzy area between the "Low Cost" and

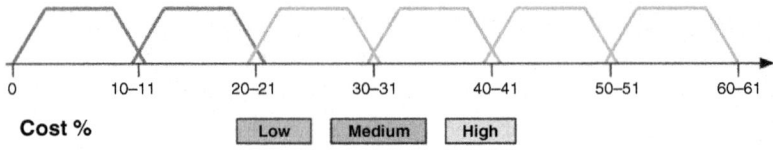

Cost variable round two Fuzzy Delphi

Fig. 6.6 Cost and lean variable round 2 Fuzzy Delphi

"Medium Cost" shown between 20% and 21% as experts shifted from low to medium. Furthermore, the fuzzy area between the "Medium" and "High" cost is shown between 40% and 41% as experts shifted towards high (Fig. 6.6). Similar to the pilot and first round, the experts' answers did not exceed the maximum scope of 60% Cost conducted in this study. Although there are small intersections with a tiny fuzzy area due to a small divergence in opinion, it is insignificant. This led the fuzzy area in the MDM model to shrink and for the four quarters (Agile, Lean, Leagile and BSC) to start merging.

The "JIT Lean" percentage developed a similar range to that of the Cost, with 0–10%, 11–20%, 21–30%, etc. The "Low JIT Lean" distinct fuzzy range became between 30–31% JIT Lean as experts opinions shifted to "Medium". Moreover, the fuzziness between the "Medium" and "High" JIT Lean is between 70–71% as the majority of experts shifted from medium to high (Fig. 6.6). The experts ranked 90% to >91% as "High" and the most favourable position. By taking the data and feedback from the last round into consideration it can be deduced that the preferred high JIT Lean lies between 90% and 98%. Similar to the "Cost" there are intersections with a tiny fuzzy area, created due to a small divergence in opinion, however this is insignificant. This also led

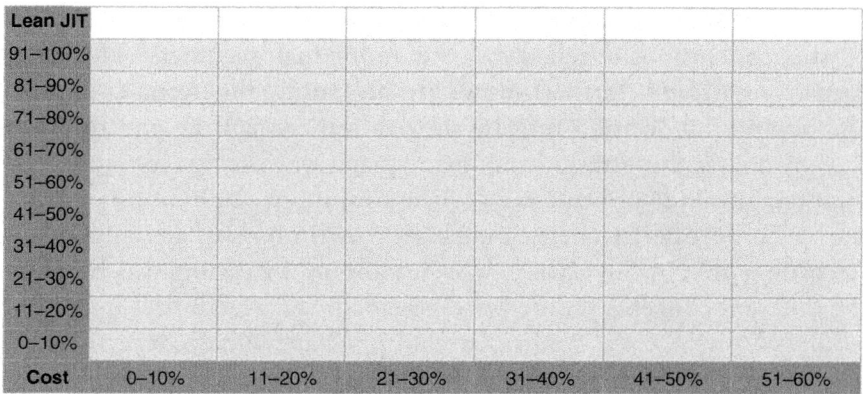

Fig. 6.7 Preliminary interactive MDM

the fuzzy area in the MDM model to shrink and for the four quarters to start merging

As consensus has been achieved in the second round of Fuzzy Delphi, the "Cost" and "JIT Lean" ranges developed will be used as a basis for the analysis and creation of the scatter diagrams which are then translated into the fuzzy rules and input into the interactive MDM. Reduced fuzziness resulted in the MDM merging into one matrix without the fuzzy area intersection present in the preliminary MDM. This resulted in the four quarters (Lean, Leagile, Agile and BSC) intersecting and merging into a single matrix, as the variables led to the supply chain strategies constantly shifting between quarters. The Cost and JIT Lean range in the preliminary interactive MDM are shown in Fig. 6.7.

Defining Consensus

Consensus measurement plays a significant role in Delphi research, as it is considered an important component for analysis and data interpretation. The term "consensus" is defined by Fowler (1995) as "a general agreement". Meanwhile Armstrong (2001) describes consensus as the agreement of collective unanimous opinion of a number of persons, indicating that a group's conclusion represents a fair summary of the conclusions reached by the individual members. However, Armstrong (*ibid.*) further shows in his study the term consensus embodying the decision-making process rather than the end result of the group, as he stresses the inadequacy of forcing consensus by increasing rounds unnecessarily when a result can be established from the panel's indecisiveness, or closes proximity to an agreement. According to Gracht (2012) it is important to distinguish between the different concepts "consensus/agreement" and "stability" in Delphi studies. Many Delphi studies have stopped the survey once a predefined level of agreement, i.e. consensus, was achieved. However Gracht (*ibid*) noted that consensus is meaningless, if group stability has not been reached beforehand; group stability is the "consistency of responses between successive rounds of a study"; thus stability is the necessary criterion defining a consensus. This stability is found in two ways, when a certain level of agreement, e.g. convergence of opinions towards consensus is found and when a complete consensus of all the panel is established (Fig. 6.8).

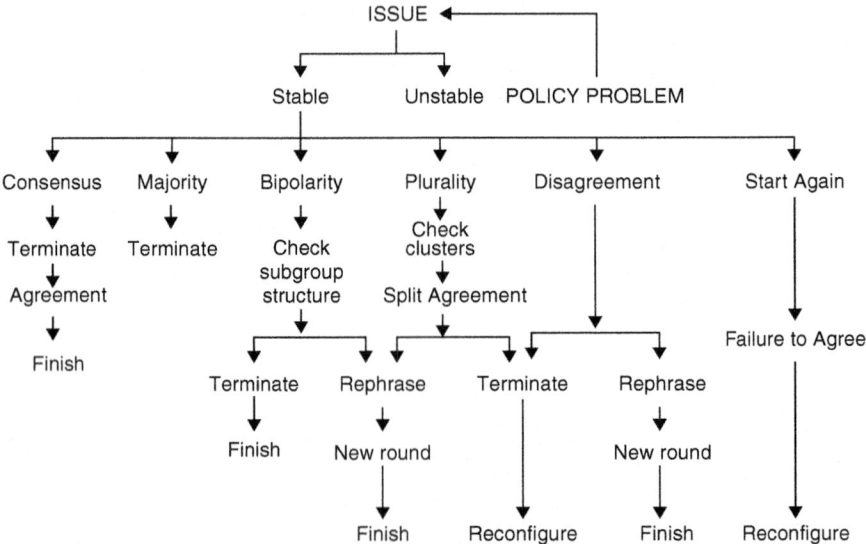

Fig. 6.8 Variety of consensus (adapted from Gracht 2012)

According to Gracht (2012), a consensus can be achieved with a certain level of agreement when a majority (>50%) of the respondents agree, referred to as a "majority consensus", while the term "plurality consensus" refers to when a larger proportion of the respondents (<50%) agree. Furthermore, Poundstone (2008) indicates the importance of these different types of consensus and to the voting system, as the outcome of an election does not depend on the choice of consensus in the voting system but on the expressed will of the voters. This means that in most cases the way people favour an option depends on how they think other people will choose. It is natural that people would try to ensure they chose the option that most other people will agree with, and identifying the best supply chain strategy is no different, as experts would choose their commodity or good, their market and choose the options based on what they think relevant companies would accept. Poundstone (2008) further explains the importance of a plurality consensus in a study, by stressing the importance of the information gained from "clones". Clones are people with similarities who find the same choices appealing. This could result in the clones splitting the results into equal halves, as any expert who likes one option will like the other nearly as much, creating an equal plurality in a study. In the second round of Fuzzy Delphi this can be seen as a group of experts generally favouring a set of strategies while another group favours another set of strategies, creating an equal plurality split. This is important in Fuzzy Delphi as it indicates that experts' choices have equal merit and can both be advisable, allowing the company to choose one of the paths that is best suited to its needs.

For example, in the variable "tactical distribution" it can be seen that some experts favour an Agile strategy while others Leagile. However, with the "innovative product" variable it can be seen that experts were grouped into favoured Leagile and BSC strategies. The same can be seen in companies as they adopt a supply chain strategy stance into their framework as part of their business structure (e.g. Jaguar Land Rover adopts a generic agile system in its business structure and management, while Toyota adopts a generic lean system within its business structure and management) (Hines 1998). Nevertheless, Poundstone (2008) further explains that a plurality consensus system is not biased in comparison to the usual first-place rankings as it takes into consideration the significance of the plurality party and interprets its impact on the outcome. Therefore, the hybrid system of making first-place choices counts as exercised within the polls and counting the plurality vote will give a more coherent understanding of peoples' choices and preferences, which fits well with this study's hybrid Fuzzy Delphi as the statements combine a multiple-choice and ranking method (Poundstone 2008). For example, the "delivery to request" variable shows that a BSC strategy came first-place, while agile and lean formed a plurality that came second and third respectively.

According to Robert's rule of Order based on parliamentary procedure which is the standard for facilitating discussions and group decision-making, commonly a majority constitutes more than half of the members (Robert 2011). However, the term plurality itself is also called "relative majority" in contrast to an "absolute majority" or "vast majority" which is more than half to almost all the members consenting. This hybrid system of first-place, majority and plurality consensus is commonly applied in cinema film awards, sports completion and parliamentary votes. Here the approaches mentioned above are used to establish a consensus system to expand on the definitions put forward by Poundstone (2008) and Robert (2011) in order to interpret the results of the second round of Fuzzy Delphi.

Interpreting Consensus

The second round of Fuzzy Delphi generated a response from 90 experts in total. In this context, a majority consensus equates to >50%, whereas an absolute majority equates to 90 to 85 (100–94.5%) experts agreeing, and all 90 experts agreeing [100%] would constitute full consensus. However, a vast majority would constitute 85–58 experts agreeing [94.5–64.5%]. The plurality consensus defined above is restrictive, hence for this study the plurality for <50% will be divided into three categories, "High, Medium and Low" consensus; the "Vast Majority consensus" when [85, 58] [94.5–64.5%] experts agree, while a "Majority consensus" is formed when [57, 46] [64.5–51.1%] experts agree, as it has to be more than half of the responses which is (90/2=45 experts, i.e. >50%). The "High Plurality" consensus is when the agreement is close to the majority, when [45, 35] [51.1, 38.9%] experts agree; as 46 experts agreeing is the fuzzy consensus area being over half (51.1%), it will be considered as a "majority consensus" in this study. The "Medium plurality" is between [34, 24] [37.7–26.7%] experts, while the "Low plurality" consensus is achieved when [23, 11] [25.6–12.2%] experts agree. Any number below 10 experts agreeing (<11%, less than 1/8th) is considered a minority and insufficient to be considered a plurality as only the highest values will be measured. Table 6.1 illustrates the calculation for each category.

From the various methods mentioned in defining consensus, it can be noted that it is one of the most contentious components of the Delphi method. The measurement of consensus varies greatly between studies (Munier and Rondé 2001) and standards for consensus in Delphi research have never been rigorously established (Gracht 2012). The literature on Delphi suggests that the stricter the criteria, the more difficult it is to achieve consensus among the expert panel. However, a majority of Delphi studies measure consensus through the use of descriptive statistics, including mean, median, standard deviation (Armstrong 2001). To avoid the trap of strict boundaries, this research used Fuzzy Delphi to allow the experts room to manoeuvre in their choices and to allow the end result to offer options as well as the recommended choice. The consensus is analysed using the question-naire tool Qualtrics, as it provides the number of responses, the mini-mum, maximum, mean, median and standard deviation, which helps analysing the establishment of consensus, majority agreement consensus and plurality consensus, which will facilitate understanding the choice of strategy selected to recommend and which is categorised as an option within the interactive MDM. These factors further indicate the advan-tage of using a Fuzzy Delphi, as any approximation in decision results in a fuzzy area that becomes an "option choice" in the MDM for the users to favour if they wish, depending on their requirements. This is crucial in creating a model that is adaptable and tailorable for supply chains.

Table 6.1 Consensus type and calculation

Type of consensus	Expert agreement for 90 experts	Formula
Vast majority consensus	When 85–58 experts agree	If [85, 58] [94.5,64.5%] experts agree, then it is called a Vast Majority
Majority consensus	When 57–46 experts agree	(90/2=45(50 %)). Therefore Majority (x) = [51.1≤ x ≤64.5 % expert, then [57, 46] [64.5, 51.1%] experts agree that it is called Majority.
High plurality consensus	When 45–35 experts agree	(90/8 =11.25 ≈ 11) (12.8%) which is 1/8 of the consensus. Then (35 + 11 = 46) is (51.1%). Therefore if [46, 35] experts agree then it is called High plurality.
Medium plurality consensus	When 34–24 experts agree	Since (90/8 = 11.25 ≈ 11) (12.8%) which is 1/8 of the consensus. Then 23 +11 = 34 is (37.8%). Therefore If [34, 24] [37.8, 26.7%] experts agree then it is called Medium plurality.
Low plurality consensus	When 23–11 experts agree	(90/8 = 11.25 ≈11) (12.8%) which is 1/8 of the consensus. Therefore If [23,11] [25.6,12.2%] experts agree then it is called Low Plurality.
Minority	When 10–1 experts agree	Below 1/8th < 11%

Part One

The first part of the Fuzzy Delphi looks at the "Cost" and "JIT Lean" of a supply chain. Using Qualtrics, a sample will be selected to illustrate how consensus has been established.

Cost Variable Function

This study chose a random sample of 0–8% Cost and 9–18% Cost to examine the established consensus from the second round of fuzzy Delphi. Figure 6.9 illustrates that 78 out of 90 (87%) ranked "0–8% Cost" as "Low". This indicates that a "vast majority" consensus has been achieved, which is when [85, 58%] experts out of 90 agree, or when [94.5, 64.5%] out of a 100 experts agree. Meanwhile, nine experts (10%) ranked it medium and 3 experts (3%) ranked it as low.

In contrast to the second example of "9–18% Cost", it can be seen there are two types of consensus, firstly a "majority consensus" with 53 members of the panel agreeing that it is considered "Low". Secondly, there is a "medium plurality" consensus where less than the majority, 29 experts have agreed that it can be considered medium (Fig. 6.9). This is shown as a fuzzy area intersection when expert opinion diverges from one range to the other. The different types of consensus are crucial in Fuzzy Delphi as it helps the creation of options and gives flexibility to the MDM to be generic and applied to a variety of supply chains. The different types of consensus with regard to the "Cost" indicates that various products or goods require different supply chain cost, as customers are willing to pay more or less depending on the value of the product or good.

JIT Lean Variable Function

A sample of the "JIT Lean" variable function has been selected. This study chose a random sample of 19–28% and 80% JIT Lean as it contains various consensus patterns.

Figure 6.10 shows that the majority consensus has been achieved with 46 experts agreeing 19–28% JIT Lean is medium. Additionally a high plurality consensus has been achieved with 38 experts agreeing that it is low. This is a fuzzy area where the experts' chosen product or commodity and their chosen distribution method to the end customer played a part in the divergence of opinion. This provides flexibility as various supply chains have different distribution methods, margins of delay, waste and delivery schedules.

Q5.   If a company's supply chain cost is 0-8% of the revenue then it is

#	Answer		Response	%
1	Low Cost		78	87%
2	Medium Cost		9	10%
3	High Cost		3	3%
	Total		90	100%

Statistic	Value
Min Value	1
Max Value	3
Mean	1.17
Variance	0.21
Standard Deviation	0.46
Total Responses	90

Cost variable function 0-8%

Q6.   If a company's supply chain cost is 9-18% of the revenue then it is

#	Answer		Response	%
1	Low Cost		53	59%
2	Medium Cost		29	32%
3	High Cost		8	9%
	Total		90	100%

Statistic	Value
Min Value	1
Max Value	3
Mean	1.50
Variance	0.43
Standard Deviation	0.66
Total Responses	90

Cost variable function at 20%

Fig. 6.9   Cost variable functions

Q14. If a company's supply chain is 30% JIT then it is

#	Answer		Response	%
1	Low Lean		38	42%
2	Medium Lean		46	51%
3	High Lean		6	7%
	Total		90	100%

Statistic	Value
Min Value	1
Max Value	3
Mean	1.64
Variance	0.37
Standard Deviation	0.61
Total Responses	90

JIT lean variable function 30%

Q19. If a company's supply chain is 69-78% JIT then it is

#	Answer		Response	%
1	Low Lean		13	14%
2	Medium Lean		8	9%
3	High Lean		69	77%
	Total		90	100%

Statistic	Value
Min Value	1
Max Value	3
Mean	2.62
Variance	0.53
Standard Deviation	0.73
Total Responses	90

JIT lean variable function 80%

Fig. 6.10 Lean variable functions

Figure 6.10 also indicates that a vast majority consensus has been achieved as 69 experts (77%) chose high Lean. However 13 experts (14%) chose low lean, while 8 experts (9%) chose medium. For certain companies, leanness is considered high when JIT Lean is > 90%. This is determined by the strategic position of the company, its product and scheduled lead-times. For example a company operating with a lean strategy, for instance Motorola Telecommunications which operates under lean six sigma has an expectation of >98% leanness, hence 69–78% JIT Lean is considered low or medium. However, other firms operating with a BSC, such as white goods, would consider 69–78% as a transitional stage between the medium and high JIT Lean range.

The vast majority consensus is achieved at the lower and high percentage ends for "Cost" and "JIT Lean". However, the middle percentages showed different ranges of consensus providing a fuzzy area as shown earlier by the intersection between sets, which allows the interactive MDM to cater for various requirements and be tailored to the specific needs of the supply chain.

Part Two

Part two has several variable functions groups that are divided into three sections. From each section a random sample will be selected and the patterns of consensus will be examined.

Section One

From the delivery group variables, the following was randomly selected:

Delivery to request. Figure 6.11 shows that a medium plurality consensus was formed for Basic, Agile and Lean supply chains. Due to the former achieving the highest number of agreements, it takes first place. Hence, it is the most advised strategy while the latter are options if the companies preferred another choice depending on their business model. This gives flexibility and freedom to choose based on the experts' preferences that will enable companies to use and tailor the MDM.

Q24. If a supply chain delivery cost is calculated by "Delivery to Request", then the supply chain is operating under:

#	Answer		Response	%
1	Lean		24	27%
2	Agile		25	28%
3	Leagile		8	9%
4	Basic supply chain strategies		33	37%
	Total		90	100%

Statistic	Value
Min Value	1
Max Value	4
Mean	2.56
Variance	1.53
Standard Deviation	1.24
Total Responses	90

Fig. 6.11 Delivery to request variable function

Section Two

From the distribution group variables the following was randomly selected:

Tactical distribution. It can be seen from Fig. 6.12 that experts' choices were formed by a medium plurality consensus for Agile, Leagile and Basic supply chains. It is evident that experts were divided into two cloning groups, the pro-Agile and pro-Leagile. This indicates that with a tactical distribution it is advised to have either an Agile or a Leagile strategy depending on the company's overall business structure, as it impacts the supply chain model, choice of product or good and market. However, companies have the option to choose a BSC strategy and tailor the tactical distribution to fit their business model depending on their market.

Q33. Tactical distribution system: creates the means by which objectives can be realised by providing balance for each function in the supply chain (e.g. inventory capacity, service, and determining...

#	Answer		Response	%
1	Lean		16	18%
2	Agile		25	28%
3	Leagile		25	28%
4	Basic supply chain strategies		24	27%
	Total		90	100%

Statistic	Value
Min Value	1
Max Value	4
Mean	2.63
Variance	1.13
Standard Deviation	1.06
Total Responses	90

Fig. 6.12 Tactical distribution variable function

From the product design group variables, the following example was randomly selected:

Innovative product. In this example there are two plurality consensus. The first is a high plurality consensus with 43 experts recommending an agile strategy, indicating a first-place agreement, recommending innovative products to have high flexibility. The second is a low plurality consensus for both Leagile and (BSC) strategies, as both equally achieved a total of 19 experts agreeing, creating two equal options (Fig. 6.13). This indicates two cloning groups where pro-Leagile experts advised that an innovative product of their choice requires high flexibility and a high lean system of waste reduction, while experts that are pro-BSC strategy advised than an innovative daily or necessity product would require a stable supply chain. By having these options a company would be able to choose the most relevant path for its innovative product's supply chain based on its market and business structure.

Q28.   According to Fisher (1997), if a company produces an innovative product, its demand is very unpredictable and in need of a responsive supply chain. If a company manufactures an innov...

#	Answer		Response	%
1	Lean		9	10%
2	Agile		43	48%
3	Leagile		19	21%
4	Basic supply chain strategies		19	21%
	Total		90	100%

Statistic	Value
Min Value	1
Max Value	4
Mean	2.53
Variance	0.88
Standard Deviation	0.94
Total Responses	90

Fig. 6.13   Innovative product variable function

Section Three

This section covers several variable functions from which one random sample was selected.

High-end products. In this example, a "high plurality" consensus was achieved with 41 experts recommending that a Leagile strategy is most suitable for a high-end product as it provides high flexibility and efficient system of waste reduction, while a low plurality consensus of 22 experts who believe that an agile strategy will provide the focus on flexibility and responsiveness that a high-end product requires (Fig. 6.14). Hence, the MDM will use the first-place method of recommending Leagile as the priority strategy, while agile will be given as an option for companies to choose if they believe it is most suitable for their market.

Q47. High-end products have a fluctuating demand, to counter this uncertainty Fisher (1997) suggested a blend of three strategies- reducing uncertainty by identifying and analysing new sources of dat...

#	Answer		Response	%
1	Lean		15	17%
2	Agile		22	24%
3	Leagile		41	46%
4	Basic supply chain strategies		12	13%
	Total		90	100%

Statistic	Value
Min Value	1
Max Value	4
Mean	2.56
Variance	0.86
Standard Deviation	0.93
Total Responses	90

Fig. 6.14 High-end product variable function

Focusing on tailoring, the emphasis on options, flexibility and suggestions is important in the establishment of a holistic model that can meet the majority of companies' supply chain needs and requirement to enable companies to diagnose the most suitable strategy for their market. The experts' answers to the statements resulted in a slight change to the MDM. The four quarters established at the preliminary MDM merged together creating a larger fuzzy area, which resulted in the quarters gradually fading and dissolving. The answers from both rounds divided the interactive MDM into a "Logistics strategy MDM" and "Supply chain strategy MDM". Although the interactive MDM is shaped into a matrix without quarters, the fuzzy area remains in the strategic recommendation and options available for the company to choose from. The quarters in the preliminary MDM provided an insight into the ranges of each supply chain strategy in terms of "Cost" and "JIT Lean". The results from round two provided basis for the variables and their importance in helping the experts identify the best suited strategy. Further explanation on the selection of these variables and their use in the study will be explained in the next section.

Fuzzy Delphi Variable Functions

The first and second round of Fuzzy Delphi introduced extra variable functions to ensure clarity and help experts answer the statements. These variable functions were selected based on the literature, theoretical framework, the panel feedback and the research conducted by several studies including Kootanaee et al. (2013) on JIT manufacturing, performance and implementation, Beamon (1999), who presents an overview evaluation of performance measures used in supply chain models with a framework for the selection of flexibility measures of performance for manufacturing supply chains that contributed to building the guidelines for the variable functions, in addition to Stevens (1989) who examined supply chain integration and control of material flow from suppliers through the value adding processes and distribution channels to customers. Meanwhile Silveira et al. (2001) examined the various methods of mass customisation and their impact on the development of production systems, also examined by Alford et al. (2000) who studied mass customisation from an automotive perspective, all of which helped establish several variable functions such as the customisation variables, integration and push system variable. Moreover, Simeonovova and Simeonov (2012) examined the lead-time reduction methods in addition to Elfving (2003), who explored the opportunities to reduce lead-times for engineered-to-order products that helped establish the manufacturing lead-time variable and shipping errors variables. Maycroft (2005) looked at consumption, planned obsolescence and waste, which helped develop the life cycle variable; while Fisher's (1997) study looked at what is the right supply chain for a product by examining Functional, Innovative and Innovative functional products which helped establish several variable functions as well as the manufacturing cost variable. Moreover, Gunasekaran et al. (2001) looked at performance measures and metrics in a supply chain environment, which also helped establish several variables such as the delivery and distribution variables and Tan *et al.* (1998, 1999) who carried out an empirical study on supplier and firm performance which helped establish several variables such as measuring output. The literature review, theoretical framework as well as additional work by Towill et al. (1992) on designing industrial dynamic models for supply chains directed the variable function parameters for the interactive MDM. However due to the scope of the study, limitations must be placed on the variable functions incorporated into the interactive MDM (Table 6.2).

Choosing the Relevant Variables

The most suited variable functions are selected from the pool of variables to be implemented into the interactive MDM. The selected variable functions will be allocated into two groups, "Logistics strategy" and "Supply chain strategy" each with its own interactive MDM. The variables that are considered most relevant are shown in Table 6.3.

Categorising the Fuzzy Variables

The Fuzzy Delphi statements of the chosen variables resulted in establishing a consensus of experts' recommendation and options. The options provide a fuzzy area that led the preliminary quarters of the MDM to merge. The (If-Then) statements created the basis for the creation of scatter diagrams. These diagrams plot the frequency number each time the supply chain variables (Agile, Lean, Leagile and BSC) were chosen. This turns the hybrid multiple-choice into a ranking process that establishes the recommendations and options incorporated into the interactive MDM. Chapter 7 examines the process of converting the data collected from Qualtrics to SPSS and to Excel, in order for the (If-Then) statements to establish the frequency tables, percentages and build the scatter diagrams. This leads to the creation of the fuzzy rule sets that builds the web-based interactive MDM for both the "Logistics strategies" and "Supply chain strategies" groups by translating

Table 6.2 Fuzzy Delphi variable functions

Variable Function	Definition	Beneficial to the experts in Fuzzy Delphi
Cost	From the stages of manufacturing (cost of production) to customer. The cost includes the supply chain sector between producing a product, logistics distribution and delivery to the customer, including the cost of lead times during that process.	Customers vary between different companies from end retail, distribution centres or end wholesaler it is important for experts to estimate the cost for their chosen products or good to be produced and distributed through the chain as it helps them understand what they believe to be the best suited strategy for companies to implement based on the cost factor they believe companies are willing to invest.
JIT Lean	Time is lean – the more time is lost the greater the waste as time is a resource. JIT Lean is defined as the development of a value stream that eliminates all waste, including time, to ensure a sophisticated level of scheduling. Therefore the assumption that time is lean is measured by JIT system, hence the term JIT Lean.	Experts establish their end customer and product or goods in addition to estimating cost. The estimation of delay is crucial in identifying the supply chain strategy that is best suited for various distribution systems. For experts to have an approximation to eliminate waste and lead time, the more they can define the best suited strategy by the JIT system, the deeper they understand the best strategy suited for waste problems in production, low inventory level, hence impacting the sourcing of raw

(*continued*)

Table 6.2 (continued)

Variable Function	Definition	Beneficial to the experts in Fuzzy Delphi
		materials, production and distribution cost, resulting in influencing sales. The JIT system requires coordination with suppliers to avoid delays in the production schedule (Kootanaee et al. 2013).
Delivery Strategies According to Gunasekaran et al. (2001) there are three types of deliveries: Delivery to request, delivery to commit date and order fill lead time.	To classify the response time between order and corresponding delivery to develop the appropriate trade-offs for the delivery system so they can be applied as a basis for planning a supply chain and delivery from manufacturing to customer (Beamon 1999).	Measuring the effects of different types of logistics on the supply chain strategy, experts choose an estimated cost which they take into consideration planning the logistics delivery from manufacturing to customer, while choosing the supply chain strategy best suited for each logistic system. Experts take into consideration the JIT lean, so that overall cost effectiveness and waste elimination is considered in choosing the best strategy.
Manufacturing Cost Is the cost of direct material, direct labour and manufacturing overheads in the fabrication, assembly and testing of an end item. This includes the utilisation of three inventory accounts: Raw Materials, Inventory,	According to Fisher (1997), if a company produces an "innovative" product, its demand is very unpredictable and in need of a responsive supply chain. According to Fisher (1997), a "functional" product is a product that people buy in a wide	It is important for companies to categorise their product type. From the literature there are three types of product. As companies categorise their market they take into consideration the cost and JIT lean to identify under which group their

Table 6.2 (continued)

Variable Function	Definition	Beneficial to the experts in Fuzzy Delphi
Work in Process Inventory and Finished Goods Inventory.	range of retail outlets that satisfies basic needs and has a predictable demand and in need of an efficient supply chain. According to Fisher (1997), an "innovative functional" product is demonstrated by the automobile industry and a functional innovative product is demonstrated by daily consumable goods such as toothpaste.	product belongs to. In order to help companies define which supply chain strategy best suits each product group, the experts were required to estimate a cost (for manufacturing) and JIT lean along with their chosen market to establish which supply chain strategy suited each product group.
Distribution Strategies Integrates manufacturing in supply chains, as the material flow must be viewed from three aspects as a whole; strategic, tactical and operational.	*Strategic distribution*: objective is expressed in terms of responsiveness, lower cost and product availability. The shape the supply chain takes is determined by the strategic location of its key facilities. The competitive aspect is integrating its manufacturing and distribution with that strategy (Gunasekaran et al. 2001). *Tactical distribution* creates the means by which objectives can be realised by providing balance for each function in the supply chain (e.g. inventory capacity, service and determining	In order to measure the material flow of components, raw materials, or commodities, between, resources, different plants, manufacturing and customer. It is important for experts to assess the best supply chain strategy that is suited for each distribution system to help companies enhance the material flow within their supply chain to create an integrated system between the different nodes in the supply chain. Focusing on the sector between manufacturing to customer the integration and

(continued)

Table 6.2 (continued)

Variable Function	Definition	Beneficial to the experts in Fuzzy Delphi
	the tools, approaches, resources necessary to manage and provide the information infrastructure for the supply chain by using (MRP, DRP, JIT) (Gunasekaran et al. 2001). *Operational distribution* concerned with the efficiency of operations by ensuring the detailed procedures of systems and appropriate controls are measured accurately in terms of supplier performance, inventory investment, service level, throughput efficiency and cost (Stevens 2007).	flow of material will be between the resources delivered to the manufacturing, distribution of components to different plants, delivery of components or materials to customers (i.e. third party logistics who may be integrated into manufacturing and warehousing during a customisation for responsiveness). Experts would estimate a cost and JIT lean as they select the best suited supply chain for each delivery system.
Measuring Output Output is measured by the number of items produced, the time required to produce a particular item and/or set of items and customer satisfaction which is measured by the number of on time deliveries and less led-time between order and corresponding delivery (Tan et al. 1998).	*Customer satisfaction:* Good flexibility and response to customer needs, good customer service and response to customer queries as well as post transaction customer service, such as problems arising from warranty claims. Less customers complaining about product features or quality, delays or shipping errors (Beamon 1999). Providing a higher service level will require higher costs (Tan et al. 1999).	The approach in measuring output is through generating more demand which is achieved when customer satisfaction is high (Tan et al. 1998). To measure customer satisfaction, the experts will be required to identify the best suited supply chain strategy that would reduce the cost and JIT lean in the customer order path, manufacturing lead time and reducing shipping errors.

Table 6.2 (continued)

Variable Function	Definition	Beneficial to the experts in Fuzzy Delphi
	Customer order path is the path that orders travel by, where time is spent in non-value adding activities, such as paperwork, checking, which can be eliminated by using JIT an EDI (Gunasekaran et al. 2001).	
	Manufacturing lead-time: Total amount of time required to produce an item or batch (Beamon 1999; Simeonovova and Simeonov 2012).	
	Shipping errors: If a supply chain focuses on customer satisfaction in the retail industry, number of incorrect shipments reflects on customer service as it is the combined effect of all functions along the supply chain (Beamon 1999; Elfving 2003).	
Measuring Product Demand By looking at the (1) End-user requirement, or (2) substitute product, or (3) competing product; then assessing the total volume of a product or service that would be bought by a consumer group where the		

(*continued*)

Table 6.2 (continued)

Variable Function	Definition	Beneficial to the experts in Fuzzy Delphi
location, time period and marketing effort are defined. **Product Life Cycle** The product life cycle has four very clearly defined stages (Introduction Stage, Growth Stage, Maturity Stage and Decline Stage), each with its own characteristics that mean different things for business that are trying to manage the life cycle of their particular products (divided into three categories).	There are three product types: *"Innovative products"* carry risk as the product has a short life cycle due to unpredictable demand, requiring a flexible supply chain with-Flexible Manufacturing System (FMS) and Computer Integrated Manufacturing (CIM) (Fisher 1997). "Functional products" have a longer life cycle of more than 2 years with an average margin forecast error of 10% (Fisher 1997). "High-end products" have a fluctuating demand, to counter this uncertainty Fisher (1997) suggested a blend of three strategies reducing uncertainty by identifying and analysing new sources of data, avoiding uncertainty by cutting lead times and incorporating flexibility and hedging against uncertainty with buffers of inventory or excess capacity	Further to measuring output by product demand, the life cycle of a product influences its demand, as it increases turnover. Products are made to expand consumption hence life cycle is crucial for planning obsolescence (Maycroft 2005). It is important for experts to choose the best supply chain strategy for each product category bearing in mind an estimated cost and JIT lean. This will help companies understand what supply chain their products require.

Table 6.2 (continued)

Variable Function	Definition	Beneficial to the experts in Fuzzy Delphi
Customisation A make-to-order lean pull system	*High-end.* If a supply chain is focused on high-end mass customisation, then it selects a relevant approach for a product that is expensive or advanced in a company's product range, or in the market as a whole. *Self-customised* enable the customer to change the product at any time to suit their own preferences (Alford et al. 2000; Silveira et al. 2001). *Collaborative customisation.* Manufacturers that involve their customers in a dialogue to identify their needs and establish their requirements are using collaborative customisation, which is specifically tailored to that specific partnership (Alford et al. 2000; Silveira et al. 2001). *Adaptive customisation* enables the user to customise the product to their requirements (Alford et al. 2000; Silveira et al. 2001). *The cosmetic customiser* presents the product differently to each customer, whether through	It is important to identify the most suited supply chain strategy for high-end products as they are the most expensive in a company's product range, they often require customisation to make the items more personalised for the customer. Hence experts estimate a cost and JIT lean for the supply chain as they choose the most suited strategy. There are different types of customisation that companies use. In order to gain variety of results and understand the best suited strategy for each, experts estimated the cost and JIT lean for each (Collaborative, Adaptive, Cosmetic and Transparent customiser) As competition is a crucial element, customisation is key. It is evident that customisation has increased as a unique selling advantage commonly through self-customisation (Silveira et al. 2001). Therefore in order to identify the best strategy, experts were asked to choose

(*continued*)

Table 6.2 (continued)

Variable Function	Definition	Beneficial to the experts in Fuzzy Delphi
	packaging or similar changes in distribution or services (Alford et al. 2000; Silveira et al. 2001). *Transparent customiser* provides unique products or services in a standard form to each customer, without the customer's knowledge that the product or service is customised (Alford et al. 2000; Silveira et al. 2001).	based on their estimated cost and JIT lean.
Push System A company makes-to-stock and maintains inventory level	*Push system.* According to Alford et al. (2000) and Stevens (1989), when a company pushes variety of goods into the market in hope that customers will find what they want.	The supply chain is divided into push and pull systems. The pull is indicated by the Lean strategy while Push can be a result of various strategies. In order to identify the best supply chain for a Push system. Experts were asked to estimate the Cost and JIT lean with regard to customisation to identify the best strategy.

the fuzzy sets into HTML and JavaScript. The chosen variable functions were divided as shown in Table 6.4.

For both groups, the interactive MDM requires the selection of the "Cost" and "JIT Lean" percentage. Once a company establishes the percentage range for its cost and lead-time, it can select a product, good or commodity and a variable from one of the groups. The interactive MDM will then diagnose the best supply chain strategy (Agile, Lean,

Table 6.3 The interactive MDM chosen variable functions

Variable Function	Why is it most relevant to this study?
Cost	Cost is one of the main variables that are crucial in the calculation of the best suited strategy for each variable. as experts aim to estimate the cost from manufacturing to customer for their chosen market and use it as a basis for selecting strategies.
JIT lean	JIT lean is also one of the main variables that is crucial in the calculation of the best suited strategy for the other variables. Experts aim to estimate the JIT lean from manufacturing to customer for their chosen market and use it as a basis for selecting strategies.
Delivery strategies group Delivery to commit date, delivery to request and order fill lead-time	Logistics elements are crucial for inter-deliveries between the supply chain and the customer. The decision-making process of selecting a suitable strategy will influence the lead times of the supply chain and its responsiveness. Hence the delivery between manufacturing through the supply chain to the end customer is a key aspect that must be included to create a holistic multi-dimensional model.
Product Strategies Labelled in the interactive MDM as "Demand approach" Is calculated by manufacturing cost. Is the cost of direct material, direct labour and manufacturing overheads in the fabrication, assembly, and testing of an end item. This includes the utilisation of three inventory accounts: Raw Materials, Inventory, Work in Process Inventory, and Finished Goods Inventory. Manufacturing cost: the manufacturing cost in production is determined	It is important for companies to understand the best supply chain strategy most suitable for their market. Therefore, by determining what product group they are manufacturing the multi-dimensional model aim aids determining the best strategy. Understanding the different costs and JIT Lean associated with each product type in terms of the best suited supply chain strategy is extremely important for companies, as it establishes the foundation on which the product type is selected, strategy

(continued)

Table 6.3 (continued)

Variable Function	Why is it most relevant to this study?
by the market the company is catering for, the market determines the product type (innovative, functional and innovative functional) which in turn determines the cost of manufacturing and production.	approach implemented and manufacturing method is built based on demand.
Distribution Strategies Group Strategic distribution, tactical distribution, and operational distribution.	It is important for companies to understand the intra-logistics distribution throughout its supply chain network. It is crucially important to determine the strategies used for intra-logistics in order to create a coherent flow of materials, components and goods.
Measuring Output There are various variables in measuring output and increase or decrease of demand. The selected variable for the scope of this study is *"manufacturing lead-time"*.	It is important for companies to reduce the time a product stays in manufacturing in order to increase turnover. Additionally lead times can be reduced by decreasing the time spent on paper work of clearing products (Simeonovova and Simeonov 2012). As companies are moving toward re-engineering their supply chain to manufacture-to-order, the manufacturing lead time has become crucial to the industry and to the scope of this study (Elfving 2003).
Measuring Product Demand A related factor to the "Demand approach" variable group, as companies must take into account the demand of the target market before selecting their product type (innovative, functional and innovative functional).	The life cycle of products in relation to their type is of crucial importance to companies, as it determines the level of output and the nature of their supply chain.
Customisation Labelled in the interactive MDM as "Demand approach" There are many type of variables for customisation as it has gained	High-end was selected to offer a variety of options to this study, as companies using the multi-dimensional model may require a high-end customisation option.

Table 6.3 (continued)

Variable Function	Why is it most relevant to this study?
popularity throughout the years. However, three variables were selected under the "Demand approach" group for the scope of this study. "High-end customisation strategy, push system and self-customisation"	As the Pull system is measured through a Lean system, it's important for the multi-dimensional model to be inclusive by having the Push system incorporated within it. Self-customisation became the most popular method of customisation, as it gives the customer control and flexibility to have the product made and customised to their specific preferences.

Table 6.4 Category groups of the chosen variables

	Logistics strategy	Supply chain strategy
Cost percentage	*Delivery strategy group*	*Product design group*
JIT Lean percentage	1. Delivery to commit date	1. Innovative
	2. Delivery to request	2. Functional
	3. Order fill lead-time	3. Innovative functional
	Distribution strategy group	*Demand approach group*
	1. Strategic distribution	1. High-end strategy
	2. Tactical distribution	2. Push system
	3. Operational distribution	3. Self-customiser
	Manufacturing lead-time	

Leagile and BSC) based on the experts' answers to the (If-Then) statements from the Fuzzy Delphi. The company can apply the recommendation or decide to implement the optional strategy. Tailoring the web-based interactive MDM can then be considered by adding further variables or changing the (If-Then) statements depending on the company's requirement to build a unique interactive MDM exclusive to its specification.

Unforeseen Obstacles

The main issue during the Fuzzy Delphi study is uncertainty with regard to the consistency in responses from experts and their commitment to stay for the whole duration of the study. The consistency issue involves the decision-making process, which can be due to little in attention to the intentions, actions, context or processes surrounding the participation of experts (Rowlands 2005), for example explanation on how these variables interact with the outside world. In addition, the commitment issue resulted in losing experts between the pilot and second round. Initially 137 experts from various academic and industrial backgrounds were contacted; the pilot Fuzzy Delphi study generated a response from 83 experts who remained for the first round but three participants dropped out resulting in 80 second round Delphi responses.

One of the major sources of error in any Delphi is non-response. Non-response errors result from participants not fully completing the questionnaire. There are several reasons why a response rate of a web-based survey decreases. These include open-ended questions, questions arranged in tables, fancy or graphically complex design, pull-down menus, unclear instructions, and the absence of navigation aids (Archer 2007). Excessive length of a questionnaire contributes to the problem, in addition to open-ended questions, both generating a higher drop-out rate.

Overcoming Issues

To ensure consistency between the Fuzzy Delphi rounds, the amendments made sure that questions were based on the theoretical framework and remained within the scope of the study to gather relevant information needed to create the multi-dimensional model (Rowlands 2005). In addition the amendments between rounds ensured that experts had a complete understanding of the problem, through adding definitions and explanation of the study's aim included in the cover letter.

Secondly, as the commitment of participants decreased throughout the Fuzzy Delphi rounds (Archer 2007) some factors can contribute to increased response rates. These include personalised email cover letters, follow-up reminders, pre-notification of the intent to survey and simpler formats. Experts that dropped out were sent a follow up reminder email. This helped regain 10 experts' interest in the study which resulted in 90 experts in total who successfully completed both rounds of the Fuzzy Delphi.

References

Alford, D., Sackett, P., & Nelder, G. (2000). Mass customisation: An automotive perspective. *International Journal of Production Economics, 65*(3), 99–110.

Archer, T. (2007). Characteristics associated with increasing the response rates of web-based surveys. *Practical Assessment, Research and Evaluation, 12*(12), 1–9.

Armstrong, J. S. (2001). *Principles of forecasting: A handbook for researchers and practitioners.* Boston, U.S.A: Kluwer Academic Publishers, 59–125.

Beamon, B. (1999). Measuring supply chain performance. *International Journal of Operations and Production Management, 19*(3), 275–292.

Davidson, P. (2013). The Delphi technique in doctoral research: Considerations and rationale. *Review of Higher Education and Self-Learning, 6*(22), 53–65.

Elfving, J. (2003). Exploration of opportunities to reduce lead times for engineered-to-order products. *Engineering-Civil and Environmental Engineering, 1*(1), 1–50.

Fisher, M. (1997). What is the right supply chain for your product? *Harvard Business Review, 1*(3), 105–116.

Fowler, H. W. (1995). *A dictionary of modern English usage.* Oxford: Oxford University Press.

Gracht, H. (2012). Consensus measurement in Delphi studies review and implications for future quality assurance. *Technological Forecasting and Social Change, 79*(1), 1525–1536.

Gunasekaran, A., Patel, C., & Tirtiroglu, E. (2001). Performance measures and metrics in a supply chain environment. *International Journal of Operations and Production Management, 21*(2), 71–87.

Herzog, N., & Tonchia, S. (2014). An instrument for measuring the degree of lean implementation in manufacturing. *Journal of Mechanical Engineering, 60*(12), 797–803.

Hines, P. (1998). Benchmarking Toyota's supply chain: Japan vs. U.K. *Long Range Planning, 31*(6), 911–918.

Jüttner, U., Godsell, J., & Christopher, M. (2006). Demand chain alignment competence: Delivering value through product life cycle management. *Industrial Marketing Management, 35*(9), 989–1001.

Kootanaee, A., Babu, K., & Talari, H. (2013). Just-in-time manufacturing system: From introduction to implement. *International Journal of Economics, Business and Finance, 1*(2), 7–13.

Mason-Jones, R., Naylor, B., & Towill, D. (2000). Lean, agile or leagile matching your supply chain to the marketplace. *International Journal of Production Research, 38*(17), 4061–4070.

Maycroft, N. (2005). *Consumption, planned obsolescence and waste.* Unpublished Paper, University of Lincoln: Lincoln School of Art and Design.

Munier, F., & Rondé, P. (2001). The role of knowledge codification in the emergence of consensus under uncertainty: Empirical analysis and policy implications. *Journal of Research Policy, 30*(1), 1537–1551.

Poundstone, W. (2008). *Gaming the vote: Why elections aren't fair (and what we can do about it).* New York: Hill and Wang. 4–258.

Robert, H. (2011). *Robert's rules of order newly revised.* Philadelphia PA: Da Capo Press. 26–202.

Rowlands, B. (2005). Grounded in practice: Using interpretive research to build theory. *The Electronic Journal of Business Research Methodology, 3*(1), 81–92.

Silveira, G., Borenstein, D., & Fogliatto, F. (2001). Mass customization: Literature review and research directions. *International Journal of Production Economics, 72*(1), 1–13.

Simeonovova, I., & Simeonov, S. (2012). Lead time reduction methods. *Institute of Production Machines, Systems and Robotics, 12*(3), 334–335.

Stevens, G. (1989). Integrating the supply chain. *International Journal of Physical Distribution and Materials Management, 19*(8), 3–8.

Tan, K. C., Kannan, V., & Handfield, R. (1998). Supply chain management: Supplier performance and firm performance. *International Journal of Purchasing and Materials Management, 34*(3), 2–9.

Tan, K. C., Kannan, V., Handfield, R., & Ghosh, S. (1999). Supply chain management: An empirical study of its impact on performance. *International Journal of Operations and Production Management, 19*(10), 1034–1052.

Terano, T., Asai, K., & Sugeno, M. (1994). *Applied fuzzy systems.* London: Academic Press Limited. 9–161.

Towill, D. R., Naim, N. M., & Wikner, J. (1992). Industrial dynamics simulation models in the design of supply chains. *International Journal of Physical Distribution and Logistics Management, 22*(5), 3–13.

7

Data Analysis for Strategic Supply Chain Management

Interplay of data

The Fuzzy Delphi gathered 12 measurement variable categories outlined in Chapter 6. Due to the substantial task of accommodating all 12 variable categories into this study, five categories in addition to the "Cost" and "JIT Lean" were chosen to be analysed and put into the interactive MDM, which is built using the Unified Modelling Language (UML). These five variable groups (Distribution strategies, Delivery strategies, Manufacturing lead-time, Product demand and Demand approach) were chosen based on their relevance and scope of the study. The experts were asked to answer the questions related to the Supply Chain and Logistics variable categories by rating which supply chain strategy they deemed most suitable for each of the variables. The experts would choose whether Lean, Agile, Leagile or Basic Supply Chain (BSC) strategy (1, 2, 3 and 4, respectively) was most appropriate for the variable in question. Furthermore, experts were asked to answer the "JIT Lean" and

© The Author(s) 2017
S. Sindi, M. Roe, *Strategic Supply Chain Management*,
DOI 10.1007/978-3-319-54843-2_7

"Cost" variable categories by rating which percentage constitutes Low, Medium and High (1,2,3, respectively).

The definition of "JIT Lean" is the delay time it takes a product to move between the resource or component plants to the manufacturing node, to assembly, handling and distributed to the warehouse, retailer or wholesaler. The definition of "Cost" is the expense of acquiring raw materials, equipment or machinery operations at the manufacturing node (excluding labour cost), distribution costs (varies on mode of transport selected) from resource or component plants to manufacturing and the overall supply chain (varies on product design and strategy) of delivering the commodity from plant to warehouse, retailer or wholesaler. The cost excludes labour, premises or equipment hire and is only the estimated cost being invested in creating the product, its supply chain and logistics. The "Cost" variable does not indicate the overall cost gained from the gross profit margin, as it could be skewed if the company sells many different products. Each product could have a different profit margin and it will be very hard to calculate the true gross profit margin.

Deduction is used to analyse the perspective, choices and conclusions of the experts in constituting the variables in question. The analysis of SPSS and Excel will create scatter diagrams that form the fuzzy rules that design the interactive codes for the MDM. The fuzzy rule codes will be input into a web page ready to be tested by a selected company, to determine its applicability.

SPSS

This section looks at the frequency tables created by SPSS. Each set of variables will be provided with their set of frequency tables and explained. Firstly, the frequency tables of the "Cost" and "JIT Lean" variables will be analysed. This will be followed by the logistics variables which include both "Distribution Strategies" and "Delivery Strategies", and finally the supply chain variables which includes the two groups, "Product Design" and "Demand Approach".

Cost Variable

In business strategy cost is crucial to the process, especially with regard to supply chains and logistics. Due to the complexity of different nodes found within the supply chain, managing cost along the entire process is extremely important. Moreover, the cost of logistics has become crucial due to the significance speed has in distribution across continents in a globalised economy and ensuring the products reach the right destination, at the right time and in the right condition.

The experts were asked to rate a recommended cost for a retail product of their own choice. This study defines "Cost" as the company's investments from the manufacturing stages (cost of production) to end-customer. Although the definition of end-customer varies between different companies, from end-customer to end-wholesaler, as the experts chose their own products they also chose what they consider an end-customer, hence the recommended cost. Therefore, deductively the "Cost" cannot be more than 60% of the total manufacturing and supply chain distribution cost, which includes producing a product, cost of lead-times during that process, logistics distribution and delivery to the end-customer.

Due to the number of frequency tables created by SPSS, this section will select the most relevant tables as an example to analyse the "Cost variables". The samples illustrate that when the cost is under/equal 10% the majority of experts chose "Low cost", indicating that it is mostly favoured for the supply chain of their product. Meanwhile, when the cost is under/equal to 20%, experts scored it as "Low cost", as it was still within their favoured region (Table 7.1). This could be due to the products chosen being within the high-end category which has a higher cost of sourcing, production and distribution, such as high-end customised cars, wedding gowns and expensive sport equipment. However, when the cost reached 30% or above, the experts' ranking dropped to between "Medium" and "High" Cost, indicating that it is not a favourable cost percentage for supply chain and logistics.

The frequency tables also show the "valid percent", which is calculated by SPSS to provide a percentage of the total cases for each variable. The valid percentage illustrates the proportion of a sample that is valid,

Table 7.1 Cost variables

	Frequency	Valid percent
If a company's supply chain cost is 0–8% of the revenue then it is		
Valid　　　Low cost	79	87.8
Medium cost	9	10.0
High cost	2	2.2
Total	90	100.0
If a company's supply chain cost is 9–18% of the revenue then it is		
Valid　　　Low cost	54	60
Medium cost	30	33.3
High cost	6	6.7
Total	90	100.0
If a company's supply chain cost is 29–38% of the revenue then it is		
Valid　　　Medium cost	51	56.7
High cost	39	43.3
Total	90	100.0
If a company's supply chain cost is 49–58% of the revenue then it is		
Valid　　　Mediumcost	10	11.1
High cost	80	88.9
Total	90	100.0

as data can be invalid for a variety of reasons. Some data are simply impossible, such as negative heights or weights, while some comparison data can be shown to be invalid when correlated with other data. Finally, some data can be identified invalid due to machine error or human entry error (Field 2009).

Just in Time Lean Variable

In addition to cost, lead-time is equally crucial to supply chains. With consumer tastes changing regularly and with expectations of products arriving as fast as possible, lead-times have become key to a successful business strategy with an orientated value chain. This study considered that the best way to measure lead-time within supply chains is assuming that time equals leanness, as examined by James-Moore and Gibbons (1997), the more time is lost the greater the waste as time is a resource. Therefore, the more a supply chain strategy moves towards Lean strategy, the less lead-time it has due to JIT, hence this assumption measures time by JIT Lean system.

To test this assumption, experts were asked to choose a percentage they deemed appropriate for deliveries to be on time. As "time" is endless, for simplicity this study ranks the JIT Lean to be from (0 – >90%), where the SPSS calculated ten frequency tables. However, three samples were selected for this analysis based on the contrast and compatibility of their data. The first example is if a company's supply chain is ≤10% JIT, indicating there is an estimation of ≤90% lead-time, the majority of experts ranked it at "Low lean" and thus not favourable. Moreover, the second example is if JIT Lean is above/below 30% where more than half of the experts reached a consensus that it is "Medium" and the others were split with 18 experts ranking it as "High" and 15 "Low"; this is due to the strategy of the business they selected, the product, distribution and end consumer they had in mind. However, the third example is when JIT Lean is above/equal to 90% meaning ≤10% lead-time, a majority of experts ranked it "High lean", indicating this is the position most companies aim to achieve. The Fuzzy Delphi study questions on JIT Lean show that time can be considered Lean and measured by JIT, as all the experts understood the concept of the questions and answered them accordingly (Table 7.2).

Logistic Variables

This section looks at the logistics variables divided into three categories: distribution strategies, delivery strategies and manufacturing lead-time. These variables are chosen due to their relevance in building the MDM and the scope of analysis to be undertaken. The logistics framework combines the planning, implementation, control, efficiency, effectiveness and storage of goods, services and related information flows from the point of origin to the point of consumption (Slack 2005). Both distribution and delivery strategy variables consist of inbound and outbound logistics. Therefore, experts select the most suitable supply chain model for the logistics distribution and delivery strategies to help improve tactical operations, reliability, reduce lead-times and maximise utilisation (Mangan et al. 2008).

Table 7.2 JIT lean variables

		Frequency...	Valid percent
If a company's supply chain is 0–8% JIT then it is			
Valid	Low lean	84	93.3
	Medium lean	4	4.4
	High lean	2	2.2
	Total	90	100.0
If a company's supply chain is 29–38% JIT then it is			
Valid	Low lean	15	16.7
	Medium ...	57	63.3
	High lean	18	20.0
	Total	90	100.0
If a company's supply chainis 29–38% JIT then it is			
Valid	Low lean	15	16.7
	Medium ...	57	63.3
	High lean	18	20.0
	Total	90	100.0
If a company's supply chain is 89–98% JIT then it is			
Valid	Low lean	2	2.2
	High lean	88	97.8
	Total	90	100.0

Distribution Strategies

The distribution strategies are divided into Operational distribution, Strategic distribution and Tactical distribution systems. They include the distribution movement of information flows and the inbound process of purchasing, movement of material parts from suppliers to manufacturing or assembly plants to warehouses (Gunasekaran et al. 2001). If it is a finished product, then distribution strategies also include the outbound process of storing and distributing the final product from the end of the production line to the end-customer which could be a warehouses, retail stores or consumers (Mangan et al. 2008).

Operational Distribution System

Experts were asked to pick a retail product and categorise which supply chain strategy best suits the operational distribution. From the SPSS analysis (Table 7.3), most experts chose BSC to be most suitable for an

Table 7.3 Operational distribution variable

Operational distribution system: concerned with the efficiency of operations by ensuring the detailed procedures of systems and appropriate controls are measured accurately

		Frequency	Valid percent
Valid	Lean	13	14.4
	Agile	18	20.0
	Leagile	26	28.9
	Basic supply chain strategies	33	36.7
	Total	90	100.0

operational distribution, while Leagile was chosen to be second most suitable making Agile the third most suitable for operational distribution. Meanwhile Lean ranked as the least likely strategy, as the level of lead-time reduction would be too complex for operational distribution, requiring time to ensure the detailed products are accurate for their customer's demand (James-Moore and Gibbons 1997). The operational distribution system is often used for customised products or mass customisation as well as products that require specific handling, packaging and distribution, all of which require predictable or flexible lead-times which contradict a Lean strategy (Swaminathan and Tayur 2003).

Strategic Distribution System

When experts were asked to categorise the best supply chain strategy for the distribution of their chosen commodity, the majority of responses were for both Agile and BSC while the rest believed a strategic distribution was more appropriate for a Lean system, while Leagile ranked last (Table 7.4). This is because an Agile system requires responsiveness to customer's needs, taste and requirements; therefore, a strategic system will allow for warehouses to be close to targeted markets to reduce lead-time (Heikkilä 2002). This is also beneficial for products that require a BSC system, such as everyday requirements of soaps, toothpaste and seasonal items (Alford et al. 2000). Additionally, the strategic system is most suitable for a Lean strategy as it focuses on reducing cost and waste as well as lead-time, the main elements of JIT, although a Leagile system

Table 7.4 Strategic distribution variable

Strategic distribution system: objective is expressed in terms of responsiveness, lower cost and product availability. The shape the supply chain takes is determined by the strategic location			
		Frequency	Valid percent
Valid	Lean	22	24.4
	Agile	25	27.8
	Leagile	18	20.0
	Basic supply chain strategies	25	27.8
	Total	90	100.0

combines both Lean and Agile's best attributes operating with a flexible production capacity to meet surges in demand (Kotzab 2003). Experts believe Leagile is least suitable, due to products requiring an innovative Leagile strategy, customised or within the high end sector, due to Leagile operating as a "postponement" strategy where products are part-assembled to forecast, then completed to order hence deferring some of the expense until a sale is assured (Swaminathan and Tayur 2003).

Tactical Distribution System

When the experts categorised the tactical distribution of their chosen commodity, a majority believed that an Agile or Leagile system is most suitable, with BSC as an option (Table 7.5). This is due to the tactical distribution strict operation guidelines that determine when day-to-day scheduling can be executed either from manufacturing or procurement (Gunasekaran et al. 2001). These key operating targets are provided with several software tools that are available to the company. An agile strategy focuses on responsiveness and knowing which processes to operate at which time (such as safety stocks, planned lead-times and batch sizes), crucial to the company's cost and getting the right product to the right customer (Naylor et al. 1999). Also a Leagile strategy relies on post-ponement strategy and a tactical distribution will help identify which components and products should be part-assembled and sent to the warehouse, while for a BSC system it is important to coordinate the daily consumer requirements across the different units within a supply

Table 7.5 Tactical distribution variable

Tactical distribution system: creates the means by which objectives can be realised by providing balance for each function in the supply chain (e.g. inventory capacity and service)

		Frequency	Valid percent
Valid	Lean	16	17.8
	Agile	25	27.8
	Leagile	25	27.8
	Basic supply chain strategies	24	26.7
	Total	90	100.0

chain (Pagh 1998). Meanwhile, the lean strategy is ranked as least suitable due to a tactical distribution requiring pre-determined and flexible lead-times (Gunasekaran et al. 2001).

Delivery Strategies

Delivery strategies are divided into three variable categories: delivery to commit date, delivery to request and order fill lead-time. Similar to the distribution strategy, experts include in their assumptions of selecting the best supply chain strategy the inbound and outbound logistic factors.

Delivery to Commit Date

Experts were asked to identify under which supply chain strategy the delivery to commit date will most likely be suitable (Table 7.6). A majority of expert opinions believe that Agile is most suitable as it caters for flexibility as well as responsiveness, which is critical for the percentage of orders that are put in place to be fulfilled on/before the original scheduled "commit date", while BSC is ranked second most suitable due to the difficulties of developing large scale integrated models, consisting of multiple entities for daily products (Lu et al. 2003). Meanwhile, Leagile and Lean are both least suitable due to delivery to commit date requirements of simplicity, flexibility and responsiveness which will be complex to implement with a Lean or Leagile strategy (Melton 2005).

Table 7.6 Delivery to commit date variable

If a supply chain delivery cost is calculated by "Deliveryto commit date", then the supply chain is operating under:

		Frequency	Valid percent
Valid	Lean	18	20.0
	Agile	33	36.7
	Leagile	18	20.0
	Basic supply chain s trategies	21	23.3
	Total	90	100.0

Delivery to Request

A majority of experts identified a BSC strategy as most suitable for delivery to request because daily products are required to be delivered as soon as the requests are sent from the retailer to the supplier (Table 7.7). Therefore, the percentage of stock level in retailers must remain constant and orders must be delivered on time to maintain inventory level with complete documentation and perfect condition (Shah and Ward 2003). The Agile strategy came second due to its responsiveness as delivery to request is usually from the warehouse or wholesaler to the retailer. This helps an Agile strategy to cope with any demand surplus or change in season or consumer habits in contrast to the former "delivery to commit date" for Agile which scored as most suitable due to it being from manufacturing to the warehouse or wholesaler. The third suitable strategy is Lean, as during shipment or distribution between warehouse and wholesaler to the retail Lean requires under

Table 7.7 Delivery to request variable

If a supply chain delivery cost is calculated by "Delivery to Request", then the supply chain is operating under:

		Frequency	Valid percent
Valid	Lean	24	26.7
	Agile	25	27.8
	Leagile	8	8.9
	Basic supply chain strategies	33	36.7
	Total	90	100.0

"deliver to request" for orders to be delivered within next day delivery of the order receipt with minimum stock and waste (Heikkilä 2002). This means orders must be filled from the warehouse or wholesaler and complete shipment or distribution within 24 hours which is a very complex and difficult requirement (e.g. Armstrong (2013) in his case study of Amazon Prime).

Order Fill Lead-Time

For "order fill lead time", experts ranked BSC as the most suitable strategy due to daily products having fewer lead-time processes checks before being sent through to distribution (Table 7.8). Meanwhile, Leagile strategy came second due to its "postponement" strategy where products are already processed with their semi-assembled, documentation and await to be put through the final stages of "order fulfilment" (Naylor et al. 1999). The Agile strategy came third as due its responsiveness of adapting to changes in demand or customer preference, products have to be designed to take less lead-time especially with documentation processes, shipments and distribution clearance. The Lean strategy came last due to its emphasis on speed, reduced stock/inventory level and waste reduction (Melton 2005). However, as products are not put through the Lean system until an order has been placed it is very difficult to plan or clear process before orders come in, hence experts believe Lean is least suitable (Naylor et al. 1999). For the "order fill lead time" to be fully utilised, efficiency is required to clear products from the system, transforming resources into goods and services

Table 7.8 Order fill lead time variables

If the supply chain delivery cost is calculated by "Order Fill Lead-Time", then the supply chain is operating under:		Frequency	Valid percent
Valid	Lean	19	2.1
	Agile	20	22.2
	Leagile	21	23.3
	Basic supply chain strategies	30	33.3
	Total	90	100.0

from the moment a customer order is received, including lead-times through to the end-customer with low/zero inventory (Lu et al. 2003).

Manufacturing Lead-Time

When experts were asked which strategy best suited manufacturing lead-time, a majority believed that Agile mostly required a "manufacturing lead time" reduction system due to its responsiveness to changes in consumer taste, having a system that favours a fast manufacturing process with least lead-time as possible that focuses on minimal time to manufacture an item, including order preparation time, queue time, setup time, run time, move time, inspection time and put-away time (Table 7.9) (Shah and Ward 2003). For a Leagile strategy, manufacturing lead-time is very important once the semi-assembled postponed product becomes activated to be launched into its final production stage, as the Lean aspect of the Leagile strategy is applied then lead-times must be reduced to a minimum for the product to reach its destination on time (Heikkilä 2002). The BSC is usually associated with daily products and make-to-stock products hence reducing lead-time in manufacturing is crucial especially for those with a short shelf life. Additionally, reducing the time of releasing an order to production and receipt into finished goods inventory for make-to-order products is crucial to maintaining stock levels (Ergen et al. 2007). The Lean strategy is least suitable because throughout the processes components are only assembled when an order is in place; therefore,

Table 7.9 Manufacturing lead-time variables

Manufacturing lead-time: is the total amount of time required to produce an item or batch. If a supply chain focuses on customer satisfaction in the retail industry, then Manufacturing lead time should be:			
		Frequency	Valid percent
Valid	Lean	14	15.6
	Agile	35	38.9
	Leagile	21	23.3
	Basic supply chain strategies	20	22.2
	Total	90	100.0

due to the efficiency and waste reduction engineered into the Lean strategy the manufacturing process is already designed to assemble components and manufacture them systematically (Simeonovova and Simeonov 2012). Within the lean strategy, the process which requires reduction in lead-time during manufacturing is quality control. As the quality control node in the manufacturing lead-time system is crucial, the JIT in Lean strategy embeds a flagging system where a component is flagged as it is manufactured if it fails quality checks. This helps lead-time reduction as the component is fixed straightaway due to the efficiency strategy of Lean. Therefore, as the make-to-order products in the Lean strategy have an in-built manufacturing Lead-time reduction system from the moment an order is released to production, manufacturing, assembling, distribution and shipment, experts believe Lean strategy did not require a "manufacturing lead time" (Lee et al. 2007).

Supply Chain Variables

While the term logistics refers to tactical and operational issues, supply chain is used to refer to strategic issues, which includes the systematic, strategic coordination of business functions and tactics across the supply chain for the purposes of improving the long-term performance of the company as a whole (Georgia Tech Supply Chain and Logistics Institute 2010). This section looks at a list of supply chain strategy variables, divided into two categories, product design and demand approach. These variables are chosen due to their importance in this study and to narrow the scope of research.

Product Design

Product design is divided into three categories, "Innovative Products", "Functional Products" and "Innovative Functional Products". Each product type will be allocated by the experts to its best supply chain strategy along with optional strategies that companies may find useful, depending on their business structure.

Innovative Products

Experts were asked to choose the most suitable strategy for an innovative product. The majority chose Agile due to innovative products requiring flexibility in understanding customer needs and reacting to demand during their creation and distribution (Sanchez and Nagi 2001) – for example accessories, fashion and household technological devices (Fisher 1997). Leagile and BSC strategy came second equally (Table 7.10). With Leagile, it can be deduced that experts believed the strategy to be complex for innovative products, as the possibilities of changes in demand once the product is made require an Agile focused approach (Agarwal et al. 2006). For example, the postponement and lean distribution system in Leagile would make it difficult to adapt the product as inventory levels cannot respond fast enough to changes in a customer's taste (Naylor et al. 1999). The BSC main focus is on daily products or product/components that are of stable or predictable demand and require simple production, handling and distribution, which does not apply to innovative products. The Lean strategy was considered less suitable due to innovative products requiring time for research and design to fully capture the consumer's requirements and hence inevitably leading to some wasted resources (Sugimori et al. 1977). Additionally, innovative products start at the high-end market with complex production, assembling, handling and distribution, making them unfit for the tight scheduling of the lean strategy (Pagh 1998).

Table 7.10 Innovative product variable

According to Fisher (1997), if a company produces an innovative product, its demand is very unpredictable and in need of a responsive supply chain.		Frequency	Valid percent
Valid	Lean	9	10.0
	Agile	43	47.8
	Leagile	19	21.1
	Basic supply chain strategies	19	21.1
	Total	90	100.0

Functional Products

For the functional product, experts chose the BSC strategy to be most suitable due to being mass-produced daily requirements of the public (Table 7.11). For example plastic utilities and stationery (Cagliano et al. 2004). Lean strategy is second most suitable, due to the functional product being mass produced with predictable demand, hence lead-times and waste reduction can be easily accounted for and scheduled with no inventory (Melton 2005). Additionally functional products usually follow straightforward production, assembling and handling, hence making distribution simple and enabling easier lead-time reduction with less labour intensive activities such as certification documents (Fisher 1997). Agile and Leagile were classed as less suitable due to their responsiveness attributes which are not required for a functional product with a predictable demand (Sanchez and Nagi 2001).

Innovative Functional Products

Experts classified Leagile strategies as most suitable for innovative functional products (Table 7.12). This is due to these products having a functional basis that can be mass produced and held at the postponement stage for the "Innovative" elements to be added at final production and assembly although Pagh (1998) states in some cases

Table 7.11 Functional product variable

According to Fisher (1997), a functional product is a product that people buy in a wide range of retail outlets that satisfy basic needs and has a predictable demand and in need of an efficient supply chain

		Frequency	Valid percent
Valid	Lean	21	23.3
	Agile	17	18.9
	Leagile	14	15.6
	Basic supply chain strategies	38	42.2
	Total	90	100.0

Table 7.12 Innovative functional product variables

According to Fisher (1997), an innovative functional product is demonstrated by the automobile industry and a functional innovative product is demonstrated by daily consumable goods such as toothpaste

		Frequency	Valid percent
Valid	Lean	20	22.2
	Agile	25	27.8
	Leagile	26	28.9
	Basic supply chain strategies	19	21.1
	Total	90	100.0

elements can be added at the handling stage before being put through a lean distribution system. Innovative functional products are usually mass customised such as cars, household furniture, laptops and personal computers. Agile strategy came second as innovative functional products can also be aimed at the high end market where demand and taste can fluctuate requiring flexibility in manufacturing and responsiveness, such as wedding gowns and professional sports equipment as well as special brands of automobiles (Silveira et al. 2001). Lean strategy was chosen third due to its difficulty for Innovative Functional products, however car manufacturers for a mass customised market such as Toyota were able to implement a lean strategy successfully (Hines 1998). This is due to their make-to-order system's fast response to orders and their tactical placement of plants around the world for quick manufacturing of components, which enables them to strategically distribute components to their assembling plants for final manufacturing and delivery to customers' request (Tomino et al. 2009). Basic strategy was chosen last as Innovative Functional products can additionally be mass produced for the day to day markets such as detergents (i.e. soaps and household cleaning equipment) and electronic accessories. These types of Innovative Functional products have a stable demand and mostly have a very similar production process with slight changes for Innovation, such as few additional ingredients/components, variety of flavours, scent and branding, hence requiring a simple assemble, handling and distribution (Tomino et al. 2009).

Demand Approach

Demand approaches are divided into three categories, high-end, self-customised and push system. Experts will examine each demand approach as they allocate the best supply chain strategy and optional strategies that they recommend for companies to implement, depending on their business structure.

High-end Mass Customisation

Experts categorised Agile strategy as most suited for "high-end" products because they are innovative with volatile demand and are characterised by changes in taste (Table 7.13). For example, sports equipment such as heartrate monitors have to undergo a series of pilot tests before consumer preference is understood (Mourtzis et al. 2008). However, once the product is manufactured, additional design information can be added depending on consumer taste. Additionally demand can fluctuate when the product has been used widely, due to consumer change in requirements or need for the product. Hence manufacturing, assembling, inventory, handling, storage and distribution must maintain its flexibility and responsiveness (Silveira et al. 2001). Experts selected Leagile as the second most suitable supply chain strategy for a high end product demand as it combines the best Lean and Agile strategy. As Mourtzis et al. (2008) state, a high-end manufactured product could require customisation at the last stage of production, such as authentic leather brief cases, personalised wedding gifts, technological accessories

Table 7.13 High-end product variables

If a supply chain is focused onhigh-end mass customisation, then its approach should be:		Frequency	Valid percent
Valid	Lean	22	24.4
	Agile	26	28.9
	Leagile	24	26.7
	Basic supply chain strategies	18	20.0
	Total	90	100.0

such as personalised keyboards and mice, also customised high-end desk chairs. For the example of a high-end leather briefcase, the Agile operation will be during the manufacturing and assembly stage of the supply chain, while any personalisation such as design or engraved initials will be done after at the holding up stage or "postponement" stage. The Lean operation will then take place at the handling and distribution stage (Naylor et al. 1999; Mourtzis et al. 2008).

Experts selected the Lean strategy third due to difficulty implementing in full throughout the high-end product supply chain. However, most innovative and high-end products have a Lean strategy for their assembly and distribution nodes as customers pay premium prices for these products (Kootanaee et al. 2013). The BSC strategy was least suitable for high-end products due to the nature of responding to demand, complexity of manufacturing, stock level, handling and in some cases distribution (Chakravarty 2014). However, some products such as wedding gowns require basic components to be manufactured using a basic supply chain, for example wedding veils, dress extension and accessories. These items can be stocked as the demand for them can be forecasted (Tan et al. 1998).

Self-Customised

Experts chose the Leagile strategy to be most suitable for self-customised products (Table 7.14); for example with a high-end laptop from Dell, sourcing and manufacturing follows an agile strategy to incorporate changes in technology, while assembly is Lean and built-to-order as customer personalisation takes place using JIT system and is distributed accordingly (Davis 2010). Agile came second as it allowed room for customisation flexibility; for example specialist mountain bikes are customised at production in accordance to the consumer's needs; if the consumer changes their mind, the supply chain must be able to adapt. The same can be applied to personal gaming computers where the consumer can build the parts of the computer they which to buy, however if they change their mind then the assembly node of the supply chain must be able to account for that (Davis 2010). The Lean strategy came third due to the difficulty of accommodating the consumer's

Table 7.14 Self-customised product variable

		Frequency	Valid percent
Self-customized goods: enable the customer to change the product at any time to suit their own preferences (Alford et al. 2000).			
Valid	Lean	17	18.9
	Agile	25	27.8
	Leagile	36	40.0
	Basic supply chain strategies	12	13.3
	Total	90	100.0

expectation of self-customised products to be delivered at the next available delivery. Therefore self-customised supply chains most likely require the assembly, handling and distribution stages to be as lean as possible (Mourtzis et al. 2008). The BSC strategy came last as most daily products do not require self-customisation but rather mass production. However, some products such as household or birthday gifts can be self-customised and require a simple basic supply chain where demand is predictable, inventory is kept stable, the goods are mass produced, and manufactured at low cost for the mass market then stocked at the warehouse to be distributed with a planned scheduled with predictable lead-time to the wholesaler, where at the retailing stage the item would be customised to the customer's request (Tan et al. 1998), for example customised jumpers, printed t-shirts and mugs.

Push System

Experts chose BSC as most suitable due to goods that require a push system usually having a predictable demand (Table 7.15) such as cutlery, stationery and school or work uniforms. These products have a stable demand and therefore have a stable inventory level that requires them to be manufactured using a push system in order for the wholesaler to maintain their predicted stock level (Cagliano et al. 2004). Leagile was chosen as the second most suitable strategy as some of these products such as work uniforms can be classified as functional innovative, where different styles and designs can be applied at the assembly stage and the

Table 7.15 Push system variable

According to Alford et al. (2000), when a company pushes.variety of goods into the market in hope that customers will find what they Want.

		Frequency	Valid percent
Valid	Lean	9	10.0
	Agile	22	24.4
	Leagile	24	26.7
	Basic supply chain strategies	35	38.9
	Total	90	100.0

products can be held at the postponement stage for seasonal purposes. However manufacturing the garments would have a system to push these products into the market (Lu et al. 2003). After the items are released from the postponement stage they are pushed to the wholesaler where inventory level has to be maintained to satisfy the forecasted demand (Alford et al. 2000). Experts chose Agile strategy as third most suitable; in the case of the fashion industry examined by Bruce et al. (2004), clothes are designed and pushed to production in preparation for different seasons, although due to customers' change in taste and unpredictable weather the Agile strategy explained by Cagliano et al. (2004) combines the push system at manufacturing with flexibility to enable the supply chain to respond to changes in the market. The Lean strategy was chosen as least suitable due to the nature of push products being made for a "make-to-stock" model rather than a "make-to-order". However, all "make-to-order" products require their basic component and parts to be manufactured and pushed into their components inventory until an order arrives for manufacturing to begin, and usually forecasting can be predicted for resources and components that are needed to manufacture the products that will be ordered (Elfving 2003).

Excel Analysis

In addition to SPSS, this study chose Excel because it is widely used and understood in addition to the simplicity of manoeuvring data. Excel was used to further explain the data collection and describe how scatter diagrams were created in order to establish the fuzzy rule sets used for building the interactive MDM.

The scatter diagrams illustrate the repetition of each relevant variable against "JIT Lean" and "Cost" which then creates the Excel frequency. For example Delivery to request versus the low, medium and high "JIT Lean" and "Cost". Extracting a scatter diagram from the variables helps creation of the frequency and percentage Excel table of the chosen variables in order to illustrate the most favoured supply chain strategy and other possible options for each node in the supply chain (Table 7.16).

The Excel spreadsheet that summarises frequency was derived by adding up the experts' opinions from Fuzzy Delphi data converted into percentages. The data collected reflects the opinion of 90 experts, hence the percentage factor is 100/90=1.11 which is then multiplied by the frequency number to gain the total percentage. For example in Table 7.16, Delivery to request = frequency of 24 Lean, hence 24×1.11=26.7%.

Margin of Error

Because the data collected the opinions of 90 experts which is relatively close to 100, it is reasonable to discuss the statistical elements in percentage terms for this section of the analysis. Some data in most surveys is likely to be inaccurate, statistically known as margin of error and which is a measure of the survey's uncertainty. Questionnaires are designed to provide an estimation of the true value of one or more variables, however when errors occur it does not render the questionnaire of no value, especially when the margin of error is insignificant in comparison to the majority who have reached a consensus (Munier and Rondé 2001). The extent of sampling error is calculated as (estimate ± margin of error) (American Statistical Association 1998). There are several factors that affect the margin of error. Firstly size: larger samples are more likely to yield results close to the target as the quantity will have smaller margins of error than modest-sized samples. Secondly, each design has a probability of having a degree of marginal error. Finally, the sampling type such as random sampling, random digit dialling and stratified sampling (American Statistical Association 1998). The Fuzzy

Table 7.16 Summary of frequency variables converted into percentages

	DELIVERY			PRODUCT DESIGN			DISTRIBUTION			LEAD-TIME	DEMAND APPROACH		
	Request	Comit Date	Order fill Lead-time	Innovative Product	Functional Product	Innovative Functional	Strategic	Tactical	Operational	Manufacturing Lead-time	High-end Strategy	Self-customised	Push System
Frequency													
Lean	24	18	19	9	21	20	22	16	13	14	22	17	9
Agile	25	33	20	43	17	25	25	25	18	35	26	25	22
Leagile	8	18	21	19	14	26	18	25	26	21	24	36	24
BSC	33	21	30	19	38	19	25	24	33	20	18	12	35
Total	90	90	90	90	90	90	90	90	90	90	90	90	90
	To change the frequency to 100 we have to multiply the figures by: 1.111												
%	26.7	20.0	21.1	10.0	23.3	22.2	24.4	17.8	14.4	15.6	24.4	18.9	10.0
%	27.8	36.7	22.2	47.8	18.9	27.8	27.8	27.8	20.0	38.9	28.9	27.8	24.4
%	8.9	20.0	23.3	21.1	15.6	28.9	20.0	27.8	28.9	23.3	26.7	40.0	26.7
%	36.7	23.3	33.3	21.1	42.2	21.1	27.8	26.7	36.7	22.2	20.0	13.3	38.9
Total	100.0	100.0	100.0	100.0	100.0	100.0	100.0	100.0	100.0	100.0	100.0	100.0	100.0

Delphi follows a random sampling as experts in supply chains were selected from random industries and institutes across the world to add background variety and different perspectives to the study.

Table 7.17 shows the Lean variable at (70%) was answered inaccurately at least once, as the number of experts choosing that "70% Lean = Low" should be less than those choosing "60% Lean = Low". The higher the percentage of Lean the less lead-time, hence more experts would move towards the high and medium variable as the percentage increases. This margin of error is highlighted in the percentage summary of 4.4%. However, a maximum of two experts made a consecutive error of choosing "Low" from 70% to 90% Lean. Therefore, the two experts equate to 2.2% marginal error out of 4.4%, while the rest will be ruled out as human error due to the experts correcting their answers in the questions that followed. Accordingly the marginal error in this case is 2.2% and can be calculated as follows:

(Estimate ± margin of error) = (88–92%) = the margin of error is –4%

Without calculating the margin of error, the statistics represented by the questionnaire would find that 2.2% of the experts believe that 70% Lean results in "more" lead-time than 60% Lean, resulting in incomplete information. However when the margin of error is specified as 2.2%, this indicates that 90% of expert opinions should be interpreted as 88–92%, giving complete information for the majority to have a consensus that 70% Lean will result in "less" lead-time.

The margin of error is usually expressed as a percentage, but in some cases, may also be expressed as an absolute number. In statistics, margin of error makes the most sense for normally distributed data such as the bell shape diagram (Chandrasekaran 2011).

The pilot Delphi was designed on the basis of experts initially identifying the relevant "Cost" and "JIT Lean" fuzzy sets. Therefore, to further illustrate their features, the "Cost" and "JIT Lean" fuzzy set variables were plotted against their frequencies. The frequencies for each "Cost" and "JIT Lean" were represented based on the number of experts choosing what percentage constitutes "High", "Medium" and "Low". Figure 7.1 shows that both the "High Cost" and the "High JIT Lean"

Table 7.17 Cost and JIT lean frequency converted into percentage

		COST						LEAN								
		0–10%	11–12%	21–30%	31–40%	41–50%	51–60%	0–10%	11–12%	21–30%	31–40%	41–50%	51–60%	61–70%	71–80%	81–>90%
Frequency	Low	79	54	17	0	0	0	84	76	39	15	5	3	4	3	2
	Medium	9	30	55	51	21	10	4	12	47	57	40	33	12	5	0
	High	2	6	18	39	69	80	2	2	4	18	45	54	74	82	88
	Total	90	90	90	90	90	90	90	90	90	90	90	90	90	90	90
Percentage	%	87.8	60	18.9	0	0	0	93.3	84.4	43.3	16.7	5.6	3.3	4.4	3.3	2.2
	%	10	33.3	61.1	56.7	23.3	11.1	4.4	13.3	52.2	63.3	44.4	36.7	13.3	5.6	0
	%	2.2	6.7	20	43.3	76.7	88.9	2.2	2.2	4.4	20	50	60	82.2	91.1	97.8
	Total	100.0	100.0	100.0	100.0	100.0	100.0	100.0	100.0	100.0	100.0	100.0	100.0	100.0	100.0	100.0

To change the frequency to 100 we have to multiply the figures by: 1.111

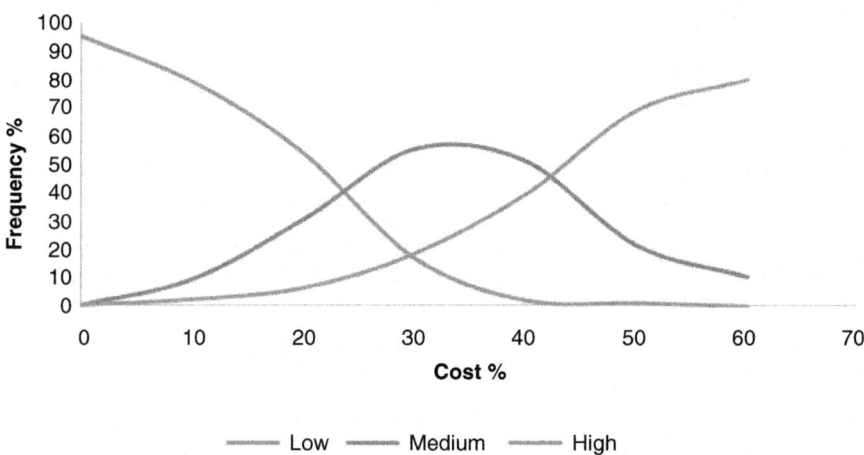

Fig. 7.1 Cost vs frequency variables

percentages are directly tangent proportional with the frequency percentage; while both the "Low Cost" and "Low JIT Lean" percentages have a negative relation to the frequency. Meanwhile, the "Medium Cost" as well as the "Medium" JIT Lean percentages have negative parabola (concave shape) with the frequency percentage, reaching its apex at ≈60% frequency with ≈34% Cost, and ≈60% frequency with ≈40% JIT Lean.

The "Cost" fuzzy set diagram illustrates a bell shape between the "Cost" trend and its frequency in relation to the "Low", "Medium" and "High" variables (Fig. 7.1). The values of the "Low" and "Medium" trends of the "Cost" percentage intersects at ≈22% cost with ≈40% frequency, while the "High" and "Medium" values intersect at ≈42% cost and ≈45% frequency. However, the trends of the "High" and "Low" of the "Cost" percentage against its frequency intersects at 30% Cost and 18 % frequency.

The "Low Cost" curve is downward-bowed, indicating decrease in a strictly concave trend, while the "High Cost" curve is upward-bowed indicating increase in a strictly convex trend. The "Medium Cost" has a bell-shaped normal distribution that intersects with both the "Low Cost" and "High Cost" trends. Each intersection shows the relationship between the "Low", "Medium" and "High" options. For example, from Fig. 7.1 it can be seen that at above/below 30% "Cost", ≈18 experts believe it is "Low", ≈60 "Medium" and ≈20 " High", indicating a very close relationship between what constitutes a "Low" or "High" Cost at 20% frequency, although most experts rank 30% cost as "Medium". However, at 40% cost a close relationship can be seen forming between the "Medium" and "High" options, which becomes less close as the cost percentage increases. This signifies a consensus in the relationship between the Cost and its frequency regardless of the marginal error. The Cost diagram illustrates two elliptical bounded areas (or fuzzy area) created by the three trends. The first has an average of 23–44% Cost and 15–58% frequency. The second has an average of 3–30% Cost and 2–40% JIT Lean. In the first elliptical bounded fuzzy area, the target of the companies should be at least >23% and <44% Cost. The second elliptical bounded fuzzy area is the target of the companies and should be at least >3% and <30% Cost. The second elliptical bounded fuzzy area is most favoured as indicated by the Fuzzy Delphi Qualtrics and SPSS consensus.

Similarly, the Lean fuzzy set diagram shows the "Low Lean" curve as downward-bowed, indicating its strictly concave decreasing trend, while the "High Lean" curve is upward-bowed, indicating its strictly increasing convex trend (Chandrasekaran 2011). Similar to the Cost, the "Medium Lean" has a bell-shaped normal distribution that intersects with both the "Low" and "High" trends. Each intersection shows the relationship between the trends, for instance at ≈40% JIT Lean, the "Low" and "High" are closer together while the majority of experts ranked it as "Medium". This is also shown at ≈50% JIT Lean between the "Medium" and "High", while the gap in the relationship becomes further apart as the JIT Lean percentage increases (Fig. 7.2). This signifies a consensus in the relationship between the JIT Lean and its frequency regardless of the marginal error. Meanwhile, the values of the "Low" and "Medium" trends of "JIT Lean" intersect at ≈28% JIT Lean and ≈43% frequency, while the "High" and "Medium" values start intersecting at ≈50% JIT Lean and at ≈45% frequency. Nonetheless, the "High" and "Low" trends of the JIT Lean against its frequencies intersects at ≈40% JIT Lean and 17% frequency. The JIT Lean has three elliptical bounded

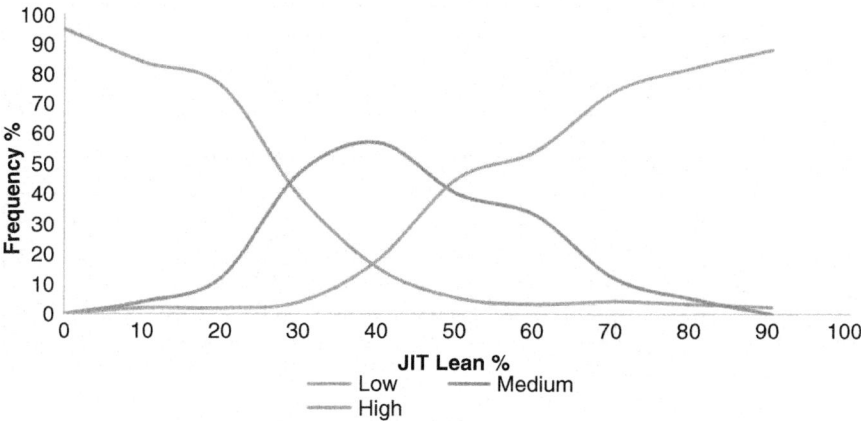

Fig. 7.2   Cost vs. frequency and JIT lean vs. frequency variables

fuzzy areas, the ft is between 17–60% frequency and ≈30–50% JIT Lean. The second is between 5–60% frequency and ≈5–40% JIT Lean. The last and most favoured elliptical bounded fuzzy area by companies as indicated by the Fuzzy Delphi consensus is for the JIT Lean to be at least >55%, hence 17–60% frequency and 40– >90% JIT Lean.

Scatter Diagram Analysis

Scatter diagrams are used to represent and compare two sets of data. For example from the logistics group variables, "Delivery to Request" was plotted against "JIT Lean" (Fig. 7.3). The scatter diagram illustrates whether there is any connection (correlation) between two sets of data, by plotting the ranges of a variable against its frequencies. The scatter diagrams show the relationship between two variables in pairs of obser-vations and may indicate a cause and effect relationship that leads to further investigation. For example the "Delivery to Request" variable is plotted by having the JIT Lean percentage (Low, Medium and High) on the horizontal axis while the vertical axis represents the supply chain strategy (Lean, Agile, Leagile and BSC) best suited for the firm.

Abbreviations		
1	**Lean** supply chain strategy	**L** **Low**
2	**Agile** supply chain strategy	**M** **Medium**
3	**Leagile** supply chain strategy	**H** **High**
4	**Basic** supply chain strategy	

Delivery to Request	0–10%	11–20%	21–30%	31–40%	41–50%	51–60%	61–70%	71–80%	81>90%
4	32 1	29 3 2	14 17 2	5 23 5	1 16 16	1 12 20	2 2 29	2 31	1 32
3	7 1	7 1	3 5	2 3 3	1 1 6	1 1 6	1 1 6	1 7	8
2	21 3 1	20 4 1	13 11 1	4 17 4	2 12 11	12 13	1 4 20	1 2 22	1 24
1	24	20 4	9 14 1	4 14 6	1 11 12	1 8 15	5 19	2 22	24
	L M H	L M H	L M H	L M H	L M H	L M H	L M H	L M H	L M H

JIT Lean%

Fig. 7.3 Delivery to request and JIT lean scatter diagram

The scatter diagrams also plot Cost against each of the variables according to the supply chain strategies. For example the "Delivery to Request" variable is plotted by having the Cost percentage (Low, Medium and High) on the horizontal axis while the vertical axis represents the best supply chain strategy in the experts' opinion based on what they constitute the best strategy for that range (Lean, Agile, Leagile and BSC) (Fig. 7.4). The scatter diagram illustrates the responses to changes between both axes, which build the structure of the fuzzy rules.

The SPSS frequency and Excel percentages formed the basis of the scatter diagrams that structured the fuzzy rules on which the interactive MDM was established. These fuzzy rules are input to the database's code system of the interactive MDM to create a tool that can be tested for validity to ensure its applicability to SMEs and industries.

Scatter diagrams were developed for all the relative groups within the logistics and supply chain variables. Each group within the logistics and supply chain variables was plotted against "JIT Lean" and "Cost" in accordance with the four supply chain strategies of Lean, Agile, Leagile and BSC. For example, from the supply chain group variables, under "Product Design", the "Innovative Product" variable was plotted against JIT Lean. Figure 7.4 illustrates that when JIT Lean is low from 11% to 20% the supply chain strategy values are highest at the "Low

Delivery to request	0–10%			11–20%			21–30%			31–40%			41–50%			51–60%		
	L	M	H	L	M	H	L	M	H	L	M	H	L	M	H	L	M	H
4	30	3		22	9	2	6	23	4	23	10		7	26		5	28	
3	6	2		5	3			6	2	1	7			8			8	
2	20	4	1	16	6	3	5	14	6	16	9		7	18		3	22	
1	23		1	11	12	1	6	12	6	11	13		7	17		2	22	

Cost %

Fig. 7.4 Delivery to request and cost scatter diagram

Lean" option, with the majority of experts choosing Agile strategy as most suitable. Meanwhile, from 31% to 50% supply chain strategy values are moving towards the "Medium Lean", with a majority of experts maintaining their choice of Agile strategy. Nevertheless, the shift in value continues towards "High Lean" from 51% to >90%, as the concave trend emerges from Lean strategy to BSC, while the majority of experts maintain the choice of Agile as most suitable (Fig. 7.5).

The scatter diagrams were used to formulate the fuzzy rules. The Cost percentage variable ranges from 0% to <60%, similar to the JIT Lean as it ranges from 0% to –>90%. Each interval has been divided into three clusters "Low", "Medium" and "High". The scatter diagram plotting the "Cost" percentage against the logistics and supply chain variable groups gives 78 scatter diagrams in which each figure (rectangle) reflects the frequency replies of the 90 participants. Meanwhile, "JIT Lean" against logistics and supply chain variable groups gives 117

Innovative product	0–10%			11–20%			21–30%			31–40%			41–50%			51–60%			61–70%			71–80%			81–>90%		
	L	M	H	L	M	H	L	M	H	L	M	H	L	M	H	L	M	H	L	M	H	L	M	H	L	M	H
4	18	1		16	3		5	14		1	14	4	1	4	14	1	2	16	1		18	1		18			19
3	18		1	16	2	3	6	12	1	1	13	5		8	11		7	12	1	3	15	1	1	17	1		18
2	39	3	1	36	6	1	22	18	3	9	26	8	3	22	18	2	20	21	2	7	34	1	4	38	1		42
1	9			8	1		6	3		4	4	1	1	6	2		4	5		2	7			9			9

JIT lean %

Fig. 7.5 Innovative product and JIT lean scatter diagram

scatter diagrams. When combined, the total scatter diagrams between the Cost against the logistics and supply chain variable groups, as well as the JIT Lean against the logistics and supply chain variable groups gives 195 scatter diagrams.

Fuzzy Rule Sets

To illustrate how the fuzzy rules were created, only a random sample of the logistics and supply chain strategy variables are selected due to the large number of fuzzy rules extracted from the data. The scatter diagrams are created from the frequency and percentage tables generated by SPSS and Excel while the fuzzy rules are created from the scatter diagrams by extracting the correlating variables of the logistics and supply chain groups against "JIT Lean" and "Cost" variables. The fuzzy rules establish a relationship between the "JIT Lean" and "Cost" using selected logistics or supply chain variables using (If-Then) and the scatter diagrams for each logistics and supply chain group against the "JIT Lean" and "Cost", then merged together (e.g. the logistics variables vs. "JIT Lean" with logistics variables vs. "Cost") to create the (If-Then) fuzzy rules of the interactive MDM. These (If-Then) fuzzy rules are then implemented in a combination of JavaScript and HTML code to create a web-based interactive system where the MDM can operate interactively. The random sample examined from the logistics variable will be "Manufacturing lead-time" while the supply chain variable will be "Innovative product".

Logistics Strategies: Manufacturing Lead-Time

The scatter diagram plots the frequency of a logistics variable "Manufacturing lead-time" generated from the SPSS and Excel against the supply chain strategy (Lean, Agile, Leagile and BSC) with regard to the "JIT Lean" (Fig. 7.6).

Figure 7.6 shows clustering of frequencies which illustrate the relationship between the manufacturing lead-time and the best suited supply chain strategy chosen by the experts in accordance with what is

Manufacturing lead time	0–10% L	0–10% M	0–10% H	11–20% L	11–20% M	11–20% H	21–30% L	21–30% M	21–30% H	31–40% L	31–40% M	31–40% H	41–50% L	41–50% M	41–50% H	51–60% L	51–60% M	51–60% H	61–70% L	61–70% M	61–70% H	71–80% L	71–80% M	71–80% H	81–>90% L	81–>90% M	81–>90% H
4	18	1	1	17	2	1	9	9	2	3	12	5	2	8	10	1	8	11	2	3	15	2	1	17	1		19
3	20	1		18	3		6	14	1	1	15	5		6	15		5	16		1	20			21			21
2	35			31	4		19	16		9	23	3	3	20	12	2	14	19	1	7	27		3	32			35
1	11	2	1	10	3	1	5	8	1	2	7	5		6	8		6	8	1	1	12	1	1	12		1	13

JIT lean %

Fig. 7.6 Manufacturing lead-time vs. JIT lean scatter diagram

considered an acceptable lead-time measured by "JIT Lean". The (If-Then) fuzzy rules that can be extracted from the scatter diagram are written:

If 0–10% JIT Lean = **Then** – Low lean, majority recommend Agile, option Leagile

If 11–20% JIT Lean = **Then** – Low lean, majority recommend Agile, option Leagile

If 21–30% JIT Lean = **Then** – Low lean, majority recommend Agile, option Leagile

If 31–40% JIT Lean = **Then** – Medium lean, majority recommend Agile, option Leagile

If 41–50% JIT Lean = **Then** – Medium lean, majority recommend Agile, option Leagile

If 51–60% JIT Lean = **Then** – High lean, majority recommend Agile, option Leagile

If 61–70% JIT Lean = **Then** – High lean, majority recommend Agile, option Leagile or BSC

If 71–80% JIT Lean = **Then** – High lean, majority recommend Agile, option Leagile

If 81–>90% JIT Lean = **Then** – High lean, majority recommend Agile, Leagile or BSC

The manufacturing lead-time scatter diagram against the "Cost" shows the clustering of frequencies of the most suited supply chain strategy chosen by the experts (Fig. 7.7).

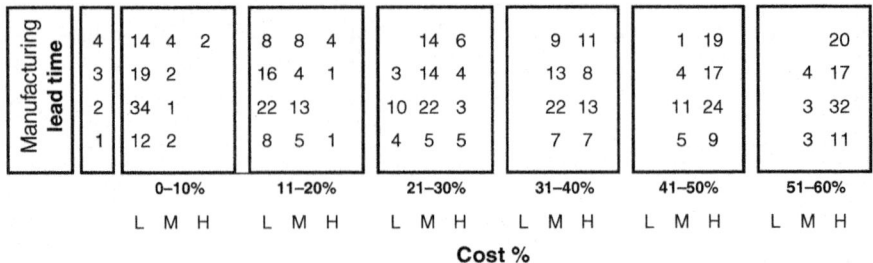

Fig. 7.7 Manufacturing lead-time vs. cost scatter diagram

The (If-Then) fuzzy rules extracted from the manufacturing lead-time against the "Cost" (Fig. 7.7), are written in the following method:

If 0–10% Cost = **Then** – Low cost, majority recommend Agile
If 11–20% Cost =**Then** – Low cost, majority recommend Agile
If 21–30% Cost =**Then** – Medium cost, majority recommend Agile, option Leagile And/Or BSC
If 31–40% Cost =**Then** – High cost, majority recommend Agile, option Leagile
If 41–50% Cost =**Then** – High cost, majority recommend Agile, option BSC
If 51–60% Cost =**Then** – High cost, majority recommend Agile, option BSC

The (If-Then) fuzzy rules have been summarised in Table 7.18 to enable easy access to the data.

Combining both "Cost" and "JIT Lean"(If-Then) fuzzy rules together, the best supply chain strategy for manufacturing lead-time can be identified (Table 7.19). This is done by taking the common factors and merging them together for every "Cost" and "JIT Lean" percentage. Since the "JIT Lean" has a range from 0% to >90% and "Cost" ranges from 0% to 60%, each combination covers every "JIT Lean" percentage for each logistic group variable.

For the example in this section, one sample of the 0–10% "JIT Lean" and 0–60% "Cost" is chosen to illustrate the combined fuzzy rules. These rules are summarised in Table 7.18.

Table 7.18 Manufacturing lead-time fuzzy rules summary

Manufacturing lead-time vs. JIT lean and cost variables

If	→	Then		
JIT%	Cost%	Favoured	Option	And/or
0–10	0–20	Agile strategy	Leagile strategy	
	21–30	Agile strategy	Leagile strategy	And/or BSC strategy
	31–40	Agile strategy	Leagile strategy	
	41–50	Agile strategy	Leagile strategy	And/or BSC strategy
	51–60	Agile strategy	BSC strategy	Leagile strategy
11–60%	0–60	Agile strategy	Leagile strategy	
61–70	0–40	Agile strategy	Leagile strategy	BSC strategy
	41–60	Agile strategy	BSC strategy	Leagile strategy
71–80	0–20	Agile strategy	Lean strategy	Leagile strategy
	21–30	Agile strategy	Leagile strategy	And/or lean strategy and/or BSC Strategy
	31–40	Agile strategy	Leagile strategy	And/or BSC strategy
	41– 60	Agile strategy	BSC strategy	And/or lean strategy and/or Leagile Strategy
81–> 90	0–20	Agile strategy	Leagile strategy	BSC strategy
	21–30	Agile strategy	Leagile strategy	And/or BSC strategy
	31–40	Agile strategy	Leagile strategy	BSC strategy
	41–60	Agile strategy	BSC strategy	Leagile strategy

JIT 0–10% Lean and Cost with Manufacturing lead-time variable:

If 0–10% JIT + 0–10% cost = **Then** – majority recommend Agile option Leagile

If 0–10% JIT + 11–20% cost = **Then** – majority recommend Agile option Leagile

If 0–10% JIT + 21–30% cost = **Then** – majority recommend Agile option Leagile And/Or BSC

If 0–10% JIT + 31–40% cost = **Then** – majority recommend Agile option Leagile

If 0–10% JIT + 41–50% cost = **Then** – majority recommend Agile option Leagile And/Or BSC

If 0–10% JIT + 51–60% cost = **Then** – majority recommend Agile option BSC And/Or Leagile

Table 7.19 Manufacturing lead-time of 0–10% JIT lean vs. cost

		MLT			Abbreviations	
JIT	Cost%	F	1	2	MLT	Manufacturing lead-time
0–10	0–10	ASC	LeSC		F	Favoured
	11–20	ASC	LeSC		1	Option
	21–30	ASC	LeSC	And/or BSC	2	And/or
	31–40	ASC	LeSC		ASC	Agile
	41–50	ASC	LeSC	And/or BSC	LeSC	Leagile
	51–60	ASC	BSC	LeSC	BSC	Basic supply chain

Table 7.20 Innovative product fuzzy rules summary

Innovative product vs. JIT lean and cost variables				
If	→	Then		
JIT %	Cost %	Favoured	Option	And/or
0–20	0–60	Agile strategy	Leagile strategy	And/or BSC strategy
21–50	0–60	Agile strategy		
51– >90	0–60	Agile strategy	BSC strategy	

These combined fuzzy rules (Table 7.20) will be translated into JavaScript code to create the interactive MDM matrix, which will be accessed via a website to be used as a tool to aid company decision making. This will improve the suitability of a supply chain strategy at each node of the business framework.

Supply Chain strategies: Innovative Product Design

As noted in the previous section, the scatter diagram of the innovative product variable will show the relationship between the "JIT Lean" and the best suited supply chain strategy for that variable (Fig. 7.8).

The (If-Then) fuzzy rules will be generated from the frequency clusters and were written as follows:

If 0–10% Lean = **Then** – Low lean, majority recommend Agile, option Leagile And/Or BSC

If 11–20% Lean = **Then** – Low lean, majority recommend Agile, option Leagile And/Or BSC

Innovative product	0–10% L	M	H	11–20% L	M	H	21–30% L	M	H	31–40% L	M	H	41–50% L	M	H	51–60% L	M	H	61–70% L	M	H	71–80% L	M	H	81–>90% L	M	H
4	18	1		16		3	5	14		1	14	4	1	4	14	1	2	16	1		18	1		18			19
3	18		1	16	2	3	6	12	1	1	13	5		8	11		7	12	1	3	15	1	1	17	1		18
2	39	3	1	36	6	1	22	18	3	9	26	8	3	22	18	2	20	21	2	7	34	1	4	38	1		42
1	9			8		1	6		3	4	4	1	1	6	2		4	5		2	7			9			9

JIT lean %

Fig. 7.8 Innovative product vs. JIT lean scatter diagram

If 21–30% Lean = **Then** – Low lean, majority recommend Agile

If 31–40% Lean = **Then** – Medium lean, majority recommend Agile

If 41–50% Lean = **Then** – Medium lean, majority recommend Agile

If 51–60% Lean = **Then** – High lean, majority recommend Agile, option BSC

If 61–70% Lean = **Then** – High lean, majority recommend Agile, option BSC

If 71–80% Lean = **Then** – High lean, majority recommend Agile, option BSC

If 81–90% Lean = **Then** – High lean, majority recommend Agile, option BSC

The second scatter diagram shows the relationship between the "Cost" and best suited supply chain strategy for the innovative product. This is illustrated in Fig. 7.9.

The (If-Then) fuzzy rules will be generated from the frequency clusters:

If 0–10% Cost = **Then** – Low cost, majority recommend Agile

If 11–20% Cost = **Then** – Low cost, majority recommend Agile

If 21–30% Cost = **Then** – Medium cost, majority recommend Agile

If 31–40% Cost = **Then** – High cost, majority recommend Agile

If 41–50% Cost = **Then** – High cost, majority recommend Agile

If 51–60% Cost = **Then** – High cost, majority recommend Agile

Combining both the fuzzy rules for the JIT Lean and Cost, the best supply chain strategy for an innovative product design can be found.

Innovative product		0–10%			11–20%			21–30%			31–40%		41–50%		51–60%	
	4	18	1		9	9	1	2	13	4	7	12	2	17		19	
	3	17	2		11	8		2	14	3	10	9	4	15		4	15
	2	35	6	2	28	10	5	10	23	10	27	16	11	32		6	37
	1	9			6	3		3	5	1	7	2	4	5		9	

0–10%	11–20%	21–30%	31–40%	41–50%	51–60%
L M H	L M H	L M H	L M H	L M H	L M H

Cost %

Fig. 7.9 Innovative product vs. Cost scatter diagram

Given the "JIT Lean" has a range up to >90% and "Cost" up to 60%, the fuzzy rule combination has to be made for each "JIT Lean" percentage against each "Cost" percentage. A sample of 0% to –>90% "JIT Lean" against 0–60% "Cost" is chosen to illustrate this combination process. From the innovative product vs. "Cost" scatter diagram variable, it can be deduced that Agile is the common factor, however from the innovative product vs. "JIT Lean" scatter diagram, the fuzzy rules gave the option of Leagile And/Or BSC, which can be combined to give a unified fuzzy rule to be input into the interactive MDM. Combining the options of the innovative product against both the "JIT Lean" and "Cost" variables, gives companies room to manoeuvre to choose what suits their business and product.

Table 7.19 illustrates the combination results between 0–>90% "JIT Lean" and 0–60% "Cost" against the innovative product variable. The (If-Then) fuzzy rules for the sample of 0–10% "JIT Lean" and 0–60% "Cost" for the innovative product were written as follows:

> **If** 0–10% JIT + 0–10% cost = **Then** – majority recommend Agile option Leagile And/Or BSC
> **If** 0–10% JIT + 11–20% cost = **Then** – majority recommend Agile option Leagile And/Or BSC
> **If** 0–10% JIT + 21–30% cost = **Then** – majority recommend Agile option Leagile And/Or BSC
> **If** 0–10% JIT + 31–40% cost = **Then** – majority recommend Agile option Leagile And/Or BSC

If 0–10% JIT + 41–50% cost = **Then** – majority recommend Agile option Leagile And/Or BSC

If 0–10% JIT + 51–60% cost = **Then** – majority recommend Agile option Leagile And/Or BSC

These combined variables are organised and summarised in order to ease access to the information and for the fuzzy rules to be easily input into JavaScript to build the interactive MDM web-based tool. This shows that the most favoured strategy at 0–10% "JIT Lean" (Low Lean) and 0–60% "Cost", is Agile with the option of Leagile strategy and/or BSC. This selection can be explained by the flexibility requirement of a product on the low Lean end which can be accommodated by an Agile strategy.

Testing the interactive MDM will examine if the matrix can help identify the appropriate supply chain strategy for the nodes related to these variables. The testing involves participation by a selected company in addition to a case study that provides examples of the implementation of the interactive MDM.

Automated Multi-dimensional Model

Once the combined fuzzy rules from the scatter diagrams are created they are translated into JavaScript creating the web-based interactive MDM. Once the coding of the fuzzy rules are complete they are then loaded onto a website using HTML.

On the website, companies can browse the variables they wish to explore and select.

The website shows two tabs one for the logistics strategy and one for the supply chain strategies (Figs 7.10–7.12). In each of the logistics and supply chain strategy tab, the variables are classified into a logistics strategies tab that include, delivery strategy group, distribution strategy group and manufacturing lead-time.

Figure 7.12 displays the Supply chain strategies that include the Product design and Demand approach group. Each group has two drop down lists, one with the "JIT Lean" percentage variable and the other "Cost" percentage variable. Once the company selects the range they want, the interactive MDM matrix will highlight the best strategy for the variable node in

Fig. 7.10   Interactive MDM home-page

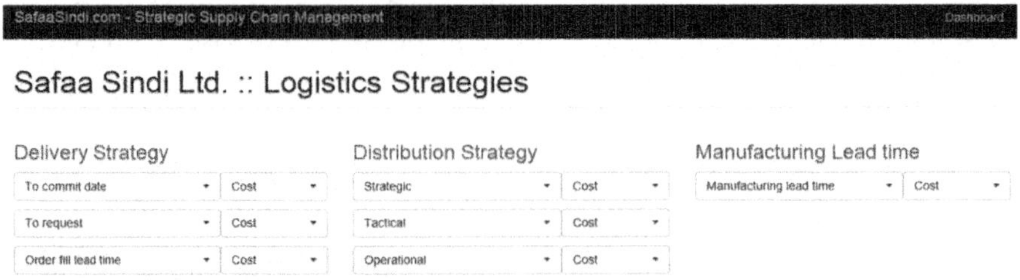

Fig. 7.11   Interactive MDM home and logistics strategy pages

accordance to that range selected. In Fig. 7.12 an example of the selected variables is shown in the supply chain category under the "Innovative product" from the product design group. The "JIT Lean" selected was 21–30% while the selected Cost was 0–10%, and the interactive MDM calculated and highlighted for this range "Agile" as a recommended supply chain strategy for an "Innovative product".

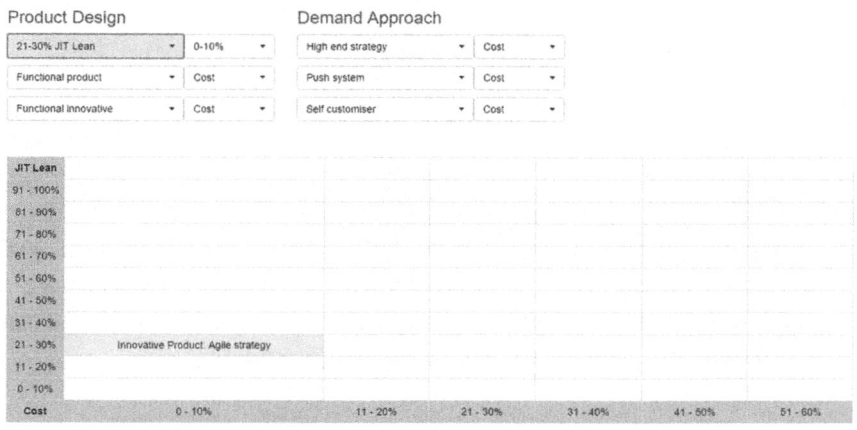

Interactive MDM (21-30% JIT vs. 0-10% Cost)

Fig. 7.12 Interactive MDM supply chain strategy and 21–30% JIT vs. 0–10% Cost

However, if the range changes to another percentage, the MDM calculation will alter to recommend another supply chain strategy. For instance, when "JIT lean" is >90% and the "Cost" is 0–10%, the MDM recommends "Agile option BSC" (Fig. 7.12).

The interactive MDM can be used as a tool for companies to select their required ranges and the recommended strategy will be highlighted for them to select the best suited option (Fig. 7.13). The interactive MDM website

Safaa Sindi Ltd. :: Supply Chain Strategies

Product Design

91-100% JIT Lean ▼	0-10% ▼
Functional product ▼	Cost ▼
Functional innovative ▼	Cost ▼

Demand Approach

High end strategy ▼	Cost ▼
Push system ▼	Cost ▼
Self customiser ▼	Cost ▼

JIT Lean						
91 - 100%	Innovative Product: Agile option BSC					
81 - 90%						
71 - 80%						
61 - 70%						
51 - 60%						
41 - 50%						
31 - 40%						
21 - 30%						
11 - 20%						
0 - 10%						
Cost	0 - 10%	11 - 20%	21 - 30%	31 - 40%	41 - 50%	51 - 60%

Fig. 7.13   Interactive MDM (>90% JIT lean vs. 0–10% cost)

will be tested in the next chapter and applied to a selected company and within a case study in order to determine its applicability in real situations. The company will use the inactive MDM website to identify the optimal supply chain strategy for coordinating their distribution. Furthermore a case study will be used to help illustrate the situations where the MDM can be used to aid companies' supply chain decision making.

References

Agarwal, A., Shankar, R., & Tiwari, M. (2006). Modelling the metrics of lean, agile and leagile supply chain: An ANP-based approach. *European Journal of Operational Research, 173*(3), 211–225.

Alford, D., Sackett, P., & Nelder, G. (2000). Mass customisation: An automotive perspective. *International Journal of Production Economics, 65*(3), 99–110.

American Statistical Association. (1998). What is a margin of error? *Section on Survey Research Methods American Statistical Association*, pp. 2–11.

Armstrong, N. (2013). Amazon case study: Part one. *Busidata, 21*(1), 2–7.

Bruce, M., Daly, L., & Towers, N. (2004). Lean or agile: A solution for supply chain management in the textiles and clothing industry?. *International Journal of Operations and Production Management, 24*(2), 151–170.

Cagliano, R., Caniato, F., & Spina, G. (2004). Lean, agile and traditional supply: How do they impact manufacturing performance?. *Journal of Purchasing and Supply Management, 10*(4), 151–164.

Chakravarty, A. (2014). *Supply chain transformation: Evolving with emerging business paradigms.* Boston: Springer. 13–21.

Chandrasekaran, V. (2011). *Convex optimization methods for graphs and statistical modelling.* Cambridge MA: Massachusetts Institute of Technology. 3–33.

Davis, M. (2010). Case study for supply chain leaders: Dell's transformative journey through supply chain segmentation. *Gartner, 1*(1), 2–11.

Elfving, J. (2003). Exploration of opportunities to reduce lead times for engineered-to-order products. *Engineering-Civil and Environmental Engineering, 1*(1), 1–50.

Ergen, E., Akinci, B., & Sacks, R. (2007). Life-cycle data management of engineered-to-order components using radio frequency identification. *Advanced Engineering Informatics, 21*(3), 356–366.

Field, A. (2009). *Discovering statistics using SPSS.* 3rd. London: SAGE Publications Ltd. 20–26.

Fisher, M. (1997). What is the right supply chain for your product?. *Harvard Business Review, 1*(3), 105–116.

Georgia Tech Supply Chain and Logistics Institute. (2010). The evolution of the supply chain and logistics. http://www.scl.gatech.edu/scl-evolution.php.

Gunasekaran, A., Patel, C., & Tirtiroglu, E. (2001). Performance measures and metrics in a supply chain environment. *International Journal of Operations and Production Management, 21*(2), 71–87.

Heikkilä, J. (2002). From supply to demand chain management: Efficiency and customer satisfaction. *Journal of Operations Management, 20*(6), 747–767.

Hines, P. (1998). Benchmarking Toyota's supply chain: Japan vs. U.K. *Long Range Planning, 31*(6), 911–918.

James-Moore, S. M., & Gibbons, A. (1997). Is lean manufacture universally relevant? An investigative methodology. *International Journal of Operations and Production Management, 17*(9), 899–911.

Kootanaee, A., Babu, K., & Talari, H. (2013). Just-in-time manufacturing system: From introduction to implement. *International Journal of Economics, Business and Finance, 1*(2), 7–13.

Kotzab, H. (2003). Value-adding partnerships and co-opetition models in the grocery industry. *International Journal of Physical Distribution and Logistics Management, 33*(3), 268–281.

Lee, H. L., Park, N., & Lee, S. (2007). Analysis of the manufacturing lead time in a production system with non-renewal batch input, threshold policy and post-operation. *Applied Mathematical Modelling, 31*(1), 2160–2171.

Lu, Y., Song, J., & Yao, D. (2003). Order fill rate, lead-time variability and advance demand information in an assemble-to-order system. *Operations Research, 51*(2), 292–308.

Mangan, J., Lalwani, C., & Butcher, T. (2008). *Global logistics and supply chain management*. Chichester: John Wiley and Sons Ltd. 57–335.

Melton, T. (2005). The benefits of lean manufacturing: What lean thinking has to offer the process industries. *Chemical Engineering Research and Design, 83*(6), 662–673.

Mourtzis, D., Papakostas, N., Makris, S., Xanthakis, V., & Chryssolouris, G. (2008). Supply chain modelling and control for producing highly customized products. *Manufacturing Technology, 57*(5), 451–454.

Munier, F., & Rondé, P. (2001). The role of knowledge codification in the emergence of consensus under uncertainty: Empirical analysis and policy implications. *Journal of Research Policy, 30*(1), 1537–1551.

Naylor, J. B., Naim, M., & Berry, D. (1999). Leagility: Integrating the lean and agile manufacturing paradigms in the total supply chain. *International Journal of Production Economics, 62*, 107–108.

Pagh, J. (1998). Supply chain postponement and speculation strategies: How to choose the right strategy. *Journal of business Logistics, 19*(2), 13–33.

Sanchez, L., & Nagi, R. (2001). A review of agile manufacturing systems. *International Journal of Production Research, 39*(16), 3561–3600.

Shah, R., & Ward, P. (2003). Lean manufacturing: context, practice bundles and performance. *Journal of Operations Management, 21*(3), 129–149.

Silveira, G., Borenstein, D., & Fogliatto, F. (2001). Mass customization: Literature review and research directions. *International Journal of Production Economics, 72*(1), 1–13.

Simeonovova, I., & Simeonov, S. (2012). Lead time reduction methods. *Institute of Production Machines, Systems and Robotics, 12*(3), 334–335.

Slack, N. (2005). The flexibility of manufacturing systems. *International Journal of Operations and Production Management, 25*(12), 1190–1200.

Sugimori, Y., Kusunoki, K., Cho, F., & Uchikawa, S. (1977). Toyota production system and Kanban system materialization of just-in-time and respect-for human system. *International Journal of Production Research, 15*(6), 553–564.

Swaminathan, J., & Tayur, S. Graves, S. C., & De Kok, A. G. (2003). *Tactical planning models for supply chain management. OR/MS handbook on supply chain management: Design, coordination and operation.* London: Elvesier Publishers. 5–30.

Tan, K. C., Kannan, V., & Handfield, R. (1998). Supply chain management: Supplier performance and firm performance. *International Journal of Purchasing and Materials Management, 34*(3), 2–9.

Tomino, T., Park, Y., Hong, P., & Roh, J. (2009). Market flexible customizing system (MFCS) of Japanese vehicle manufacturers: An analysis of Toyota, Nissan and Mitsubishi. *International Journal of Production Economics, 118*(3), 375–386.

8

Testing and Implementing the Strategic Supply Chain Model

In this chapter the interactive MDM will be tested through a renowned international automobile manufacturing company to determine its usefulness and application. Additionally case studies will be used to compare two types of supply chain structures (push and pull). The testing was done using a semi-structured interview conducted during a three-month internship at Jaguar Land Rover (JLR) in the UK.

Jaguar Land Rover (JLR)

Testing was conducted with the automotive industry with special attention placed on JLR as it had an interesting recent history of moving from one parent company to another (Ford Motor to Tata Motors). After the recent world economic downturn, JLR was relatively unaffected with continual stable sales of its target prime market of high-end products. The recession had little effect on the high-end consumers interested in JLR vehicles, as they could still afford high range products. This contrasted to the middle market automotive companies, whose target markets suffered a severe decrease in sales. Currently, JLR is attempting to

© The Author(s) 2017
S. Sindi, M. Roe, *Strategic Supply Chain Management*,
DOI 10.1007/978-3-319-54843-2_8

Table 8.1 Major automotive companies manufacturing in the UK (adapted from Automotive Council UK, 2016)

Company	Plant	Production
Bentley Motors (2014–present)	Crewe	10,014
Ford of Britain (2007–present)	Southampton	75,662
General Motors Company (2014–present)	Luton	74,000
Honda of UK (2014–present)	Swindon	237,783
Jaguar Land Rover (2014–present)	Castle Bromwich, Solihull and Halewood	288,677
Toyota of UK (2014–present)	Burnaston	277,637
Vauxhall Motors (2007–present)	Ellesmere Port	115,476

compete in both markets to strengthen its strategic position against other major automotive companies that manufacture in the UK such as Ford, BMW, Honda and Toyota (Table 8.1). The testing was conducted using semi-structured interviews during a three month internship working with the Global Material Planning and Logistics department of JLR in Solihull (Birmingham) in the UK. The interactive MDM was considered by the EU distribution team and the strategic planning division.

Background

The foundations of JLR are modelled around the purpose of combining both the features of the earlier companies of Jaguar and Land Rover and were explored through a series of unstructured interviews. The strategic planning supervisor of the EU distribution team stated that marketing the name Jaguar aims to make a person feel "alive" as it is all about the experience and luxury of life, while Land Rover has the marketing image of "overcoming barriers" as they are built to be robust to tackle any obstacles. According to the strategic planning supervisor both Jaguar and Land Rover have a shared vision of quality and high-end mass customisation production that follows a "Push system". The semi-structured interviews found that JLR's push system model starts by the car dealer forecasting average sales and then putting in a request order. The average turnover for a vehicle completion in production is estimated to be six months. To ensure JLR delivers its promises of quality, heavy investments are made and time is taken to ensure that the product reaches the standard required. This contrasts with Toyota's lean-pull manufacturing system where information is fed through to the supply chain from a bottom-up approach (Jayaram et al. 2010).

The operations specialist of the EU distribution team stated that the car company has an economic cycle; for example sales peak in April due to it being the beginning of the fiscal year and the end of the winter months, when JLR sees a reduction in stock and an increase in demand. The operations specialist of the EU distribution team further explained that during the recession the company continued to sell cars to its high-end target market despite its slow progress at producing newer cars. Furthermore, the new vision of JLR aims to produce mass customised production of 50 new vehicle models in the next five years to overcome the lag during the recession.

During testing the interactive MDM this study worked closely with the EU distribution team and the strategic planning division of finished goods. This department looks at the vehicles distributed from manufacturing to the customer; this is divided into two segments, the "distribution team" in charge of operations and the "strategic planning division" in charge of logistics and supply chain strategy and planning. Firstly, the "strategic planning" division takes charge of the vehicle from manufacturing in a process called Accepted By Sales (ABS) where it becomes the responsibility of the EU distribution team and the supply chain strategy shifts from "Agile" during manufacturing to "Lean" for distribution. This transfer phase is crucial as any defect or issues that arise from that stage will be the responsibility of the distribution team. Secondly, both the operations manager and operations specialist of the EU distribution team stated that their responsibility as part of the "distribution team" in charge of operations, is to ensure the continuous flow of logistics distribution of the vehicle from "Port of exit" to the dealer. They further investigate if the designated market is suitable for the vehicle or not and if it is not, their duty is to assess the reasons and certify the vehicle's documents to enable them to enter the market before shipping. They also ensure that the invoices indicate that the vehicle has been sold to the right place/customer (dealer), as well as check the amount of vehicles being sold is correct. According to the strategic planning supervisor of the EU distribution team, JLR has 20 suppliers including logistics carriers that liaise with the distribution department; these suppliers get reviewed every six months for their performance in terms of quality agreements, achieving targets, costs and reducing lead-times. If the suppliers underperform on any of these terms, they are notified.

The semi-structured interview with the logistics co-ordinator specialist further explained the distribution operation. The EU distribution team has responsibility to ensure that vehicles are moving with less lead-time by monitoring the vehicles as they go on the distribution line. This includes forecasting manufacturing in order to predict the ABS point at the dispatch stage, where the responsibility switches to the distribution team as they are required to predict the time when the vehicles arrive at the "Port of exit". During the switch of responsibility, the distribution team is in charge of how long the vehicle dwells in the port, when the port transports the vehicles, if the vehicle has been transported by the right method and if a warning occurs (e.g. weather, strikes or theft, etc.), what other methods of transport can or cannot be approved and if a route change is required. If another route is the best option then the distribution team looks at short sea shipping, trucks and various hub solutions. In most cases trucks are used despite them not being the most sustainable, due to their land efficiency. Although the distribution team has the responsibility from the ABS point, the carriers share that responsibility as the vehicles are being transported by them.

Centralised Logistics

JLR has a centralised strategy with its headquarters in the UK, yet it has a market of 28 countries for the EU department alone. Therefore flexibility, speed and reliability are of great importance. Hence, the distribution team has the vital role or reporting to JLR carriers all the schedules required for the vehicles, as each of the carriers have their own system to monitor and dispatch their transportation to deliver the vehicles to the port and reduce lead-time. Therefore JLR implements a predominantly Agile strategy to move the vehicles from plant to car centre then customer. However, JLR is looking to incorporate a Lean strategy to help reduce lead-times. The interactive MDM will examine which strategy best suits JLR that can be efficiently incorporated. Furthermore, in dealing with their centralised logistics, JLR are looking into introducing new modes of transport, such as air freight for the "special moves" VIP operations, especially to the Middle East, where a large volume of high-end vehicles are delivered. In addition, transhipments are helpful in dealing with JLR's centralised position as it reduces cost when volumes fluctuate in different markets. The current Agile strategy helps JLR deal with the volume fluctuation by moving the vehicles' final destination by the use of transhipments, to satisfy changes in demand. However, to reduce lead-time, JLR are looking for leaner solutions to add into their business structure. The Lean solutions that JLR are hoping to incorporate are further rail networks and inland waterways such as barges. To be able to accommodate both modal options, the interactive MDM will be tested to identify the best strategy that will enable JLR to benefit from both its Agile and newly introduced Lean solutions to help further strengthen their business structure.

Working with the senior logistics co-ordinator of the EU distribution team and the distribution strategic planning specialist, the interactive MDM was applied to JLR's EU distribution. The interactive MDM is built for the generic use of the retail industry but here will be focused on JLR. The interactive MDM was tested with >90% JIT Lean and with <10% Cost. Within JLR's framework 95–98% JIT Lean must be maintained by their carriers; the contractors are paid regardless to deliver within that range. The issues facing JLR are with short-distance distribution as the service cost remains the same regardless of the distance; hence it is calculated to be cheaper for long distance distribution. Therefore JLR believes that a Leagile strategy per mile is more worthwhile than an Agile strategy per vehicle; however the switch is a slow process. Therefore, changing the system from carriers charging per vehicle to charging per mile, will make the delivery process "Low Cost≤10%" with "High JIT Lean>90%", to match JLR's chosen parameters for the interactive MDM. The aim of testing the interactive MDM is to help establish if the model can diagnose and recommend the best logistics and supply chain strategy JLR requires in their delivery operations with regard to (Low Cost, High JIT Lean) and how can they efficiently moving towards the recommended strategies.

Testing

When using the interactive MDM, companies are required to identify several factors before accessing the web-based model. The interactive MDM is a tool, which requires the user to:

1. choose the product, commodity or good they wish to diagnose;
2. establish if it is "Innovative", "Functional" or "Innovative functional";
3. examine if it is most likely to follow a "High-end", "Push system" or "Self-customised" strategy;
4. decide if their distribution of components from allocation of plant or warehouses follows a "Strategic," "Tactical" or "Operational" system; and
5. analyse if their delivery system is likely to follow a "Delivery to Commit Date", "Delivery to Request" and "Order Fill Lead-time".

Once the company has clarified these factors it can use the interactive MDM to diagnose which is the best strategy for each relevant node of its supply chain. The company can chose between the "Logistics strategy" and "Supply chain strategy" tabs on the website. If the logistics strategies option was chosen then three categories will be visible; if the company chooses supply chain strategy then two categories will be visible. For both tabs, the "Cost" and "JIT Lean" options need to be determined by clicking on the drop down boxes as the MDM uses them to determine the range to calculate the best suited logistics and supply chain strategy.

Implementation

The distribution strategic planning specialist defined the manufacturing of automobiles as "Innovative Functional" products, as they are a commodity that everyone needs, with similar attributes, yet require differentiation (Novack and Simco 1991). The interactive MDM was put forward to JLR's EU distribution department for testing on their Invoice triggers. These triggers determine the stages the automobile has to go through before reaching the market. Within the EU, JLR has three essential markets: firstly the National Sales Countries (NSC), which are countries that are part of the EU; secondly the countries that have joined the EU market but do not have JLR presence; lastly importing counties that are considered in the European zone but are not part of the EU market.

Testing National Sales Countries NSC

This begins with the NSC, which are the EU importing countries with JLR presence or headquarters. The presence of JLR is vital with regard to quality control or damage issues as maintenance can be undertaken quickly and efficiently, reducing lead-time rather than having the vehicle recalled back to the UK to be fixed. The testing of the interactive MDM will be on the supply chain segment between the component stocks (inventory of automobiles and parts) to the "Port of entry" at the designated country. The distribution strategic planning specialist at JLR was asked to use the interactive MDM to identify if it can diagnose the most suited strategy for each node, starting with the "Components Stock", "Off Assembly", "Accepted By Sales (ABS)", "Available For Delivery", "Gate Dispatched", "Port of Exit" to "Arrived at Port of Entry" (Fig. 8.1).

The testing commenced with the "Supply chain strategies" groups, where the "Product design" was set to "Innovative Functional" in the interactive MDM. Looking at the "Components stock" node, JLR

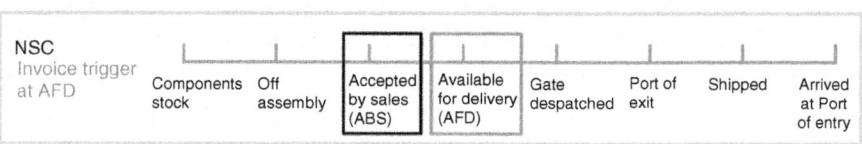

Fig. 8.1 NSC invoice trigger nodes

is required to coordinate all the inventory for the automobile across all plants and supplies. For the NSC most automobiles follow a "Push system" selected from the "Demand approach" group with the "Cost" of production and stocking of components being ≤10% while the "JIT Lean" is >90%, the interactive MDM generated "Leagile option Agile" as the best strategies (Fig. 8.2). However, due to the type of push system in JLR, the distribution strategic planning specialist chose Leagile as the best recommended strategy from the interactive MDM.

Currently, JLR is moving towards a make-to-order pull strategy for some of its models that require customisation (which is a self-customised strategy from the Demand approach group in the interactive MDM): the options given by the interactive MDM with the same range (≤10% Cost and >90% JIT Lean) are "Leagile option Agile". Hence, the distribution strategic planning specialist chose Agile as the best recommended strategy from the interactive MDM to be the most appropriate. This can be explained, as customisation of a high-end product requires flexibility to be a priority which is a core element catered for by the Agile strategy (Fig. 8.2).

Testing the "Logistics strategy" for the "Components stock", the distribution strategic planning specialist chose the "Order Fill Lead-time" from the "Delivery strategies" (as it was the most relevant group to this node) to be ≤10% "Cost" with >90% "JIT Lean", as the components must move quickly from the plants or suppliers to manufacturing in order to fulfil the inventory component level for the push or pull system products. The choices given by the interactive MDM were "BSC option Leagile", where the distribution strategic planning specialist chose Leagile due to the need for components to be cleared quickly from the inventory system, especially clearing pull products from the moment a customer order is received (Jüttner et al., 2007). The distribution strategic planning specialist stated that Leagile will accommodate the Lean factor for the push forecasted components, while Agile will accommodate any change in customisation for the pull components (self-customised) (Fig. 8.2). Moreover, the Leagile strategy with its Lean and Agile characteristics would also account for the high-end products for JLR's VIP customers, labelled "special moves".

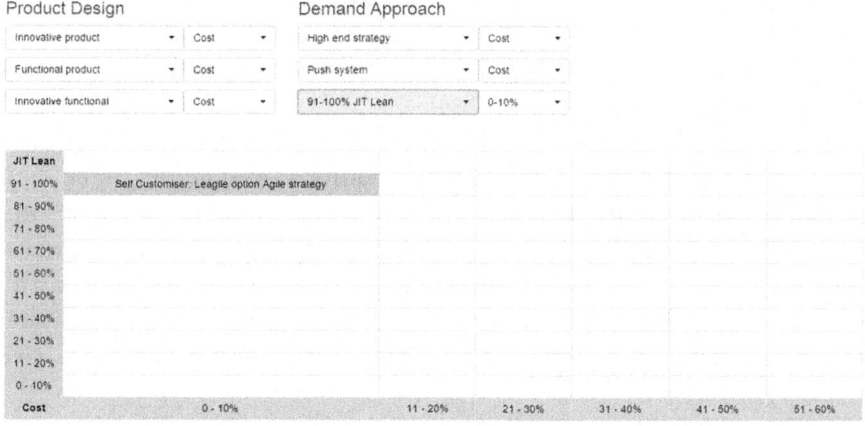

Safaa Sindi Ltd. :: Supply Chain Strategies

Product Design

Innovative product	▼	Cost	▼
Functional product	▼	Cost	▼
91-100% JIT Lean	▼	0-10%	▼

Demand Approach

High end strategy	▼	Cost	▼
Push system	▼	Cost	▼
Self customiser	▼	Cost	▼

NSC with≤10% Cost and >90% JIT Lean

Safaa Sindi Ltd. :: Supply Chain Strategies

Product Design

Innovative product	▼	Cost	▼
Functional product	▼	Cost	▼
Innovative functional	▼	Cost	▼

Demand Approach

High end strategy	▼	Cost	▼
Push system	▼	Cost	▼
91-100% JIT Lean	▼	0-10%	▼

NSC self-customisation with ≤10% Cost and >90% JIT Lean

Fig. 8.2 NSC strategies

Safaa Sindi Ltd. :: Logistics Strategies

Delivery Strategy			Distribution Strategy			Manufacturing Lead time		
To commit date	▼	Cost ▼	Strategic	▼	Cost ▼	Manufacturing lead time	▼	Cost ▼
To request	▼	Cost ▼	Tactical	▼	Cost ▼			
91-100% JIT Lean	▼	0-10% ▼	Operational	▼	Cost ▼			

JIT Lean	
91 - 100%	Delivery on Order fill lead time: BSC option Legile strategy
81 - 90%	
71 - 80%	
61 - 70%	
51 - 60%	
41 - 50%	
31 - 40%	
21 - 30%	
11 - 20%	
0 - 10%	
Cost	0 - 10% 11 - 20% 21 - 30% 31 - 40% 41 - 50% 51 - 60%

Order fill lead-time with ≤10% Cost and >90% JIT Lean

Fig. 8.2   (Continued)

The next node to be tested by the interactive MDM is the "Off Assembly", where the automobile is manufactured, assembled and leaves the production phase. At this node the invoice for the vehicle is created and awaits to be triggered (Fig. 8.3).

However it is still under the responsibility of the manufacturing department, as they are in charge of any faults or mishandling including any added customisation similar to the previous node, and when testing the "Supply chain strategy" the "Product design" of the interactive MDM is set to "Innovative Functional". The testing is done on the "Self-customised" strategy from the "Demand approach" group, where the "Cost" remains ≤10% and the "JIT Lean" >90%, the interactive

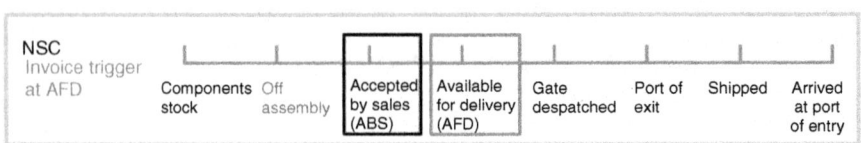

Fig. 8.3   NSC, testing "off assembly" node

MDM generated "Leagile option Agile". The distribution strategic planning specialist chose Leagile to be most suitable for push products and Agile for the pull products.

When testing the "Logistics strategy" the distribution strategic planning specialist chose the "Manufacturing lead-time" to be the most suitable group for this node. The "Cost" would be ≤10% and "JIT Lean" is >90%, the option given by the interactive MDM is "Agile option Leagile option BSC", where the Leagile was chosen to be the most suitable (Fig. 8.4). In addition to the reasons mentioned in the previous node, the Leagile will allow for fast and responsive quality control checks where any faults can be quickly rectified before the vehicle is "Accepted By Sales". This is not only crucial for the NSC markets who have JLR presence who can deal with issues promptly, but for the new countries in the EU market and European zone countries where a Leagile strategy would suit vehicle re-calls and dispatch.

The next node is "Accepted By Sales" (ABS) which is important as it is the switching point where the responsibility shifts from the manufacturing department to the EU distribution department; hence it is highlighted in Fig. 8.5.

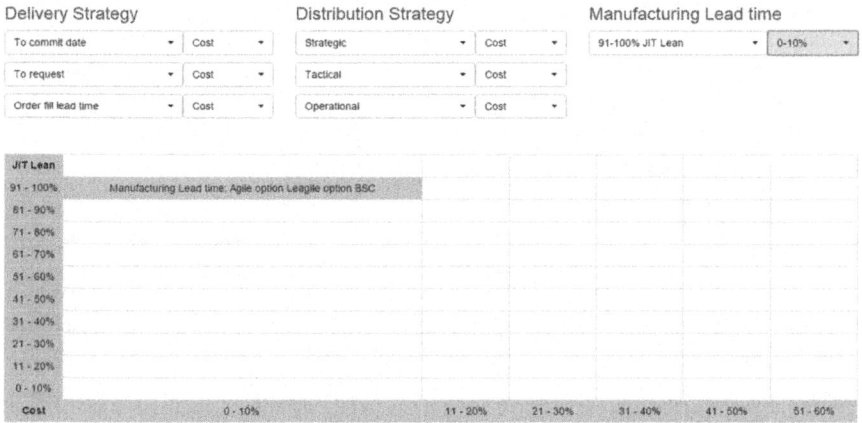

Fig. 8.4 Manufacturing lead-time ≤ 10% cost and >90% JIT lean

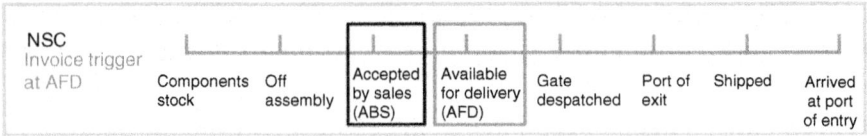

Fig. 8.5 NSC, testing "accepted by sales"

When testing the "Supply chain strategy", the options given by the interactive MDM were similar to the previous node where the "Product design" is set to "Innovative Functional", where the "Cost" is ≤10% and "JIT Lean" is >90%. The testing is done for both pull and push systems where the push system is tested via selecting "Push system" from the "Demand approach" group, resulting in the interactive MDM generating "BSC option Agile And/Or Leagile" (Fig. 8.6).

Meanwhile, testing the pull systems was done via selecting "Self-customiser" from the "Demand approach" group with the same range for "Cost" and "JIT Lean", where similar to the previous nodes, the interactive MDM generated "Leagile option Agile" strategy. The distribution strategic planning specialist chose Leagile as the most suitable strategy for both the pull and push systems, as not only is it the common factor but at the ABS point the priority is to identify the best transportation method and carriers that can quickly move the vehicles to the right destination with the least lead-time. Therefore, at ABS the ability to reduce lead-time in getting the vehicles to the port of exit requires leanness and the ability to quickly adapt to changing situations by flexibly using different distribution modes requires agility. Hence, the choice of Leagile is due to both leanness and agility being crucial at the ABS point regardless of the pull or push systems.

Moreover, in testing the "Logistics strategy" for the ABS node, the distribution strategic planning specialist selected "Operational distribution" from the group "Distribution strategy" to be most suitable for this node. Currently JLR operates under an operational distribution where their "Cost" is ≤10% and "JIT Lean" is >90%. Their carrier companies must achieve 98% "JIT Lean" for an operational distribution or they will be notified of under-achieving. Therefore, to ensure the vehicles reach their destination without any delay the

Safaa Sindi Ltd. :: Supply Chain Strategies

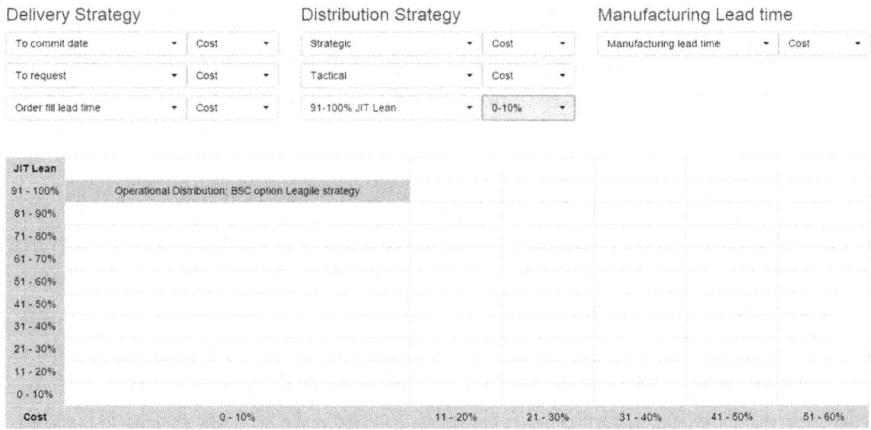

Product Design

Innovative product	▾	Cost	▾
Functional product	▾	Cost	▾
Innovative functional	▾	Cost	▾

Demand Approach

High end strategy	▾	Cost	▾
91-100% JIT Lean	▾	0-10%	▾
Self customiser	▾	Cost	▾

JIT Lean	
91 - 100%	Push System: BSC option Agile And/Or Leagile strategy
81 - 90%	
71 - 80%	
61 - 70%	
51 - 60%	
41 - 50%	
31 - 40%	
21 - 30%	
11 - 20%	
0 - 10%	
Cost	0 - 10% 11 - 20% 21 - 30% 31 - 40% 41 - 50% 51 - 60%

Push system with≤ 10% Cost and >90% JIT Lean (sources, author)

Safaa Sindi Ltd. :: Logistics Strategies

Delivery Strategy

To commit date	▾	Cost	▾
To request	▾	Cost	▾
Order fill lead time	▾	Cost	▾

Distribution Strategy

Strategic	▾	Cost	▾
Tactical	▾	Cost	▾
91-100% JIT Lean	▾	0-10%	▾

Manufacturing Lead time

| Manufacturing lead time | ▾ | Cost | ▾ |

JIT Lean	
91 - 100%	Operational Distribution: BSC option Leagile strategy
81 - 90%	
71 - 80%	
61 - 70%	
51 - 60%	
41 - 50%	
31 - 40%	
21 - 30%	
11 - 20%	
0 - 10%	
Cost	0 - 10% 11 - 20% 21 - 30% 31 - 40% 41 - 50% 51 - 60%

Operational distribution <10% Cost and >90% JIT Lean

Fig. 8.6 Supply chain and logistics strategies. Push system and operational and strategic distribution

Safaa Sindi Ltd. :: Logistics Strategies

Strategic distribution <10% Cost and >90% JIT Lean

Fig. 8.6 (Continued)

distribution strategic planning specialist chose Leagile from the recommendations given by the interactive MDM which were "BSC option Leagile", due to the fast, reliable and responsive attributes of this strategy (Fig. 8.6).

For example, during the testing period with JLR, several rail and truck strikes occurred which delayed the vehicles; however by having a Leagile strategy this situation can be rectified by changing the mode of transport, route, scheduling and carrier companies. The agile aspect of this strategy would aid flexibility, while the leanness aspect would ensure minimal lead-times regardless of any disruptions. However, JLR is attempting to move towards a "Strategic distribution" as part of their "Hubs" project, which would require them to investigate different modal options such as barges, several closed wagon rail options and acquiring more car centres in various countries with quality control checks in order to deal with maintenance issues, preventing lead-time recalls. By switching to a "Strategic distribution" with ≤10% "Cost" and >90% "JIT Lean", the options generated by the interactive MDM are "BSC option Agile And/Or

Leagile" illustrated in Fig. 8.6, where the distribution strategic planning specialist stated JLR would use either Agile for the pull products or Leagile for the push products.

Once the different carrier companies, modes of transport from "Component stock" at the plant to port of exit, port of entry and to the NSC dealer are identified, the shipment scheduling is then made and the vehicle is moved to the "Available For Delivery" (AFD) node. At this node the invoice for the vehicle is triggered, and as previously, under the "Supply chain strategy", the "Product design" is set to "Innovative Functional" for both pull and push systems, and tested with less ≤10% "Cost" and >90% "JIT Lean". The testing of AFD for push products by selecting the "Push system" from the "Demand approach" group generated "BSC option Agile And/Or Leagile" while testing the AFD for pull systems was done by selecting "Self-customiser" from the "Demand approach" group and generated "Leagile option Agile". The distribution strategic planning specialist selected Leagile strategy as best suited for the process throughout to the "Port of Entry" node.

Testing the "Logistics strategy" at this node takes into consideration that carriers are required to deliver the vehicles to the "Port of Entry" on the contracted date. Therefore, the distribution strategic planning specialist selected "Delivery to commit date" from the "Delivery strategy" group, as it is the aim of the logistics planning conducted at this node. With the "Cost" and "JIT Lean" remaining the same, ≤10% and >90% respectively, the interactive MDM generated the following "Agile option BSC" (Fig. 8.7). The distribution strategic planning specialist chose Agile as at this stage the scheduling of the vehicle must be adjustable to accommodate any disturbance; hence, using different flexible modes to ensure the vehicle arrives on the agreed day.

This strategy remains until the vehicle arrives at "Port of Entry"; at this node "Delivery to Request" is chosen with ≤10% "Cost" and >90% "JIT Lean", where the interactive MDM generated "BSC And/Or Lean And/Or Agile" (Fig. 8.7). The distribution strategic planning specialist chose Lean as the most suited strategy, as once the vehicles reach the port of entry they must be distributed quickly to their dealers, as any delay will reduce customer satisfaction. Throughout this process the supply chain push system with the Leagile strategy still holds, as it accounts for

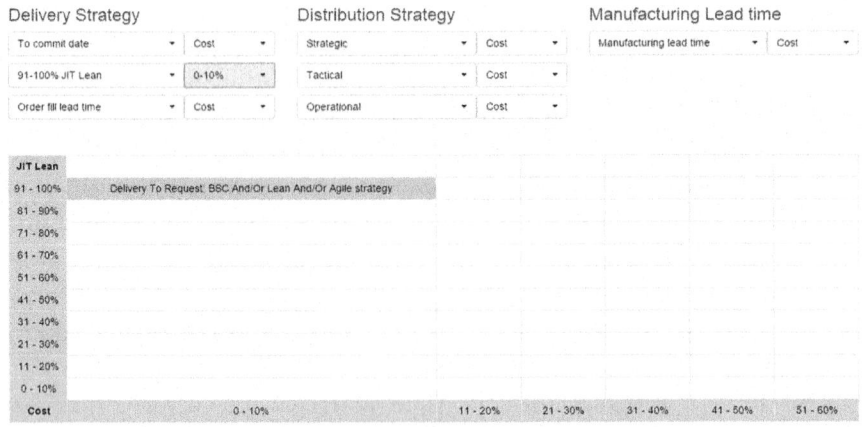

Delivery to commit date <10% Cost and <90% JIT Lean

Delivery to request <10% Cost and >90% JIT Lean

Fig. 8.7   Delivery to commit date and delivery to request

both the "Delivery to commit date" with Agile and "Delivery to request" with its Lean strategy.

Testing Importing Non-EU Countries Within the EU Zone

The next example to be tested is the invoice trigger from the importing non-EU countries that are within the European zone, such as Turkey. These countries import JLR vehicles to supply their own customers or are used as a base for the vehicles to pass onto another country. There are no JLR headquarters but rather only dealers and car centres where the vehicles await shipment to the next country. The supply chain and logistics leg that is being tested will be from the "Component Stock" to the "Arrival at Port of Entry" nodes where the vehicle goes to the dealer or the car centre. The leg where the vehicles move from the car centre to another country is not included, as it is the responsibility of the dealers in these designated countries. The EU distribution department at JLR is only responsible for delivering the vehicles to the dealer or car centre of the contracted country and ensuring that the vehicles move from the car centre within the designated time frame, to allow room for the next arriving batch.

The supply chain and logistics strategy for the components stock for this invoice trigger is similar to the previous one. The difference between the NSC and the Importer non-EU countries is the "Off Assembly" node, although for both the invoice is created and awaits to be triggered; for importer non-EU countries a "Performa" must also be generated in order to be sent to the dealer or attached to the vehicle's paper work. The "Performa" is the paperwork necessary to allow a vehicle to enter a country, custom cleared with all the information relevant to the vehicle enclosed (Fig. 8.8).

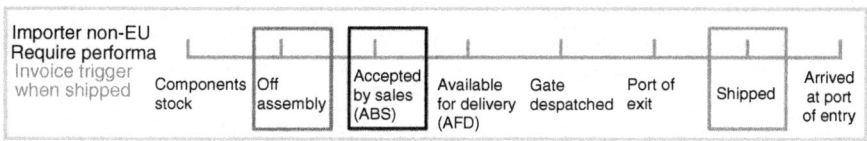

Fig. 8.8   Importer Non-EU countries invoice trigger

Testing "Supply chain strategy" remains the same, with "Product design" set to "Functional Innovative" and the "Cost" ≤10% and "JIT Lean" >90%. The testing of "Push system" and "Self-customiser" generated the same recommendations by the interactive MDM, where the distribution strategic planning specialist chose Agile strategy for pull products (labelled self-customisation) and Leagile for the push products, with similar justifications as the previous NSC sector.

While testing the "Logistics strategy", the distribution strategic planning specialist selected "Manufacturing lead-time", with "Cost" ≤10% and "JIT Lean" <90%, resulting in "Agile option Leagile option BSC". The distribution strategic planning specialist selected Leagile as best suited for the "Off Assembly" manufacturing lead-time in order to reduce the lead-time creating and clearing the "Performa" necessary for the vehicles.

The ABS node is crucial as it is where the responsibility shifts from manufacturing to the EU distribution department. Here the distribution strategic planning specialist selected the same options as the previous NSC and chose the same strategies throughout the "Port of Entry" node. The sole exception is the invoice being triggered to the dealers once the vehicle is "Shipped" rather than at AFD as is the case with the NSC market. After the vehicle is shipped the dealers will then communicate with the finance department to pay the outstanding balance within a designated time frame, at which the vehicle must be sold.

Testing Importer EU Countries

The last example to be tested is the importer European countries that do not have JLR headquarters but are members of the EU. Similar to the previous importer non-EU, they do not have the capability to handle maintenance for quality or damage issues (Fig. 8.9). However, due to these countries being members of the EU they do not require a "Performa" to enable the vehicle to enter the country or pass customs. Similar to the NSC, they only require an invoice trigger.

The supply chain and logistics strategy for the importer EU countries have the same range as the previous two, ≤10% "Cost" and >90% "JIT

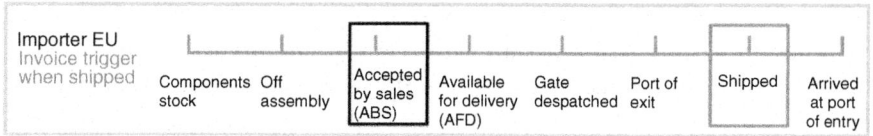

Fig. 8.9   Importing EU invoice trigger

Lean". The distribution strategic planning specialist selected the same options as the previous NSC and importer non-EU, and selected the same strategies for each node through to "Port of Entry". Similar to the importer non-EU, the invoice is triggered once the vehicle is "Shipped" as the dealers communicate with the finance department and the vehicle must be sold within the designated time frame.

From the testing, the distribution strategic planning specialist and the EU distribution department stated that the interactive MDM is of use as a diagnostic model that will help companies identify the strategies that they are currently using along with the option to change them if they wish. By identifying each strategy that is suitable for every node the company can understand their supply chain framework better and diagnose the nodes that require improvement. The EU distribution department noted that the interactive MDM is a useful tool that would further aid their strategic planning in designing new logistics routes to reduce lead-time, and planning a better robust supply chain structure that can adapt to changes.

Case Study – Toyota

In this section the interactive MDM will be tested on the case study of Toyota automobiles to draw a comparison between JLR and Toyota's logistics distribution (plant to dealer) and their supply chain system (manufacturing to dealer).

In 1950, Toyota adopted the concepts of continuous material flow, process standardisation and waste elimination. This created the foundation of its success and the movement towards a "pull system" supply chain. After refinement, the "push system" and Just-In-Time (JIT) were combined to create the Toyota Production System (TPS) (Hines 1998).

The traditional concept was that only mass production could reduce manufacturing costs (Elfving 2003). However, Toyota managed to achieve low cost manufacturing with smaller volume, higher complexity and shorter lead-times by implementing waste elimination, efficiency and durability throughout their value chain (Tomino et al. 2009). This system worked for Toyota due to the fundamental changes built into the enterprise's long term framework and engraved within its culture, while other automobile companies struggled with the same implementation (Wee and Wu 2009).

Toyota's Supply Chain

Within the Toyota supply chain, the term "Lean" means a series of activities or solutions to eliminate waste, reduce Non-Value Added (NVA) operations and improve Value Added (VA) operations. Value Stream Mapping (VSM) is a lean supply chain tool used by TPS to identify the necessary value-adding activities from the wasteful ones in order to eliminate them (Elfving 2003). VSM begins by listing all operations and classifies them into VA and NVA, as well as the status of their lead-times from incoming parts to finished goods delivery. The VA activities are those that customers are willing to pay money for tangible goods or intangible functions, while the NVA are the activities that increase lead-time without positive output (Wee and Wu 2009). By using the Kanban system that links assembly lines tightly to suppliers, Toyota succeeded in limiting the costs and the risks in the wider supply chain (Ludwig 2013).

In testing the "Supply chain strategy" of the interactive MDM the automobile is classified as an "Innovative/Functional" product (Jayaram et al. 2010). Therefore, as Toyota operates under waste elimination, then "Cost" would be ≤10%, while "JIT Lean" would be >90%. Using the interactive MDM, selecting "Innovative Functional" from the "Product design" group this generated "Leagile option Agile", which would be chosen to accommodate Toyota's Lean production system. The choice of Leagile would allow Toyota to have the responsiveness it needs when creating car models and leanness it requires to get the car design into production.

When testing the "Demand approach" group there are two applicable options, the "High-end" or the make-to-order pull system labelled "self-customiser". Due to Toyota's Lean strategy, "Cost" will be ≤10% while "JIT Lean" is >90%. Firstly for "High-end" products, the interactive MDM generated "Agile and/or Leagile option Lean", which is in accordance with Toyota's system and the importance of a "High-end" product, Lean would be chosen to ensure the least amount of waste and lead-time to manufacture a vehicle and send it through the supply chain to the dealer. Secondly, for the "self-customiser" for pull products, the interactive MDM generated "Leagile option Agile". In this case, Leagile would be the most suitable option as the make-to-order push system indicates that an automobile is manufactured when an order is put through from the customer. However, tastes and needs change and the push system would be required to adapt to these changes in customisation (Jayaram et al. 2010). Hence, by having a Leagile system, Toyota can benefit from having a waste reduction Lean system as well as a responsive Agile system embedded into one strategy.

Centralised and De-centralised Logistics

JLR logistics followed a centralised system contrasting to that of Toyota which follows a de-centralised system, where each plant is a separate entity that can manufacture, assemble and distribute up to 12 vehicle models (Tomino et al. 2009). For example, in North America Toyota spends about US$26 billion each year on parts and US$1.5 billion on services from 660 suppliers. About 75% of its inbound material is sourced in North America, while a large concentration of suppliers are situated around the Midwest states of the USA (Ludwig 2013).

In obtaining raw materials for its plants, they contract with third parties to supply small parts such as seats, steering wheels and tyres. However the important aspects of the vehicle such as the machine engine are imported from Japan, making the logistics for it centralised (Ludwig 2013). The reason for the centralised system for the engine is to maintain the quality and Japanese manufacturing in-house. Having a de-centralised plant system situated across the globe in every accessible market Toyota can create a sophisticated distribution system by benefiting from the local market's transportation networks (Elfving 2003). Creating a foothold in every market, this allows plants to produce accurate volumes and respond faster to changes in demand within their region, as well as enabling them to deliver the vehicles straight to the dealer using trucks or trains, reducing lead-times (Lee 2004).

In testing the "Logistics strategy", the "Manufacturing Lead-time" was chosen as most irrelevant to Toyota's production due to its lean system, which is sophisticated with its automation operations throughout the entire manufacturing, assembly, quality checks and vehicle tracking to minimise lead-time and human error. Although employees oversee the entire operation from plant to dealer, Toyota's full integration of an automated system within their supply chain has reduced lead-times, especially within manufacturing and assembly (Jayaram et al. 2010). With "Cost" ≤10% and "JIT Lean" >90%, the interactive MDM generated "Agile, option Leagile, option BSC", where Leagile is considered the most suited for Toyota's reduction of manufacturing lead-time. The combination of Agile and Lean will increase flexibility to solve any issues of quality, assembly and certifying vehicles, in addition to eliminating any NVA activities to reduce lead-times.

The remaining two groups "Delivery and Distribution strategies" are relevant to Toyota's logistics system, with the latter being applied to the distribution between the acquisition of raw materials from second and third party suppliers to the plant and then to its distribution through the region (Sugimori et al. 1977).

From the "Distribution strategy" group, as Toyota has a de-centralised plant system it follows a "Tactical Distribution" with "JIT Lean" > 90% and "Cost" ≤10%, in order to incorporate Toyota's waste reduction and in house-distribution. The interactive MDM generated the following "Agile And/Or Leagile And/Or Basic" (Fig. 8.10). Leagile is chosen to be most suitable as it will support both the centralised and de-centralised distribution of Toyota. The engines follow a centralised distribution from Japan, so the Lean characteristics in Leagile will help engines reach the plants with minimal lead-time to enable speedy

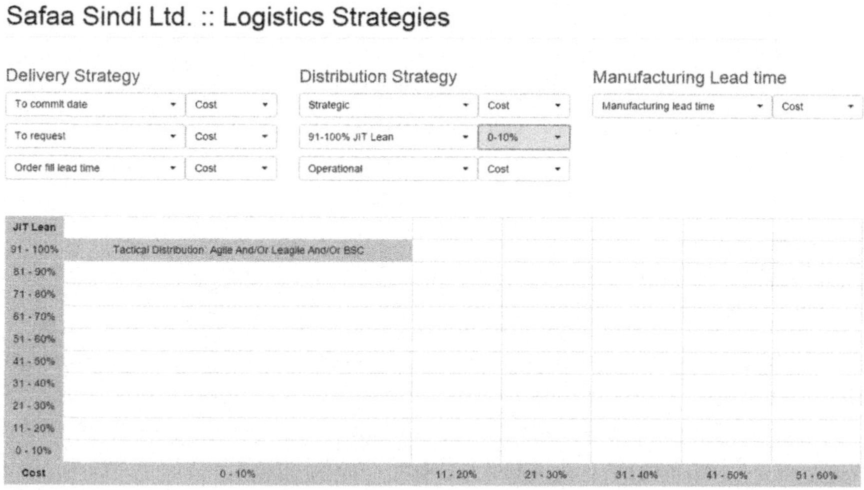

Safaa Sindi Ltd. :: Logistics Strategies

Fig. 8.10   Tactical distribution <10% cost and >90% JIT lean

production (Ludwig 2013). In addition the Agile characteristics of Leagile suits the de-centralised distribution by supporting the second and third party supplies to respond faster to low stock of component parts. Hence, the suppliers need to be flexible in distributing these parts to all the plants across the region (Jayaram et al. 2010). The Agile characteristics will help plants understand the shift in demand in their local market and communicate changes to their supplier who in turn are able to react to the shifts. Having a Leagile strategy the plants would be able to satisfy the demand of their region by increasing or decreasing their volumes, automobile design and fast and reliable distribution of vehicles to their dealers.

From the "Delivery strategy", the "Delivery to request" is chosen to best represent Toyota's transportation of Make-to-order (pull system) vehicles from its holding centre to the dealer. With "Cost" ≤10% and "JIT Lean" >90%, the interactive MDM generates the following "Basic And/Or Lean And/Or Agile". Toyota's system implements a sophisticated transportation network that uses the local region's road and rail to its advantage as well as waste reduction that implies a quick turnover of a few days in its warehousing car centres due to low inventory levels (Hines 1998). Therefore, the best suited strategy would be Lean in order to ensure Toyota's business structure maintains its JIT demeanour.

Conclusion

The testing concludes that the deductive reasoning behind the experts' opinions is valid as it shows that the interactive MDM is a useful tool although firms may find it hard to implement different strategies for each node due to their established business structure and the cost of change. For example, JLR has a mainly push Agile/Leagile system, with centralised production and distribution that is hard to change into a pull make-to-order Lean/Leagile system such as Toyota with a de-centralised production and distribution system. The change would not only require a shift in the business framework, but a switch in business culture as well, which is time consuming and costly.

From this testing, it has been established that the interactive MDM is able to aid companies in diagnosing and recommending the logistics and supply chain strategies most suited for them. Additionally, as JLR is looking to expand globally to build assembly plants in regional markets internationally, the interactive MDM will help JLR diagnose which strategy is most useful in their new venture of adding a pull system within each market. This will help JLR identify the most suited strategy that will help transfer information faster in every regional market to their designated plant, in order to respond to demand and customise the vehicles accordingly.

References

Elfving, J. (2003). Exploration of opportunities to reduce lead times for engineered-to-order products. *Engineering-Civil and Environmental Engineering*, *1*(1), 1–50.

Hines, P. (1998). Benchmarking Toyota's supply chain: Japan vs. U.K. *Long Range Planning, 31*(6), 911–918.

Jayaram, J., Das, A., & Nicolae, M. (2010). Looking beyond the obvious: unravelling the Toyota production system. *International Journal of Production Economics, 128*(3), 280–291.

Jüttner, U., Christopher, M., & Baker, S. (2007). Demand chain managementintegrating marketing and supply chain management. *Industrial Marketing Management, 36*(4), 377–392.

Lee, H. L. (2004). The triple-a supply chain. *Harvard Business Review*, December, 1–11.

Ludwig, C. (2013). Toyota's total supply chain vision. http://www.automoti velogisticsmagazine.com/interview/total-supply-chain-vision

Novack, R. A., & Simco, S. W. (1991). The industrial procurement process: A supply chain perspective. *Journal of Business Logistics, 12*(1), 145–167.

Sugimori, Y., Kusunoki, K., Cho, F., & Uchikawa, S.. (1977). Toyota production system and Kanban system materialization of just-in-time and respect-for human system. *International Journal of Production Research, 15*(6), 553–564.

Tomino, T., Park, Y., Hong, P., & Roh, J. (2009). Market flexible customizing system (MFCS) of Japanese vehicle manufacturers: an analysis of Toyota, Nissan and Mitsubishi. *International Journal of Production Economics, 118* (3), 375–386.

Wee, H., & Wu, S. (2009). Lean supply chain and its effect on product cost and quality: A case study on Ford Motor Company. *Supply Chain Management: An International Journal, 14*(5), 1–5.

9

Conclusions – What Next for Strategic Supply Chain Modelling?

Both SMEs and larger corporations are facing challenges in determining the best supply chain strategy for every node of their business framework. To analyse this further and to help in the search for an appropriate supply chain strategy for their business structure, the first stage was to identify existing supply chain strategies and allocate them into "Eras". This was done by determining the emerging supply chain definitions in each era and highlighting the issues faced by companies. These strategies were then selected from each era and incorporated into a Multi-Dimensional Matrix (MDM). The MDM was created and tested in its ability to help firms identify and allocate their strategy in accordance with their speciality and market.

Furthermore, the testing has helped to understand the interactive MDM's capability to help firms shorten their lead-time by choosing a suitable strategy for the tested node in addition to helping them understand which node can add value and reduce costs, as the MDM acts as a diagnostic tool that can generate recommendations as well as options for the firm to choose from. Moreover, the interactive MDM has sufficient capabilities to survive in a digitalised era indicated by its interactive capacity which can be tailored by companies adding

© The Author(s) 2017
S. Sindi, M. Roe, *Strategic Supply Chain Management*,
DOI 10.1007/978-3-319-54843-2_9

variables and truth functions to create a model that is unique to their business structure and framework.

Research into the development of models for supply chain management is significant in a number of ways. Firstly it provides an overview of how supply chains have developed through time, the strategies created to counter the difficult issues that have been identified and the evolving definitions of the concept. Secondly, allocating each evolution of supply chain into Eras and highlighting the overlap between each evolution, the expansion of the concept and the new developments helps to highlight future needs. Thirdly, it identifies a range of variables to measure the supply chain issues faced by companies and establish the most suited strategy for each in addition to the new concept of measuring the significance of time to supply chains by using the JIT system and Lean strategy. Furthermore, the development of the interactive MDM provides a tested platform that illustrates the issues companies face in assessing supply chain strategy, as well as a tool which they can use to mitigate difficult issues, and most importantly can be further developed and tailored to suit the needs of the user.

What Comes Next?

Much more remains to be done. The interactive MDM can be developed to accommodate reasoning capability by learning from errors. The interactive MDM tool can be improved to synergise human-like reasoning such as learning capability by including heuristic learning and neural networks (Burney and Mahmood 2006). Furthermore, the interactive MDM can be developed to face external influences such as those emanating from the political environment. The extent of these influences can be examined using game theory and the study of strategic decision-making to minimise these influences on the proposed recommendations of the MDM. Heuristic learning enables the addition of more variables to be used in the interactive MDM model, which will give it a wider outlook on recommending the best supply chain and logistics strategy. Adding game theory, heuristic learning and neural networks to the interactive MDM will provide a synergy of methods that can establish whether the recommended strategy will be accepted and applied by the majority of firms or suppliers or whether some will firms refuse to cooperate in the hope of gaining more by acting independently and thus affecting the overall welfare of the industries. Game theory's ideology is that people and organisations act in their best interest while at the same time this behaviour can be predicted (Fox 2006). Adding game theory to the interactive MDM will allow companies to analyse their suppliers' desired goal, their flexibility, their attention to the problem and their influence (Summer 1994). The game theory element will not only allow the interactive MDM to recommend options but will also determine their likely course of action and evaluate their ability to influence others as it predicts the course of events by the help of heuristic learning. If a human mediator is not available or is distrusted, the heretic learning and game theory equations can offer reliable strategic solutions. The use of game theory will give the interactive MDM the capability to analyse human behaviour, which is important for strategic prediction (Lange et al. 1990).

Game theory has had a deep impact on the theory of industrial organisation. According to Fudenberg and Tirole (1987) it forces economists to clearly specify the strategic variables, the timing of the variables and the information structure of the firm. Thus, game theory can be used to identify the influences placed on the experts' opinions, as it allows the researcher to learn as much from constructing the model as from solving it because in construction, one is led to examine the available realistic options (Fox 2006). The drawback is the freedom given by game theory as the modeller can choose any variables with no constraints. This drawback can be a positive in the field of supply chains, as without constraints there would be more room for adaption and tailoring to the firms needs and the market requirements (Fudenberg and Tirole 1987) (Table. 9.1).

The use of heuristic learning and neural networks as a hybrid method helps classify the prioritisation of a recommended strategy and the feasible path a firm can take (Bakheet 1995). This can be done by establishing which recommendation and course of action is classified as standard or high risk. This suggests that neural networks can be used as a means to identify which supply chain strategy companies should be

Table 9.1 Advantages and disadvantage of game theory (adapted from Foss 1999)

Advantages of game theory	Disadvantages of game theory
1. A prime tool for modelling and designing automated decision-making processes in interactive environments. The automation of strategic choices enhances the need for these choices to be made efficiently, and to be robust against abuse. Game theory addresses these requirements.	1. Branches of game theory differ in their assumptions. The right branch and assumption must be chosen accurately and in relation to the objective of the question researched. A central assumption in many variants of game theory is that players are rational. This rationality assumption can be relaxed, in different branches of game theory.
2. As a mathematical tool for decision-makers, the strength is its capability to provide structure to strategic problems.	2. Getting an accurate prediction, the parameter of the equation has to be simplified.

incorporated from the MDM model, as it can highlight which strategy has the most risk associated with it and with heuristic learning the MDM can learn to improve future recommendations (Table 9.2).

Supply chains have been analysed from the 1940s to the early twenty-first century. The factories of the future have been examined and their focus on mass customisation with the use of various technologies such as: clever software, web-based services, novel materials, automation, new technology including three-dimensional printing and a range of processes aimed at tailoring each product precisely to each customer's taste. With inevitable challenging economic climates and increasing competitive pressures, Eras six and seven were imagined directed towards the creation of an interactive web-based MDM which SMEs and large firms can incorporate into their strategy for supply chains. These models were tested with a major international automobile company (JLR) and yet at the same time can be tailored to any business structure to provide them with a uniquely diagnosed solution for each node of their supply chain. In addition, the interactive MDM can be improved further by combining the advances in information technology to enable fast and reliable communication between different nodes as well as stages in a supply chain by the use of neural networks, heuristic learning and

Table 9.2 Advantages and disadvantages of hybrid intelligent systems

Technology	Advantages	Disadvantages
Neural networks	1. A computational structure with learning and generalisation capabilities (Rosenblatt 1959). 2. Conceptually, it stores knowledge acquired by learning with known samples (Shapiro 2002). 3. Operationally, it uses a set of samples that consist of input and output relationships to create learning algorithms that perform optimisation (Widrow and Hoff 1960). 4. Has the advantage of adaption, learning and approximation (Werbos 1974).	1. Relatively slow convergence speed (Rosenblatt 1959). 2. The negative attribute of unforeseen problems or difficulties arising from the use of complex strategies especially when using complex mathematical formulae requiring a computer. This results from lack of transparency in a model or strategy (Shapiro 2002).
Genetic algorithms – "Heuristic Learning"	1. Suitable to perform randomised global search, as each fitness value and its function is evaluated on the basis of its performance. By using a genetic algorithm the best value is evolved into the next generation value with better functioning solutions (Holland 1975). 2. Has the advantage of random systematic search and derivative-free optimisation (Holland 1975).	1. It is difficult to tune the values in accordance with the function's performance (Holland 1975). 2. It has no convergence criterion. The ideal convergence criterion for a genetic algorithm would guarantee each and every parameter converge independently (Beasley et al. 1993). This is demanding and results in over-iteration, hence relaxed convergence criteria are usually employed.

game theory. The interactive web-based MDM can be incorporated into a cyber-network that links the whole supply chain together as well as comparing the firm's supply chain with its competitors. This in turn might help many industries including those with automated products and facilities to unify their supply chain and mitigate human error.

References

Bakheet, M. T. (1995). *Contractors risk assessment system (surety, insurance, bonds, construction, underwriting)*. Ph.D. Thesis. Georgia Institute of Technology, pp. 50–200.

Beasley, D., Bull, D., & Martin, R. (1993). An overview of genetic algorithms: Part 1. Fundamentals. *University Computing, 15*(2), 58–69.

Burney, S., & Mahmood, N. (2006). A brief history of mathematical logic and applications of logic in CS/IT. *Karachi University, Pakistan. Journal of Science, 34*(1), 61–75.

Foss, N. (1999). Austrian economics and game theory: A stocktaking and an evaluation. *Department of Industrial Economics and Strategy*, Copenhagen Business School, Denmark. *1*(1), 1–23.

Fox, C. (2006). Content analysis: Methods and mentoring. SLA NorthWest Regional Conference. http://units.sla.org/chapter/cwcn/conference/nwrc2006/chiarafox.pdf.

Fudenberg, D., & Tirole, J. (1987). Understanding rent dissipation: On the use of game theory in industrial organization. *The American Economic Review, 77*(2), 176–183.

Holland, J. H. (1975). *Adaptation in Natural and Artificial Systems*. Cambridge, MA: MIT Press. 10–83.

Lange, P., Liebrand, W., & Kuhlman, M. (1990). Causal attribution of choice behavior in three N-Person prisoner's dilemmas. *Journal of Experimental Social Psychology, 26*(1), 34–48.

Rosenblatt, F. (1959). Two theorems of statistical separability in the perceptron. In *Mechanization of thought processes, symposium held at the National Physical Laboratory* (pp. 421–456). UK: HM Stationery Office.

Shapiro, A. (2002). The merging of neural networks, fuzzy logic and genetic algorithms. *Insurance: Mathematics and Economics, 31*(1), 115–131.

Summer, M. (1994). Principal-agent problems from a game-theoretic viewpoint. *Institute for Advanced Studies, Research Memorandum, 347*(1), 1–18.

Werbos, P. (1974). *Beyond regression: New tools for predictions and analysis in the behavioral science*. Ph.D. Thesis. Harvard University, Cambridge, MA, U.S.A. pp. 50–130.

Widrow, B., & Hoff, M. E. (1960). *Adaptive switching circuits*. IRE Western Electric Show and Convention Record, Part 4, pp. 96–104.

Appendix 1: Era Definitions

Era 1: Definitions

Supply chains require traditional separate material functions to report to an executive responsibility to coordinate the entire material process and to require joint relationships with suppliers for multiple tiers. Supply chain is a concept, whose primary objective is to integrate and manage the sourcing, flow, and materials' controlling using the systems perspective across multiple functions and multiple tiers of suppliers. Business relation and coordinating materials flow are the essence of supply chain (Monczka et al., 1998).

Supply chain management deals with the flow of materials from suppliers through end users. Supply chain was created as an approach to control the flow of raw material from the start point of suppliers to the end point of consumer consumption, by dealing with the planning and control of the materials flow from suppliers to end users (Jones and Riley, 1985).

Supply chain management is an integrative philosophy to achieve the flow of a distribution channel from supplier to the ultimate user. Supply chain manages the flow of goods from the suppliers to consumers (Cooper et al., 1997).

Supply chains organise the purchasing of raw materials and goods, as well as ensure quality control standard are in place and establishes business long-term and short-term relationships with suppliers and consumers (Shukla et al., 2011).

Supply chains create different links from the start of the raw material handling to the end selling point to consumers (Scott and Westbrook, 1991).

(continued)

© The Author(s) 2017
S. Sindi, M. Roe, *Strategic Supply Chain Management,*
DOI 10.1007/978-3-319-54843-2

A network of entities that starts with the suppliers' suppliers and ends with the customer's custom; the production and delivery of goods and services. Supply chains create a network that combines the first suppliers of raw materials and second suppliers (i.e. manufacturing) and ends with the retailers and the delivery processes of goods or services (Lee, and Ng, 1997).

Era 2: Definitions

A set of firms that pass materials forwards. Supply chain is forward integration which passes materials in one direction from suppliers to consumers. Supply chain integration aims at creating long-term agreements by establishing trust and commitment to share demand and sales data in an attempt to forecast possible logistic changes (La Londe and Masters 1994).

Supply chain management is the network of facilities that produces raw materials, transforms them into intermediate goods and then final products to be delivered through a distribution system. Supply chains are an integrated network of different suppliers from raw material providers to manufacturers to retailers who supply the market through a distribution system and thus satisfy consumer needs (Lee and Billington, 1995).

Supply chain is the alignment of firms that bring services or products to the market and finally to the consumer. Firms utilise their suppliers' processes, from original source of raw materials, through the various firms network of manufacturing and distribution (Lambert et al., 1998).

The integration of the processes, systems and organisations that controls the movement of goods from the supplier to a satisfied customer without waste. Therefore, it improves the efficiency of the processing systems which organise and control the flow of goods. Supply chains integrate upstream and downstream processes to create a value chain which offers a high-quality goods or value and services with less supply chain operation cost (Shukla et al., 2011).

Using inter-organisational systems in supply chain practice such as EDI (Electronic Data Integration) and elimination of excess stock levels by postponing customisation towards the end of the supply chain. Integrating systems such as EDI that speeds data exchange between companies and within the internal framework of a firm, in order to mitigate stock waste as a result of delays in supplying customers (Kotzab, 2003).

Six elements of supply chain practice (using factor analysis): supply chain integration, information sharing, supply chain characteristics, customer service management, geographical proximity and Just In Time (JIT) capability. A more efficient supply chain system can be established that mitigates delays and provide customer orientated products while reducing stock levels (Cooper and Ellram, 1993).

Supply chain management covers the flow of goods from supplier through manufacturer and distributor to the end-user. A supply chain integrates three main chains (manufacturer, distributer and user) by passing materials forward

(*continued*)

in a network of facilities, alignment of nodes, to interconnect strategically in long-term agreement. Integrating upstream and downstream will integrate various functional areas within an organisation, eliminating excess stock and enhance information sharing, customer service, geographical proximity and JIT capability (Novak and Simco, 1991).

Era 3: Definitions

Supply chain is viewed as a single process, where responsibility for various segments is not fragmented; it depends on strategic decision-making of a shared objective of overall costs and market share. It calls for a different perspective on inventories where a new approach is required to integration rather than interface (Houlihan, 1988).

Supply chain is crucial to globalisation as it connects the organisations through upstream and downstream processes within a marketing area regardless of their different activities to increase the value of the product or service to consumers worldwide (Christopher, 1999).

Networks of manufacturing and distribution sites that procure raw materials, transform them into intermediate and finished products, and distribute them to customers. Creating a global supply chain with multi-national suppliers from raw materials to finished goods and finally to be distributed to the consumer (Lee and Billington, 1995).

Supply chains aim at building trust, exchanging information on market needs, developing new products, and reducing the supplier base to release management resources for developing meaningful, long-term relationships. In the global economy companies are faced with extra competition in developing new products, therefore the information exchanged based on market needs is crucial in determining the most suitable supply chain by combining manufacturing processes with management resources in order to develop long-term relationships (Berry et al., 1994).

The functions within and outside a company that enable value chains to make and provide products to the customer. Global supply chains are faced with challenges to add value to the end products distributed to the consumer (Cox, 1996).

Supply chain practice includes supplier partnership, outsourcing, cycle time compression, continuous process flow and information sharing. Global supply chains require the outsourcing of business services to second-hand partners multi-nationally, resulting in the need to improve information flows. Global supply chains aim at reducing supplier cost by developing long-term relationships and involving expert teams to measure the buyer–supplier relationship (Chen and Paulraj, 2004).

A supply chain must incorporate the complex nature of the global market and include all the processes that are linked with the product development to fulfil a customer's request (Chopra and Meindl, 2007).

(continued)

Era 4: Definitions

Specialist supply chain is to synchronise the requirements of the customer with the flow of materials from suppliers to effect a balance between what are often seen as conflicting goals of high customer service, low inventory management and low unit cost (Stevens, 1989).

Specialisation links each element of manufacturing and supply process from raw materials to end user. Specialised supply chains tailor their manufacturing processes and choice of materials to encompass the regulations of the boundaries the organisation is dealing with. Specialised integrates customer satisfaction with value chain in order to provide specialised goods to the end consumer (Lummus and Vokurka, 1999).

Specialised supply chains collaborate between the intra-elements of a company and the intra-elements such as trading partners in order to optimise efficiency (Tan et al., 1999).

Integration activities take place among a network of facilities that procure raw material, transform them into intermediate goods and then final products and deliver them to customers through a distribution system. Specialised supply chain divided their facility in order to incorporate specialised intermediate goods to produce specialised products to their consumers (Lee and Billington, 1995).

Specialised supply chains actively manage channels of procurement and distribution, adding value along product flow from original raw materials to final customer. Specialised supply chain management coordinates the channels of acquiring goods or services and their distribution to ensure specialised materials and methods of manufacturing are used in order to add value to the specialised products for their consumers (Cavinato, 1992).

There are seven elements of specialist supply chain practice: agreed vision and goals, information sharing, risk and award sharing, cooperation, process integration, long-term relationship and agreed supply chain leadership (Min and Mentzer, 2004).

Era 5: Definitions

The integrating of the globalisation within a supply chain will aim to create a network of specialised global products with a global specialised network of supply. This is initiated by creating long-term relationships and trust between companies and suppliers. The systemic, strategic coordination of the traditional business functions within the supply chain, improves the long-term performance of the individual companies and the supply chain as a whole (Mentzer et al., 2001).

A globalised and specialised network of supply chain requires a sophisticated network of information flows to reduce the occurrence of error in product development due to the mishandling of information from different parts of the world (Handfield and Nichols, 2004).

(continued)

Supply chains are networks of facilities and distribution options performing procurement of materials that transform into finished products, then distributed to customers. A specialised globalised chain aims at providing an agile method of production and distribution as demand shift are fast in the global market (Ganeshan and Harrison, 1995).

Supply chain is a system that constituent parts of material suppliers, production facilities, distribution services, and customers link together via the feed forward flow of materials and the feedback flow information. Globalised and specialised supply chains incorporate an upstream and down-stream flow of information that helps coordinate the flow of raw materials, production and delivery of goods in a fast shifting global market (Towill et al., 1992).

Appendix 2: Panel Contact Details

Institution	Expertise
Hull University Business School	EDF Energy: innovative transport and deployment systems
Birmingham City University	Senior lecturer: procurement and Operations Management
Cranfield University	Senior lecturer: logistics and supply chain management
Newcastle University	Lecturer: operations management
Newcastle University	Senior lecturer: logistics and supply chain management
World Maritime University	Senior lecturer: maritime logistics
Incept Consulting	Supply chain costing
University of London/Royal Veterinary College	Senior lecturer: business/livestock supply chains
Hull University Business School	Senior lecturer: global logistics and supply chain management
Arizona State University	Senior lecturer: supply chain design and network structures
Lexmark International Technology Switzerland	Logistics procurement manager
Coastalwise Shipping and Logistics	Maritime shipping and logistics

(continued)

© The Author(s) 2017

261

S. Sindi, M. Roe, *Strategic Supply Chain Management*,
DOI 10.1007/978-3-319-54843-2

Institution	Expertise
University of St.Gallen	Lecturer: logistics management
Information Security Forum	Global supply chains: principal research analyst
Aston University	Senior lecturer: logistics and supply chain management
University of Manchester	Lecturer: supply chain management
University of Aalborg	Senior consultant in logistics and supply chain management
University of Antwerp	Transport and regional economics
Heriot-Watt University	Supply chain management
University South of Wales	International logistics and supply chain management
North Carolina Central University	Senior lecturer: supply chain and economics
Michigan State University	Supply chain management
Auckland University of Technology	Operations/supply chain/logistics
University of Liverpool	Agility of supply chains for SMEs
Harper Adams University	Systems and their role in the supply chain
Boart Longyear	Supply chain project manager
SIG Distribution	Supply chain director
Commercial at Leyton UK	Supply chain cost optimisation, R and D management and financing
Sheffield Hallam University	Senior lecturer: international business
TNO Sustainable Transport and Logistics	Consultant freight transport and logistics
Auxilium Management	Managing director: supply chain benchmarking
Eagle Shipping International	Senior claims handler; setting the supply chain's KPIs
Harper Adams University	Senior lecturer: food marketing and supply chain management
The Chartered Institute of Logistics and Transport (CILT[UK])	Business development manager
Summit Selling Systems	Director of operations
Anglers Choice Marine	Shipping and receiving
Optum	Regional account manager
Smith Sorensen Nutraceuticals	Procurement manager
University of Pittsburgh	Manager of corporate relations
EAP	Expediting manager

(*continued*)

Institution	Expertise
Private consultancy	Web-based modelling for optimising and benchmarking supply chains
Power Tools LLC	Logistics modelling and benchmarking manager
SABIC- Diversified manufacturing of industrial polymers	Supply chain consultant
Hillman consulting	Supply chain consultant
Agricultural municipality	Chief of agricultural supply chain
Chiarini and Associates	Director of operations management
Independent distributor	Logistics coordinator
CFT – Transportation and Logistics company	Logistics market leader
Owner of a small business – SME	Supply chain and logistics specialist
Toyota	Supply chain procurement specialist
Toyota	Quality control
Health sector	Medical equipment distribution
Mercy Health	Medical equipment distribution
Omega Healthcare	Medical equipment distribution
Owner of a small company – SME	Supply chain consultant
Walmart	Procurement
Walmart	Procurement
Web service marketing provider	Director of procurement
MTB INC.	Production safety/high-end sports equipment
Owner of a small business - SME	Logistics coordinator
ICAP Shipping	Financial advisor and procurement specialist
ICAP Shipping	Logistics coordinator
ICAP Shipping	Specialises in ERP and APS systems
Harris Corp.	Quality control
Carrier company for specialist goods	Operation specialist
Owner of a small interior design company– SME	Supply chain and operations director
Conover Inc.	Procurement specialist
Chas. S. Ashley and Sons	Cargo insurance manager
Chas. S. Ashley and Sons	Financial advisor and procurement specialist
Helios management and technology consultancy	Operations specialist
Manufacturing sector	Quality control
GB Rail-freight	Logistics operations manager

(continued)

Institution	Expertise
Energy sector	Sustainable supply chain analyst
Interior design company	Lean systems analyst
Landscaping and building supplies	Procurement specialist
CLdN – ro-ro Agencies Carrier company for specialist goods	Automotive, logistics and solutions manager
Woolf Aircraft, Inc. fabrication pipeline manufacturer	Operations specialist
El Camino College	Lecturer: economics and corporate strategy
UPS carrier	Distribution specialist
GAC – Logistics carrier company	Logistics operations manager
Manufacturing interior products	Operations specialists
Delancey Art Galleries Dealers	Supply chain operation
IKEA	Strategy and planning specialist
Industrial manufacturing	Logistics modelling specialist
Manufacturing building supplies	Distribution and material handling specialist
Aerospace	Expediting and procurement manager
A-S-I Anglo Spanish Imports	Distribution coordinator
Supplier of building material and construction – SME	Director of operations
Maritime sector	Shipping manager
CC. Johnson and Malhotra Co.	Material planning and distribution consultant
JLR – EU Distribution Team, Planning and Strategy division of Outbound Finished Vehicles	Strategic planning supervisor of the EU distribution team
JLR – EU Distribution Team, Planning and Strategy division of Outbound Finished Vehicles	Operations specialist of the EU distribution team
JLR – EU Distribution Team, Planning and Strategy division of Outbound Finished Vehicles	Senior logistics co-ordinator of the EU distribution team
JLR – EU Distribution Team, Planning and Strategy division of Outbound Finished Vehicles	Distribution strategic planning specialist
JLR – EU Distribution Team, Planning and Strategy division of Outbound Finished Vehicles	Logistics co-ordinator specialist

(*continued*)

Institution	Expertise
JLR – EU Distribution Team, Planning and Strategy division of Outbound Finished Vehicles	EU distribution operations manager
JLR – EU Distribution Team, Planning and Strategy division of Outbound Finished Vehicles	Manger of the EU distribution team and the strategic planning division
JLR – EU Distribution Team, Planning and Strategy division of Outbound Finished Vehicles	Head of global material planning and logistics department

❖ *The Fuzzy Delphi panel consists of 90 experts. However, the semi-structured interview panel is not part of the Fuzzy Delphi, in order to avoid biased judgements. The semi-structured interview panel consists of 8 experts from JLR's EU Distribution Team, Planning and Strategy division of Outbound Finished Vehicles.*

Index

A

Advanced Planning And Scheduling
(APS), 10, 34, 75
Agent, 86–88
Agile Leagile, 43, 56, 57, 143, 144,
159, 179, 205, 206, 208,
209, 246
Analytic Hierarchy Process
(AHP), 122–123
Automated Supply Chain Configurer
(ASCC), 87, 88

B

Barriers, 28, 44, 45, 48, 69
Basic, 15, 17, 30, 31, 42, 43, 52–57,
79, 88, 101, 158, 194,
196, 198
Border, 48, 50, 51, 55, 56
Bullwhip effect, 73, 86

C

Collaborative Planning Forecasting
And Replenishment
(CPFR), 49, 71
Competitive advantage, 11, 12, 20,
31, 38, 39, 42, 43, 51, 54, 56,
57, 69, 80
Conceptual framework, 4, 22,
27–90, 102
Configuration, 50, 58–64, 75
Consensus, 109–117, 120, 126,
134–136, 142, 143, 147,
149–155, 158–161, 164, 183,
199, 201, 204, 205
Continuous-replenishment
model, 64–65
Craft production, 83
Crisp, 103, 124, 132–134
Customer Relationship Management
(CRM), 40, 71

© The Author(s) 2017
S. Sindi, M. Roe, *Strategic Supply Chain Management*,
DOI 10.1007/978-3-319-54843-2

Customisation, 2, 17, 18, 28, 29, 35,
    71, 75, 80, 81, 139, 147, 163,
    185, 195–197, 230, 232,
    243, 252
Cycle time, 17, 46, 56, 63

D

Data collection, 4, 53, 76, 77, 80, 82,
    84, 103, 106, 109–128, 198
Decentralised, 50, 56, 60–65, 244
Decision Delphi, 124
Decoupling, 12, 17–18, 57–59, 61,
    65, 66, 71, 80, 83
Delivery strategies, 139, 143, 144,
    146, 179, 180, 183, 187–191,
    215, 230, 237, 245
Delphi, 101, 103, 104, 106,
    109–127, 131–176, 179, 183,
    199, 201, 204, 205
Dimensions, 21, 22, 36, 42, 48, 79,
    89, 134
Disaggregative Delphi, 124
Disintermediation, 85, 86, 88, 89
Distribution Resource Planning
    (DRP), 32, 43
Distribution strategies, 139, 146,
    179, 180, 183, 184, 244
Downstream, 12, 17, 30, 31, 34, 53,
    55, 58, 59, 71, 74, 83, 87

E

E-Delphi, 124
Efficient Consumer Response
    (ECR), 71
Electronic Data Interchange
    (EDI), 32, 34, 43, 53, 58, 75

E-marketplace, 85
End customer, 74, 80, 133, 139, 140,
    142, 145, 155, 181, 184, 190
Enterprise Resource Planning
    (ERP), 9, 10, 34, 53, 58,
    72, 75
Era, 3, 4, 11, 19, 22, 28, 29, 31, 35,
    42, 43, 54–56, 69, 70, 73–75,
    84, 86, 249
Error tolerance, 85–89
Ethical supply chain, 47
Excel, 72, 103, 104, 138, 147, 164,
    180, 198–199, 206, 208
Experts, 3, 22, 103, 106, 109–117,
    119, 120, 121–124, 126, 127,
    131–140, 142–148, 151–153,
    155, 158–164, 176, 179–181,
    183–193, 195–199, 201, 204,
    206–209, 251
Exploitation, 47, 85

F

Feedback, 39, 40, 110–112, 114,
    115, 117, 120, 124, 126, 127,
    142, 143, 147, 148, 163
Flexibility, 11, 19, 20, 28, 30, 34, 36,
    43, 46, 50, 55, 58, 59, 61, 62,
    68–69, 75, 81, 83, 85, 89, 131,
    136, 155, 158, 160–163, 187,
    192, 194–196, 198, 215, 226,
    230, 236, 244, 251
Flexible Manufacturing System
    (FMS), 11, 60
Frameworks, 3, 4, 15, 21, 22, 27–90,
    101, 102, 134, 151, 163, 164,
    176, 183, 212, 227, 241, 242,
    249, 250

Fuzziness, 78, 83, 103, 122, 124, 131, 132, 133, 136, 148, 149

Fuzzy, 78, 79, 82, 84, 88, 89, 101, 103, 104, 106, 122–127, 132, 133, 135–138, 140–143, 149–153, 155, 158, 162, 164, 172, 180, 199, 201, 203–215

Fuzzy Delphi, 103, 104, 106, 121–124, 126, 127, 131–176, 179, 183, 199, 204, 205

G

Game theory, 250–251, 253

Global Commodity Chains (GCC), 52, 54

Globalisation, 10–14, 18, 19, 21, 29, 33, 43, 44, 46–48, 50–56, 59, 60, 63, 69, 90

H

Heuristic learning, 250–252

Hybrid intelligent system, 253

I

IBM, 13, 53, 54, 114

If-then, 79, 116–117, 124, 126, 133, 138, 140, 144, 147, 164, 175, 208–210, 212–214

Information technology, 14, 43, 58, 74, 80, 84, 85, 252

Innovative, 15, 16, 35, 42, 43, 53, 55, 56, 59, 60, 65, 66, 69, 70, 75, 81, 83, 87, 137, 138, 139, 147, 160, 163, 186, 192–197, 212–214

Integration, 2, 8–12, 17, 18, 20, 30–36, 38–40, 42–43, 45, 47–49, 53–55, 60, 69, 71, 74, 79, 85, 122, 163, 244

Internet, 14, 44, 71, 86

Inventory, 8, 10, 11, 13, 14, 17, 20, 29, 32, 36, 39, 46, 49, 51, 53–56, 58, 59, 61, 62, 64, 67, 68, 70, 71, 75, 81, 86, 87, 89, 146, 188–190, 192, 193, 195, 197, 198, 229, 230, 246

J

Jaguar Land Rover (JLR), 151, 223–230, 233, 234, 236, 237, 239, 240, 241, 243, 252

Just In Time (JIT), 32, 34–36, 46, 66, 67, 75, 80, 81, 140, 146, 163, 182, 183, 185, 191, 196, 242

L

Lead time, 4, 9, 12, 13, 29, 33, 34, 49, 51, 55, 59, 61, 64, 67, 69, 72, 73, 75, 80–82, 87, 135, 137–140, 145, 158, 163, 172, 179, 181–183, 185–187, 189–191, 193, 197, 201, 208–210, 215, 226–229, 234, 236, 240–244, 249

Lean, 12, 43, 47, 56, 57, 60, 63, 64, 66, 67, 69, 70, 73, 74, 80, 83, 133, 134, 137–140, 142–144, 147–149, 158, 164, 172, 179, 182, 185–196, 201, 204–208, 225, 227, 228, 230, 237, 242–246, 250

Lean production, 11, 63, 83, 242

Logistics, 1–3, 7–22, 28–31, 34,
39–41, 44–46, 48, 50, 51, 54,
55, 60, 64, 70, 71, 73, 75, 80,
88, 89, 103, 112, 113, 132,
136, 139, 140, 145, 179, 180,
181, 183, 191, 205, 206–208,
215, 216, 225–228, 237,
239–241, 243, 244, 250

M

Manufacturing, 2, 4, 10–13, 17, 18,
20, 28, 31–33, 36, 40–42, 46,
48, 54, 56, 59, 61–64, 66–68,
70, 72, 74, 83, 89, 133, 139,
144–146, 163, 180, 181, 183,
184, 186, 188, 190, 191,
194–196, 198, 208, 210, 215,
223, 225, 226, 228, 230, 232,
233, 240, 242, 244

Market qualifiers, 72, 73, 74, 79, 81

Market winners, 72, 81

Mass production, 1, 2, 28, 83,
197, 242

Material flow, 1, 17, 32, 50,
163, 241

Material Requirement Planning
(MRP), 8, 9, 29, 30, 32–34, 43

Materials handling, 1, 7, 8, 28,
30, 44

Modified Delphi, 122, 124

Multi-Dimensional Matrix
(MDM), 3, 4, 18, 21, 22, 28,
73–84, 86–90, 102, 103, 106,
125, 126, 138, 140, 141,
146–149, 153, 155, 158, 161,
162, 164, 172, 175, 179, 180,
183, 199, 206, 208, 212,
214–218, 223–225, 227–230,
232, 233, 234, 236, 237, 240,
241–245, 249–253

Multi-dimensional model, 3, 127,
140, 176, 215–218

N

Networks, 10, 29, 34, 38, 46, 52, 84,
227, 244, 250, 251, 252

Neural networks, 250–252

Non-response, 106, 126–127, 176

O

Outsourcing, 10–12, 14, 17, 39, 47,
48, 50, 54, 63, 74, 133

P

Plurality, 151–153, 155, 158–161

Policy Delphi, 118

Postponement, 71, 186, 189, 192,
193, 196, 198

Price, 11, 33, 46, 49, 51, 61, 62, 64,
65, 81, 196

Processes, 1, 3, 8, 11, 15, 17–21, 27,
29–31, 33, 35–40, 42, 43, 49,
51, 53–56, 58–63, 67–69,
72–74, 80, 83–85, 103, 112,
163, 176, 186, 189, 190, 252

Production, 1, 2, 7–9, 11, 17, 19, 20,
28, 32, 34–36, 39, 40, 44,
46–50, 52, 55, 57, 63–66, 68,
70, 72, 80, 83, 86–88, 133,
139, 146, 163, 181, 184, 186,

190–192, 194–198, 224, 225,
    230, 232, 242–245
Progressive-flow, 58, 59
Pull, 17, 18, 55, 56, 60–66, 147,
    223, 230, 233, 234, 237, 240,
    243, 245
Purchasing, 20, 31, 32, 39, 40, 54,
    73, 75, 184
Push, 16–18, 55, 57, 58, 60, 61, 139,
    147, 163, 195, 197, 198, 223,
    224, 230, 233, 234, 237, 240,
    242, 243

Q

Quality, 11, 20, 29, 30, 34–36, 43,
    46, 49, 51, 54, 55, 63, 64, 68,
    70, 71, 75, 81–83, 89, 126,
    131, 191, 224–226, 229, 233,
    236, 240, 244
Qualtrics, 124, 128, 138, 147, 153,
    154, 164, 204
Quick Response Manufacturing
    (QRM), 67

R

Real time Delphi, 118, 124
Re-engineering, 69, 73, 74, 87
Relationship marketing, 34
Research angle, 102
Research paradigm, 27, 102
Research philosophy, 102
Reverse logistics, 12, 41, 50
Risk, 11–13, 18, 21, 32, 33, 35,
    46–48, 51, 53–55, 58, 87,
    90, 120, 123, 242,
    251, 252

Rounds, 101, 106, 110, 114–116,
    120, 122, 132, 134, 138, 139,
    150, 162, 176

S

Shipping, 2, 10, 67, 139, 163,
    225, 226
Soft Systems Methodology
    (SSM), 102
Software, 2, 3, 10, 13, 14, 19, 21, 34,
    43, 53, 72, 85, 86, 88, 103,
    186, 252
Specialisation, 43, 54, 56, 57, 69
Speed, 14, 16, 20, 30, 43, 55, 60, 62,
    64, 66, 72, 75, 88, 89, 181,
    189, 226, 244
Strategy, 3, 4, 11, 12, 14–16, 18–22,
    27, 28, 31, 34, 36, 39, 45, 46,
    47, 49, 50, 54, 56, 57, 59, 60,
    63, 66, 67, 69, 70, 71, 73, 74,
    75, 76, 79–84, 87, 89, 90, 110,
    112, 117, 127, 134, 137–140,
    144, 146, 147, 151–153,
    158–164, 172, 175, 179–199,
    206–210, 212, 213, 215,
    216, 218
Subsidies, 44, 51
Supply chain, 1–4, 7, 9–22, 27–59,
    63, 66, 68–76, 79–81, 83–85,
    87–90, 101–106, 109–128,
    131–176, 179–218, 223–246,
    249–253
Supply chain models, 3, 22, 27, 30,
    74, 101, 163
Supply Chain Operations Reference
    Model (SCOR), 49, 50
Sustainability, 2, 28, 47

T

Tariffs, 28, 44, 45, 51
Technological Delphi, 118
Three-dimensional printing, 2, 252
3D printer, 2
Toyota, 34, 35, 46, 63, 66, 146, 151, 194, 224, 225, 241–246
Trade, 28, 44, 45, 50, 51
Transparency, 47, 53, 79
Transportation, 2, 8, 13, 18, 28, 30, 45, 50, 51, 53, 85, 87, 226, 234, 244, 245

U

Uncertainty, 15, 18, 40, 51, 59, 69, 72, 73, 78, 103, 122, 123, 124, 175, 199
Upstream, 12, 17, 18, 30, 31, 53, 55, 74, 83, 87, 88

V

Value, 3, 4, 11, 13, 15, 16, 20, 21, 30, 31, 36–38, 40, 42–44, 51–57, 59–61, 63–65, 70, 74, 77, 79, 80, 83, 123, 125, 140, 155, 163, 182, 199, 207, 242, 249
Value chain, 15, 42, 44, 52–57, 59–61, 75, 182, 242
Vendor Managed Inventory (VMI), 36, 49
Virtual, 59, 60, 64, 70, 71, 79, 84
Visibility, 13, 18, 21, 32, 33, 34, 36, 53, 54, 58, 61, 72, 83, 90

W

Waste, 11, 13, 20, 35, 60, 63, 66, 67, 70, 71, 75, 80, 83, 133, 138, 140, 155, 160, 161, 163, 182, 185, 189, 191–193, 241–245

Printed by Printforce, the Netherlands